GENDER, RELIGION, AND RADICALISM
IN THE LONG EIGHTEENTH CENTURY

*This book is dedicated to the memory of my mother,
Dorothy Hornsby Jennings Hornsbeck*

Gender, Religion, and Radicalism in the Long Eighteenth Century
The 'Ingenious Quaker' and Her Connections

JUDITH JENNINGS
Kentucky Foundation for Women, USA

LONDON AND NEW YORK

First published 2006 by Ashgate Publishing

Reissued 2018 by Routledge
2 Park Square, Milton Park, Abingdon, Oxon OX14 4RN
605 Third Avenue, New York, NY 10017

First issued in paperback 2021

Routledge is an imprint of the Taylor & Francis Group, an informa business

© Judith Jennings 2006

Judith Jennings has asserted her moral right under the Copyright, Designs and Patents Act, 1988, to be identified as the author of this work.

All rights reserved. No part of this book may be reprinted or reproduced or utilised in any form or by any electronic, mechanical, or other means, now known or hereafter invented, including photocopying and recording, or in any information storage or retrieval system, without permission in writing from the publishers.

A Library of Congress record exists under LC control number: 2005032500

Notice:
Product or corporate names may be trademarks or registered trademarks, and are used only for identification and explanation without intent to infringe.

Publisher's Note
The publisher has gone to great lengths to ensure the quality of this reprint but points out that some imperfections in the original copies may be apparent.

Disclaimer
The publisher has made every effort to trace copyright holders and welcomes correspondence from those they have been unable to contact.

ISBN 13: 978-0-8153-8918-7 (hbk)
ISBN 13: 978-1-3511-5760-5 (ebk)
ISBN 13: 978-1-138-35697-9 (pbk)

DOI: 10.4324/9781351157605

Contents

List of Illustrations vi
Acknowledgements vii

Introduction 1
1 Radical Self-Representation 7
2 Matrimony, Monarchy, and Fame 27
3 Confronting Samuel Johnson 49
4 Revolutionary Politics and Literary Skirmishes 73
5 Defying James Boswell 99
6 The French Revolution and a New Note 121
7 "Help Me To Pray" 145
Conclusion 165

Bibliography 177
Index 189

List of Illustrations

1. Mary Morris Knowles, *George III* [after Zoffany]
   The Royal Collection © 2005, Her Majesty Queen Elizabeth II 37

2. Mary Morris Knowles, *Portrait of George III*
   (after a painting by Zoffany)
   Victoria & Albert Museum © V&A Images 76

3. Mary Morris Knowles, *Mary Knowles at her embroidery*
   The Royal Collection © 2005, Her Majesty Queen Elizabeth II 77

4. (first name unknown) Mackenzie, *Mrs. Knowles*
   Haverford College Library Haverford Pennsylvania
   Quaker Collection, col. no. 860 152

5. (artist unknown) *Mrs. Knowles*
   Haverford College Library, Haverford, Pennsylvania
   Quaker Collection, col. no. 860 153

Acknowledgements

Thanks first to the teachers who offered historical training, models of scholarship, and enlightened civility in the best eighteenth-century style. Professor Carl B. Cone at the University of Kentucky and Professors Ian Christie and John Dinwiddy at the Institute of Historical Research maintained the venerable tradition of gentleman scholars and always had time for an encouraging word and sound advice in graduate school and beyond. Thanks also to Quaker scholar Kenneth L. Carroll, who literally helped me find the way to the new Public Record Office.

Many friends and colleagues offered assistance and encouragement from the very beginning of this research and writing process. Dr. Jim Klotter, an ally since graduate school, read an entire draft of an early version and unfailingly continued to offer sound advice whenever asked. Dr. John Inscoe and Professor Vincent Carretta helped more than they knew just by believing that this project could turn out to be interesting and useful. My long time dear colleagues Anne and Don Ritchie always offered good advice, friendly assistance, and just the right amount of relaxation when needed most.

Librarians and archivists are essential to all forms of historical research, and this book would not have been possible without the able assistance of many dedicated professionals on both sides of the Atlantic. The staff of the London Library of the Religious Society of Friends always went the extra mile to help. Former directors Ted Milligan and Malcolm Thomas offered many key suggestions for new sources and answered scores of questions. Jon North, and his wife Mary, provided continuous assistance and encouragement over many years. Josef, Peter, Sylvia, and Tabitha never seemed to tire of delivering documents and answering queries.

Because of the many interests and talents of Mary Morris Knowles, this research took me to palaces and museums as well as to libraries and archives. Thanks to Christopher Lloyd, Surveyor of The Queen's Pictures, The Royal Collection Trust, for obtaining permission from Her Majesty the Queen to view the Zoffany portrait in Buckingham Palace. Thanks to Christopher Stevens, Superintendent Royal Collection, Hampton Court Palace, The Royal Collection Trust, for permission to view the needle painting of George III in temporary storage at Hampton Court Palace.

Matthew Winterbottom, Research Assistant at the Picture Library for the Royal Collection Trust, provided helpful early advice. Shruti Patel, Head of Photographic

Services and especially Miss Karen Lawson, Senior Picture Library Assistant, Royal Collections Enterrprises, Ltd., provided photographic images and speedy advice when needed.

Clare Browne at the Victoria & Albert Museum arranged a showing of Knowles's and other needle paintings there and made many useful suggestions and connections. Martin Durrant at V & A Images was always helpful and prompt in answering requests.

On this side of the ocean, Diana Franzusoff Peterson, Manuscripts Librarian and College Archivist at Haverford College Library, never failed to provide requested information and support. In Indiana, Elizabeth Powers and Cinda May were extraordinarily generous with their time and resources. Edward Ball and Patricia Bennett at the Charleston Library Society promptly and graciously provided a key piece of information. Robert Byrd and William Ewing at the Perkins Library at Duke University were always courteous and kind as well as tremendously helpful.

This project allowed me to make new friends who generously shared their research. Many thanks to Mary DeLacy for providing information about Jonathan Binns and other eighteenth-century medical men. Tom Jackson helped track down subscription lists. Philip Nelson sent information about London addresses and Swedish/English connections, and always added kind and encouraging words, too.

Finally, many friends and coworkers made the timely completion of this book possible through their assistance and support. Colleagues from the University of Louisville provided much encouragement and advice, including Lida Gordon, who helped me understand more about the history and art of textiles. John Cumbler, Mary Ann Stenger, and Catherine Fosl read parts of this work in draft and spurred me on to make it clearer and better. Cate Fosl also responded quickly and graciously to a request for advice on the final draft.

The Kentucky Foundation for Women provided a generous grant in support of this research, before I became the director. Since I have been director, the KFW staff, Amy Attaway, Sherry Hurley, and Sue Massek, and board members have been wonderfully supportive and patient in every way.

Professor Andelys Wood at Union College in Barbourville deserves great thanks for her friendship and generosity throughout the entire life of this project. She believed in this project from the first and really helped make it happen. She listened to unending recitals of research and always seemed interested and happy to hear more. She tracked down resources in London and helped solve word puzzles. She joined me in the treks to the V & A and Hampton Court Palace, and she accompanied me to view the paintings in Buckingham Palace. Even more, she read the entire final draft of the typescript without ever once complaining and offered many substantial suggestions as well as myriad points of punctuation.

Special thanks to Erika Gaffney, Senior Editor at Ashgate, and all the friends, named and unnamed here, who helped make this book possible. I couldn't have done it without you.

Introduction

Connections

In 1949, as Britons recovered from the ravages of World War II, Queen Mary assembled an exhibition of Georgian art in the Royal Collection. According to Bernard and Therle Hughes, British art experts, two pieces in that exhibition stood out as exceptional. Both were needle paintings, a new form developed in the late eighteenth century. Both were by Quaker artist Mary Morris Knowles. One image recreated a portrait of King George III in needlework. The other, remarkable for its content as well as its skill, presented a self-portrait of the artist.[1] These two images point to unexplored connections linking this Quaker woman to the king, the creation of a new art form, and self-representation as a radical female practice.[2] A close examination of Knowles's life thus offers new ways to explore the connections linking religion, gender, and radicalism in the long eighteenth century.

One purpose of this study is to recover the life story of this influential woman, honored in the royal exhibition and famous in her lifetime, but never before extensively researched and presented for full historical consideration. A larger purpose is to situate her life story in relationship to, rather than separate from, multiple historical currents and associations, which both reflected and shaped life in the Georgian Age. While theories about separate public and private spheres inhabited by males and females have produced much fruitful scholarship over the past few decades,[3] that is not the framework employed here. By examining and contextualizing the intersections of gender with religion and radicalism as revealed through the life of Mary Morris Knowles, this study focuses on the connections, rather than the separations, interlacing social, religious, and political realms.

Closely examining Knowles and her connections calls into question narrow ideas of separate spheres, confining constructions of gender differences, fixed concepts of *public* and *private*, limited definitions of political participation, and strict notions of *black* and *white* ethnicity. This study indicates instead the importance of religious and intellectual interactions among women and men, the possibilities of female authorship and political participation, and the diversity of active social networks. It is important to ask how Knowles viewed marriage, motherhood, and domesticity, for example. Yet it is equally important to ask how she, as a woman, became publicly known for her Quaker beliefs, expressed and acted on her political opinions, and influenced religious change.

Knowles offers an exceptionally rich case study for revealing how gender intersected with religion and politics because of the wide range of her friendships and associations. Throughout her life, Knowles established important relationships with a number of key figures in Georgian England, most notably Samuel Johnson and James Boswell. Because she confronted Johnson about his views on women and Quakers, and defied Boswell's presentation of her, her story provides new insights into these much studied men.

The research presented here is based on the belief that to understand fully the rich particularities of Georgian culture, historians must examine the concepts and experiences of the women and men who made history, not just accept the categories and assumptions of those who study it. In this view, the lived experiences of individuals provide the framework to inform larger historical concepts, theories, and understandings. The biographical business of unearthing and interpreting information is the beginning but not the end of this approach.

By examining the full range of her relationships and activities, Knowles's life story becomes a window into the shared experiences of a wider range of women and men in eighteenth-century England. Placing her in larger historical contexts and focusing on connections rather than separations sheds new light on three fundamental themes. These themes can be briefly stated as: 1) the changing role of Quakers in the long eighteenth century; 2) how gender functioned, especially but not exclusively in relation to middling females; and 3) the persistence of radical political associations, ways of thinking, and activities by females, from the English Civil Wars to the eve of the Victorian Age.

Despite recent studies such as Rebecca Larson's *Daughters of Light*, focusing on women ministers,[4] there is a dearth of information concerning eighteenth-century British Quakers, male and female. Quakers of the Georgian Age are often eclipsed by the fervor of the founding Friends and the good works of the respectable reformers of Victorian times. Examining the life story of Mary Morris Knowles and her connections, not only to fellow Friends but also to Anglicans, Unitarians, Deists, Jews, and Catholics, indicates how eighteenth-century Quakers became integrated into the English social fabric under limited toleration. By developing new forms of polite Quakerliness, prosperous Friends like Knowles helped facilitate the transformation of Quakers from a peculiar sect to a Christian denomination[5] and from radical sectarians to respectable reformers.[6]

Looking at the connections linking Knowles to her female and male peers provides new insights into how gender functioned in Georgian society, including how gender intermeshed with ethnicity, authorship, fame, and social status. The friendship between Knowles and the Jamaican-born Jane Harry provides new insights into gender and the "politics of complexion."[7] Knowles's lively relationship with Anna Seward demonstrates how they discussed literary ideas and politics despite their religious differences. Knowles produced manuscripts, which became social texts, publications, and artworks that led her, like Seward, to fame; and both women commented on their public reputations. Knowles's highly charged public disputes with Samuel Johnson and James Boswell demonstrate how attitudes toward gender, religion, and radicalism became entangled not only in the eighteenth century but also in subsequent scholarship.

Closely examining the evidence relating to Knowles's political views and activities contributes to the developing scholarship on women and radicalism in the Georgian Age.[8] This set of connections is, however, sometimes elusive for Quakers, like Knowles. As religious scholar Rosemary Moore observed, by the late seventeenth century, most Quakers stopped expressing radical political opinions in print in order to survive. Moore suggested that some Quakers continued to express radical opinions, but only in oral forms, more difficult to trace by contemporaries and also by scholars.[9]

Moreover, since women could not vote or hold office, records and concepts concerning female political participation are sometimes scarce and hard to find. Historian Amanda Vickery argued for extending to women fellow historian John Brewer's definition of political participation to include: "developing political attitudes, engaging in political argument, and giving forceful expression to political views."[10] That definition is used here, along with evidence showing how Knowles, like contemporary elite women, used her social connections to exercise influence.[11]

Using this expanded definition of participation and examining manuscripts, social networks, and material culture, as well as printed sources, demonstrate how Knowles consistently supported liberty. In London, she associated with male and female radicals, including John Wilkes, Catharine Sawbridge Macaulay, and Richard Price. Tracing her radical views through the American Revolution, the origins of the campaign to abolish the slave trade, and the era of the French Revolution provides insights not only into her political ideas but also expands historical understanding of the range of civic activities available to women and men during these highly contested periods of British politics.

Exploring the connections between Knowles and these larger themes requires the use of a variety of primary sources. Quaker birth, death, and burial records provide important demographic information. Family histories, memoirs, and anecdotes reveal personal assessments and attitudes about her. Her relatively small collection of letters offers valuable first person information, especially when supplemented by correspondence written to and about her. The poems, inscriptions, and visual art she created portray her ideas and aesthetics but also provide new insights into the relationships among art, religion, and politics in the Georgian Age.

Drawing on a range of resources and interdisciplinary concepts, this study is constructed as a double-layered narrative. One layer traces the life story of Mary Morris Knowles, while the other uses her story as a lens to examine larger national and international developments affecting the lives of both women and men. The baseline narrative provides concrete examples marking the intersections of gender, religion, and radicalism. Her life is reconstructed in these pages as completely as possible, not only because she achieved fame and celebrity, but also as a way of unpacking three important themes at work in Georgian culture. The larger analytical context includes the closely interrelated cultural themes and social connections as clusters of concerns and activities rather than as distinct realms separated from her daily life and actions.

The seven chapters presented here comprise three main parts. The first part focuses on Knowles's early life. Chapters One and Two trace her development as a religious writer, advocate for women, embroidery artist, and member of the polite middling classes of Staffordshire, Warwickshire, Birmingham, and London. In the nearly four decades between her birth in 1733 and her great artistic accomplishment in 1771, she lived as a comfortably well-off country Quaker. Yet during this time, she also interacted with people from a wide variety of religious and social backgrounds. During these decades, she became noted among Quakers for resisting a secondary role for women, insisting on choosing her own husband, defending her faith, and practicing her art despite the disapproval of some Friends.

The next three chapters, forming the second part, provide a close analysis of her participation in the political and cultural life of London, as well as of her maturing religious views and writings. Chapter Three looks at her friendship with Jane Harry and whether Knowles influenced Harry's decision to become a Quaker. This chapter also examines Knowles's interactions with Boswell and Johnson. When Knowles confronted Johnson about his treatment of Harry, she and Boswell differed about Johnson's response. It is important, therefore, to compare Boswell's journal entry to Knowles's account of her confrontation with Johnson.

Chapter Four explores Knowles's interactions with a wide variety of literary, religious, and political acquaintances in London as the American Revolution presented new challenges to British radicals. She served as an important link between Anna Seward in Lichfield and literary circles in London, while Seward gained a national reputation as writer. Seward, too, wrote an account of Knowles's confrontation with Johnson, which is examined here.

Chapter Five focuses on Knowles's widowhood, continued friendship with Seward, participation in radical causes, and public dispute with Boswell. She and Seward exchanged letters about literary developments, their fame, and important political issues, such as the abolition of the slave trade and the French Revolution. Both women became part of the public controversies surrounding the publication of Boswell's *Life of Johnson* in 1791. Boswell's published account of Knowles's confrontation with Johnson is compared here to his journal entry to see what he changed and why. Knowles's letter to *Gentleman's Magazine* accompanying her account is analyzed to understand her strong reactions to Boswell's publication.

The third part, encompassing the final two chapters, details her persistent challenges to Boswell's *Life* against the backdrop of the deepening divisions caused by the French Revolution and the schisms among British Quakers. Chapter Six demonstrates the process through which her semiprivate conversation with Johnson became a matter of public debate with the publication of her rejoinder to Boswell. For Boswell, the controversy centered on the legacy of Johnson. For Knowles, the issues at stake involved the identity of Quakers as Christians and the liberty of Jane Harry to choose her religion. As the French Revolution polarized people in England, the controversy took on even greater social and philosophical significance for both female and male readers.

Throughout her final years, examined in Chapter Seven, Knowles steadfastly insisted on the accuracy of her version of her confrontation with Johnson. She also maintained her interest in public affairs and continued to practice her art. Religion, always a primary concern for her, became even more important in her last years as she approached death and British Quakers faced difficult internal divisions. In her dying days, she struggled with self-doubts and viewed her accomplishments as possible impediments to her salvation.

The Conclusion examines disconnections and reconnections in the family memories, Quaker histories, and scholarly studies relating to Knowles after her death. Some Quaker descendants, family friends, and popular publications celebrated her contributions, while others questioned her Quakerliness and expressed differing views concerning race and gender. As Boswell's text entered the canon and Johnson's life became a monument, Knowles and her account became disconnected from this dominant narrative. Yet memories and scholarly interest concerning her endured because her life explored questions that continue to challenge women and men today. The Conclusion ends with suggestions for further research on some of the important historical, literary, artistic, religious, and social questions raised by her life story.

Taken as a whole, this chronological and critical analysis of the life and connections of Mary Morris Knowles strives to present her honestly, judge her fairly, and portray her in ways she would recognize herself. For that reason, her thoughts and ideas are presented, as much as possible, in direct quotations from her and her contemporaries in order to recapture the language and concepts of their time. This approach honors the terms and concepts used by Knowles and her contemporaries and highlights the issues and concerns of importance to them.

This double-layered analysis seeks to explore the connections between her individual actions and the social changes in Britain transforming Georgian culture, juxtaposing the personal and the public, specific gender issues, and overarching developments in religion and politics. The integrated approach questions old categories and offers new information about how this influential woman constructed circles of sociability, furthered and limited religious toleration, and participated in politics and culture. This analysis of her life and connections is presented as a way to help develop fresh understandings and inform new and more inclusive theories about continuity and change in the long eighteenth century.

Notes

1   Bernard and Therle Hughes, "An Artist in Needlework," *Country Life*, 105/2714 (January 21, 1949): 138–9.

2 Eileen Jones Yeo, ed., *Radical Femininity: Women's Self-Representation in the Public Sphere* (Manchester, 1998).
3 See for example, Robert B. Shoemaker, *Gender in English Society: The Emergence of Separate Spheres?* (London, 1998). Yeo, *Radical Femininity*. Elizabeth Eger, Charlotte Grant, Cilona O'Gallchoir, and Penny Warburton, *Women, Writing and the Public Sphere* (Cambridge, 2001).
4 Rebecca Larson, *Daughters of Light: Quaker Women Preaching and Prophesying in the Colonies and Abroad, 1700–1775* (New York, 1999).
5 Adrian Davies, *The Quakers in English Society, 1655–1725* (Oxford, 2000).
6 Richard L. Greaves, "Seditious Sectaries or 'Sober and Useful Inhabitants?': Changing Concepts of Quakers in Early Modern Britain," *Albion*, 33/1 (2001): 24–50.
7 Felicity Nussbaum, "Women and race: 'a difference of complexion,'" in Vivien Jones, (ed.), *Women and Literature in Britain, 1700–1800* (Cambridge, 2000).
8 For example, Amanda Vickery, ed., *Women, Privilege and Power: British Politics 1750 to the Present* (Stanford, 2001). Kathryn Gleadle and Sarah Richardson, eds, *Women in British Politics, 1760–1860: The Power of the Petticoat* (London, 2000). Judith S. Lewis, *Sacred to Female Patriotism: Gender, Class, and Politics in Late Georgian Britain* (New York, 2003). Barbara Taylor, *Mary Wollstonecraft and the Feminist Imagination* (Cambridge, 2003).
9 Rosemary Moore, *The Light in Their Consciences: The Early Quakers in Britain, 1646–1666* (University Park, Pa, 2000), p. 65.
10 Vickery, *Women, Privilege and Power*, p. 79.
11 Elaine Chalus, "'To Serve my Friends': Women and Political Patronage in Eighteenth-Century England," in Vickery (ed.), *Women, Privilege and Power*, pp. 59–87.

Chapter 1

Radical Self-Representation

Religious convictions, gender expectations, and radical politics all played a part in the family history and early life of Mary Morris. Her ancestors embraced Quaker beliefs, and their descendants struggled to reconcile religious radicalism with social respectability, as tensions developed between Quakerism and Quakerliness. Living under limited toleration, Morris fused seventeenth-century religious ideals with the polite practices of the eighteenth century to fashion new forms of socially acceptable Quaker behavior. As a prosperous and educated provincial woman, she gained a regional reputation for her beauty and defended her beliefs in polished poetics. Furthermore, she described herself as an artist, resisted a Quaker authority, and wrote a satirical autobiography as a form of radical self-representation.

Family memoirs record how her ancestors suffered with the first Friends during the civil wars. William Sikes of Leeds, her earliest recorded relative, married Grace Jenkinson, and the two moved to Knottingly, in Yorkshire, where he worked as a merchant. Descendants described Sikes as a Puritan, noting that he refused to pay the required tithes to the Anglican Church. In 1652, local authorities imprisoned him, along with other dissidents, in York Castle. Sikes's cellmates included members of an emerging religious group who called themselves Friends but whom others derisively dubbed Quakers. Sikes died a prisoner in York Castle, leaving £5 to the Friends "as a sign of his love."[1]

After her husband's death, Grace Jenkinson Sikes became a Friend. Guided by their visionary leader, George Fox, Friends believed that "every man was enlightened by the divine light of Christ." Fox taught that women had souls and experienced the saving power of Christ within, just as did men. Some women Friends became important organizational leaders, while others were recognized as ministers. Female converts like Grace Jenkinson Sikes contributed to the fast growing numbers of Friends, increasingly called Quakers, nationwide.[2]

After Parliament restored the Stuart monarchy and the Anglican Church, fears of treason prompted periodic Quaker arrests. Following the failure of a plot in 1684, local authorities arrested 240 Quakers in Yorkshire, including the aging Grace Sikes. In 1685, according to family records, Grace Jenkinson Sikes "Died a prisoner for her Testimony" in York Castle, where her husband had perished more than 30 years before.[3]

While William and Grace Sikes died for their beliefs, their descendants faced the challenges of living as Quakers. After the accession of William and Mary to the throne, Quakers achieved a measure of religious toleration, if not full social and political integration, in a series of Parliamentary Acts. The Toleration Act of 1689 recognized Quakers as Dissenters, allowing them to gather in registered meetings for worship and affirm their loyalty instead of swearing the oath, which violated their beliefs. The Test Act, however, prohibited Quakers from holding office or attending universities. Like other Dissenters, Quakers thus occupied an ambiguous place in the nation, legally tolerated but within limits.

Sarah Sikes, the daughter of William and Grace, became a Friend and married William Storrs, also a Quaker. The couple moved to Chesterfield, where he worked as a draper. Before toleration, Sarah Sikes Storrs and her husband, like her mother and father, were imprisoned for their beliefs. Yet, Sarah and William lived to raise their daughter, Esther Storrs, under limited toleration.[4]

By the late seventeenth century, as Esther Storrs and other Friends of her generation grew up, Quakers began developing survival tactics. Adopting such strategies, which included moderating their social and political activities, enabled many Quakers both to practice their beliefs and prosper under limited toleration. Yet this "metamorphosis," as described by Quaker scholar Rosemary Moore, also resulted in continuing and sometimes serious tensions between religious radicalism and social respectability.[5]

The potentially precarious relationship between revelation and reason constituted one source of these ongoing tensions. Faith in the guidance of the divine light within remained the bedrock of Quaker belief. Yet, Robert Barclay, in his influential *Apology for the True Christian Divinity, as the same is held forth and preached by the people called, in scorn Quakers*, first published in English in 1678, explained that "inward revelations do not contradict scripture or reason." Barclay wrote that, "God gave two great lights to rule the outward world." The sun, the greater of the two, represented divine light, while the moon, borrowing "her light from the sun," represented enlightened reason.[6]

Despite this balance proposed by Barclay, the stress on the primacy of individual revelation continued to cause schisms within the Quaker organization. George Fox articulated the concept of "unity" to underscore the importance of the collective whole, while his convert and later wife, Margaret Fell, helped develop the system of local, regional, and national meetings to consider matters of collective faith and governance. Local meetings also appointed "elders," charged with counseling wayward Friends to maintain unity.[7]

Esther Storrs also grew up during a time of increasing tensions concerning the roles of women within the Quaker organization. While Quakers continued to stress the spiritual equality of women and honor them as ministers, female Friends in England were not incorporated into two emerging national decision-making bodies. Most local groups included women's meetings for business, which served important functions in approving marriages and administering charity. However, the national Meeting for Sufferings and Yearly Meeting, formed in the late seventeenth century, included no women. Quakers in the colony of Pennsylvania and New Jersey had formed a Women's Yearly Meeting by 1681, and the lack of a similar body in the mother country constituted a continuing source of irritation for some English and American Friends for the next 100 years.[8]

Quaker precepts about plain living also became another source of tensions after toleration as some Friends became more prosperous. Fox taught that Quakers should forsake "vain traditions" and social practices inimical to the guidance of their inward light. He warned Friends not to "use the world's salutations, nor fashions, nor customs."[9] The aristocratic Barclay further advised Quakers about suitable "Salutations and Recreations," but he allowed wealthy Friends some leeway in their dress and practices. "If a man dresses quietly and without unnecessary trimmings," he wrote, "we will not criticize him if he dresses better than his servants." In general, according to Barclay, "although by our principles the use of anything which is merely superfluous is unlawful, this does not deny the enjoyment of luxury for those who are accustomed to it."[10]

Esther Storrs sought to balance prosperity and the Quaker practices of her parents and grandparents when she married and moved to Staffordshire. She wed Richard Morris in 1699, and they settled in Rugeley,[11] midway between Lichfield and Stafford. A resident later wrote that, "Rugeley was a small but exceedingly neat town with some good inns, and ... upon the whole it is as agreeable a little town as any in these parts."[12] Registration records document Quaker meetings in 11 towns throughout Staffordshire in the early 1700s.[13] Richard Morris noted that one such meeting was held at his and Esther's home in Rugeley.[14]

Richard Morris prospered as a surgeon, while he and Esther developed domestic practices suitable to their economic status and religious beliefs. He wrote a treatise on the importance of spiritual guidance in understanding the scriptures.[15] She provided religious instruction to members of their household, which included more than one maid, and, when needed, a midwife and nurse. Richard later recalled that Esther wore plain apparel, favored simple furniture, and eschewed some popular customs, such as women "making presents, one to another (where it was no act of charity)."[16]

Richard and Esther raised four children, and their fourth, Moses Morris, became the father of Mary.[17] Richard and Moses Morris played a role, although not an unfailing one, in upholding Quaker practices in Staffordshire. A contemporary later described going to a rented room in Stafford with a Friend who wished to declare his intention of marriage before the men's meeting, as required by Quaker practice. When the two arrived, they found "nobody there but the old woman who lives in the house." The man who accompanied the intended groom added, "Whether Richard and Moses Morris had forgot the appointment I can't tell." Undaunted, the determined groom declared his intention of marriage to his friend "and the old woman."[18]

Moses Morris married a Quaker named Alice, probably from Birmingham or Wigginshill, a nearby village in Warwickshire.[19] By 1730, Moses and Alice Morris had settled in Rugeley. In the years following, they had three surviving children, Joseph, born in 1731, Mary in 1733, and Esther in 1737.[20] Close and loving throughout their lives, the children became affectionately known as Joe, Molly, and Etty.

By the time of Mary Morris's birth, some prosperous young metropolitan Quakers had abandoned their beliefs to follow fashion, according to one famous observer. François Voltaire described London Friends in the first four of his *Letters Concerning the English Nation*, published in 1733. Noting increasing disparities between Quaker prosperity and precepts about plain living, he wrote, "The children made rich by the industry of their fathers, want to enjoy themselves, to acquire honors, buttons, and cuffs." According to Voltaire, "They are ashamed to be called Quakers, and are turning Anglican to be in style."[21]

Voltaire's observation illustrates the differences between Quakerism and Quakerliness. Following the distinctions described by religious scholar, Emma Lapsanksy, Quakerism denotes the basic religious beliefs of Friends, inspired by Fox and other early leaders and systematized by Barclay. Quakerliness refers to the behaviors and attitudes considered appropriate for Friends, or "ways of looking, behaving, *being*" a Quaker.[22] While Quakerism is an unchanging set of beliefs, standards of Quakerliness have varied over time and place and often been contested by both Friends and observers, like Voltaire.

Growing up in a prosperous provincial family in the first half of the eighteenth century, Mary Morris experienced the tensions between Quakerism and Quakerliness. Her father died young but seems to have provided well for his family. Quaker registers record the death of Moses Morris at age "37 and one halfe," sometime between 1739 and 1741.[23] Although the emotional cost may have been great, the family remained financially comfortable. Tax records for Rugeley show an assessment of £12 on a house and land belonging to "Mrs. Morris," for example, at a time when many cottages there were assessed at £1.[24]

A popular women's magazine later reported that, "Her parents being of the Society of Friends," Mary "was carefully brought up in substantial and useful knowledge."[25] Quakers had long valued practical education for both girls and boys. Without paid clerics, Friends needed to know how to read the Bible, keep meeting records and track group finances. Before her marriage, Esther Storrs Morris, Mary's grandmother, had taught at a Quaker school, where she combined literacy skills with domestic training, instructing "the Children of Friends to read, Knit, or sew plain work."[26]

Mary's education, like that of some other prosperous Quaker contemporaries, included a broad range of secular subjects. Another Quaker girl living in the country, for example, recorded reading philosophy, history, poetry, and classical texts in English translation.[27] Morris, herself, as will be seen, learned to write poetry, cite the classics, employ Latin phrases, and analyze current scientific theories. In addition, she wrote a fine hand, learned to paint and draw, understood botany, and seemed to be fluent in French. She was also familiar with *The Tatler,* still a popular text for polite women and men.[28]

Mary Morris grew up as a prosperous and well-educated member of the second generation of Quakers born under limited toleration. Historian Adrian Davies found a remarkable degree of social assimilation of Quakers in Essex by the early eighteenth century.[29] Morris's experience indicates that the same could be true in Staffordshire. She did not confine her friendships to her co-religionists in Rugeley. As a young woman, for example, she formed a lasting friendship with Anna Seward, the daughter of an Anglican cleric in Lichfield.

Morris and Seward most likely met in Lichfield, seven miles from Rugeley. As a lively provincial center offering several bookstores, a lending library, and a range of social activities, Lichfield often attracted visitors from the country,[30] which could have included Morris and her family. Seward later described Morris, nine years her senior, as one "with whom I have maintained the most intimate connection from my earliest youth."[31]

Anna's father, the reverend Thomas Seward, Canon of Lichfield Cathedral, strongly supported education for girls in the ongoing debates concerning the proper curriculum for females. When Anna was young, her father wrote a poem entitled, "Female's Right to Literature." In it, he linked female education to British liberty and national wellbeing. Anna, like Mary, studied science and English translations of the classics while also learning to write poetry and well-turned letters.[32] The strong friendship between these two young women indicates how shared secular education could overcome religious differences and suggests one way Quakers became integrated into polite society.

Anna Seward's letters, published much later, provide glimpses of the young Morris at odds with some seventeenth-century precepts of Quakerliness. While Seward's letters must be approached carefully as historical sources, as explained in Chapter Four, they provide colorful, if opinionated, first-hand observations of her friends. Seward later recalled Morris describing herself by saying that, while growing up in Rugeley, some people considered her "a romantic chatter-brain."[33] This facetious self-description contradicts Fox's dictum that a Quaker's words should "be few and seasoned" and Barclay's stress on "serious conversation."[34]

The use of the word *romantic* is also revealing. Even in the mid-eighteenth century, the word conjured up associations with imagination and sensibility. As feminist scholar Barbara Taylor pointed out, "The imagination was a controversial faculty in the eighteenth century."[35] It became even more problematic when set against the increasing stress some eighteenth-century Quakers placed on restraint and moderation.

Moreover, Seward later reported that, as a young woman, Morris "was stiled the beauty of Staffordshire."[36] In repeating this information, Seward seems to have approved her friend's countywide reputation based on her physical appearance. While Morris may not have intentionally cultivated this public reputation, being known for her beauty must have strained against Barclay's warnings to women to avoid vanity and maintain their modesty.[37]

While Morris became friends with Seward, she also developed close connections with the Quaker Lloyds of Birmingham. Sampson Lloyd II, a contemporary of her parents, developed the family business as an iron merchant and began what later became a banking dynasty. She referred to members of this wealthy and prominent family as her cousins and may have been related to them through her mother.

A family story indicates how Sampson Lloyd III, Mary's contemporary, experienced tensions between Quakerism and Quakerliness. A descendant described the young Lloyd as handsome, well-educated, and fond of fashionable clothes. Later in his life, Lloyd gave up his fashionable dress. Yet, according to his descendant, Lloyd put on plain clothes "as if they were his coffin."[38]

In the 1750s, Sampson Lloyd II acquired a 56-acre rural retreat, known simply as Farm, outside Birmingham. The senior Lloyd refurbished the house and set about improving the grounds. Farm quickly became a favorite gathering place for the large extended family, including Mary Morris.

According to Lloyd family memoirs, Morris, then in her twenties, designed some of the gardens at Farm. "The pleasure garden was laid out" by Morris, a Lloyd descendant later reported. "One choice summer arbour … was placed by the pond," according to this family member, "and another was also erected, in a more secluded situation, lighted by a window containing blue, green, yellow, and purple panes of glass."[39]

This description not only indicates the Lloyds' affluent lifestyle but also demonstrates Morris's appreciation of color, eye for spatial effects, and knowledge of gardening. Robert Barclay included gardening as an approved form of "innocent recreation" for Quakers.[40] While some Quaker males became famous for their gardens,[41] less is known about the botanical activities of Quaker women. As botany became fashionable for polite women,[42] Morris participated in this genteel pastime by designing the gardens at Farm while maintaining her commitment to Quaker principles.

Although the Lloyds prospered in Birmingham, Quakers there and elsewhere still suffered from popular distrust, especially in times of war. During the tumultuous seventeenth century, Quaker leaders taught that "the Spirit of Christ which leads us into all truth, will never move us to fight and war against any man with outward weapons."[43] A hundred years later, during the protracted struggles of the Seven Years War, this belief led some Quakers to decline to follow the popular practice of illuminating windows to mark military victories. In 1759, rioters smashed the darkened windows of Friends in Birmingham who refused to light candles in celebration of a British victory over the French in Canada.[44]

In 1762, as the Seven Years War continued, Morris engaged in a poetic dispute concerning her religious beliefs. Her antagonist was a man using the pseudonym "Clericus."[45] A manuscript note in a later publication identified Clericus as an

"Anglican clergyman named Rand from Coventry."[46] Debating with clerics was a well-established Quaker tradition. Religious scholar Rosemary Moore showed how early Friends defended their beliefs in written disputations with Anglican priests.[47]

With Morris approaching 30 and still unmarried, however, this dispute became complicated by gender. A nineteenth-century Quaker journal reported that Morris and the clergyman "are said to have felt a mutual attachment to each other; and that the only obstacle to a union was a conscientious objection, on each side, on account of different religious sentiments."[48] Moreover, Clericus addressed Morris as "Lavinia," further supporting the possibility of a romance.

This name probably refers to the character in the popular poem "Autumn" by James Thomson, first published in 1730 as part of his cycle on the seasons. In Thomson's poem, "The lovely young Lavinia" lived, like Morris, "with her widow'd mother ... in a cottage far retir'd." Moreover, Lavinia possessed "A native grace" whose "loveliness / Needs not the foreign aid of ornament."[49] Morris's reputation as a beauty paralleled this description of Lavinia.

In the first five of his 24 lines of heroic couplets, Clericus called on Lavinia to change her beliefs. He portrayed a herald from Christ urging her to "'Repent and be baptiz'd.'" By so doing, he focused on baptism as the sacrament considered most essential to salvation for many Christians.

In the sixth line, however, he introduced the possibility of romance by asking, "Will my *Lavinia* unconverted prove / Rebel to God and faithless unto Love?" Moreover, the cleric indicated he had personal knowledge concerning his Lavinia, further asking, "Say, shall a *parent's* absolute command / The mighty voice of God himself withstand?" Quakers who married members of other religions were disowned as Friends, so marriage outside their faith was strongly discouraged. Morris's mother, as a single parent, could well have prohibited Mary from considering marriage to a non-Friend.

After his brief digression, Clericus questioned Quaker beliefs as articulated by Fox and Barclay. "Shall *human* wit Omniscience engage," he asked, "And *Barclay* endless war with *Jesus* wage?" He continued, "Must each *apostle* waive his claim to merit / That Fox may shine first martyr to the spirit?" He concluded by suggesting that Quaker stress on the spiritual rather than the historical Christ undermined the power of the crucifixion. In his last line, he stated, "Then in the letter *double* death we find, / And *Christ* in *figure* only, sav'd mankind!"[50]

Morris, as Lavinia, answered in 58 lines of heroic couplets, using the same poetic form to dispute his arguments. She made no references to their personal relationship, however, nor did she indicate any attachment to him. Instead she focused exclusively on her religious beliefs.

Morris began by referring to her "*Christian* heart," underscoring that Quakers, like Anglicans, were Christians. Yet she also pointed out their differences, based on the Quaker belief in the divine power of Christ within. "But here a different zeal excites," she wrote, "You plead for *outward*, we for *mental* rights." Speaking for Quakers, she explained, "*We* think the gospel's hallow'd page inspires, / Superior efforts, nor *one* type requires." Believing, as did Fox, and Barclay, that the spirit must precede and inform scriptural understanding, she continued, "No mode of *words* can heavn'ly grace impart, / To an infantile and *unconscious* heart."[51]

Morris portrayed Fox as freeing religion from Catholic hierarchy and Jewish practice, reflecting her commitment to liberty, as well as her own religious biases. Liberty of conscience remained a core concept for Friends, summed up by Fox's statement that, "the ministry of Christ Jesus, and his teaching, bringeth into liberty and freedom."[52] She argued that without Fox's teaching "Enslav'd by canons, and the various rules, / Of councils, synods, colleges and schools, / Thus might mankind, (for priests an ample field), / To circumcision's ancient custom yield."[53]

Morris defended Quaker views on baptism by citing New Testament scriptures, also used by Barclay, supporting the symbolic meaning rather than the literal requirement of baptism for Christians. "Christ was baptized," she acknowledged, "but his apostles thro' the world he sent, / With a baptizing *power* beyond mere element." She reminded her opponent that Matthew wrote, "'He shall baptize you with an holy flame.'" While she conceded that water baptism "was in use," among early Christians, she argued, "Yet *no* dependence plac'd therein you'll see / Both *Paul* and *Peter* in this point agree." Linking Quaker leaders with these apostles, she observed, "Fox preach'd this doctrine to a seeking age," adding, "It shines in *Barclay's* unrefuted page."

Morris not only defended Quaker beliefs, however, she went on the offensive by repeating long-standing criticisms of the paid priesthood, even though she addressed a clergyman. She praised the unpaid religious services of Fox and Barclay, saying, "Simple *their* scheme, no mean self-love they knew / But *freely* preach'd without a sordid view." In even stronger words, she implicitly compared these unpaid Quaker leaders with paid priests. "With hearts devoted, gospel Truths display'd," she continued, "And scorn'd to make divinity a *trade*."

Like Fox, she deemed the ministrations of priests unnecessary. She interpreted Romans 1:19 to mean "Tis grace *alone*, we by experience find / Imparts instruction to th' attentive mind." She believed the inward operation of divine grace "Convicts of error and restrains from sin." Priests were not needed, she argued, "For what these *are*, it manifests *within*."

In conclusion, she confidently reasserted a spiritual definition of baptism. She described the soul being "Cleans'd of its stains, and *sprinkled* from above, / With pure descendings of atoning Love/ A baptism *this*!" She felt no need to observe the outward sacrament because, "This, then, alone my spirit craves." In her final line, she cited Ephesians 4:5, implicitly reaffirming Quakers as Christians, "Since but *one* Lord, *one* faith, *one* baptism saves."[54]

In her reply to Clericus, Morris ably defended her Quaker beliefs. Her citations show she had deeply studied the Bible, the teachings of Fox, and Barclay's *Apology*. She clearly understood the scriptures she cited and appeared adamantly self-determining in her own convictions. Her words demonstrated her knowledge of Quaker theology and her commitment to Christian liberty.

Yet, like earlier Friends, Morris defended Quakers by disparaging the beliefs of others. She distanced Quakers from Catholics and Jews by describing them as slaves. In this way, she also implicitly reinforced Quaker identity as Christians by distinguishing them from Catholics and Jews. She also used strong words to condemn paid clerics of all religions.

By writing in heroic couplets, Morris reflected changing traditions of Quaker disputation. Earlier Friends created poems to explain their beliefs and defend their ideas but favored the spontaneous creation of verses over time consuming revisions, which they felt indicated too much concern for human approbation.[55] By the early eighteenth century, however, Morris and other well-educated Friends wrote about their religious beliefs in the heroic couplets popular at the time,[56] evincing evolving standards of Quaker self-expression.

Although apparently not originally intended for publication, both the clergyman and Morris clearly meant for their poems to be read, at least by each other. Their manuscript verses constituted a social text, serving an intermediate function between public and private, written neither for purely personal reasons nor primarily for print publication.[57] The exchange of manuscripts like this constituted a form of "scribal publication" and remained an important venue for women writers even as print became more popular.[58] Moreover, as will be seen, these particular verses later appeared in a wide variety of printed formats.

In this poetic exchange, Morris explained and defended Quaker beliefs, even though not a minister. While women ministers had recognized religious, social, and public roles in explicating Quaker beliefs, Morris, too, as a well-educated and sincerely devout woman, served as a Quaker spokesperson in this instance. More case studies are needed to assess the social and theological impact of eighteenth-century Quaker women outside the ministry.

Morris seemed able to expand her autonomy by adapting practices considered acceptable for Quaker women ministers. Throughout the eighteenth century, for example, female ministers often traveled on religious visitations. Although not a minister, Morris traveled to London, accompanied by her brother Joseph, for social as well as religious purposes. By adopting this behavior considered acceptable for ministers, Morris enjoyed more mobility than some other provincial females.[59]

In London, Mary and Joseph Morris often called on Jonathan Fry, a cheese monger in Whitechapel, where Mary also first met James Jenkins. Jenkins later recalled how Morris "condescended to notice, and to denominate me a smart little boy," beginning a lifelong friendship between the two. The natural son of a country Quaker and his servant, Jenkins came to the city as a young boy to live with his uncle. Jenkins later made notes, usually highly opinionated, about scores of contemporary Friends. His published *Records and Recollections* serve as a rich, but not unbiased, compendium of information about eighteenth-century Quakers.[60]

Jenkins praised Morris for her intellectual abilities and polished manners. "She'd had been favour'd with a tolerable share of education," he later wrote, "and by dint of exertion greatly augmented the natural store of intellectual riches." He described her as an especially agreeable guest at the "supper parties (so common in those days)" at the Fry's home. He noted her "fine flow of spirits, unfailing wit, and conversational powers." Borrowing a description of a later leading female, he portrayed her as "'The life, grace, and ornament of the company.'"[61]

Jenkins described how Morris combined religious beliefs with popular social practices to develop new forms of polite Quakerliness. He vividly remembered her "voice uncommonly sweet" and how "she charmed every company of which she formed a part." She had a "capacity for mimicry," he recalled, and "had it been her choice, she might have become an Actress of the first eminence." He recounted how Morris recited the "cradle hymn" by Isaac Watts "with great sweetness, and to the delight of the company."[62]

By reciting religious poems at dinner parties, Morris combined Quaker seriousness and sociability. By adapting her amateur theatrics to theological purposes, she melded popular social practices with serious religious sentiments. Jenkins's vivid memories and positive descriptions indicate that the London Friends whom she visited responded positively to this form of polite Quakerliness.

Extending her travels, in the winter of 1764–65, Morris paid a lengthy visit to her Birkbeck relatives in Settle, Yorkshire. William Birkbeck, her uncle by his first marriage, had wed, as his second wife, Deborah Wilson of Kendal. Deborah Wilson's mother, also named Deborah Wilson, served as a respected local minister, and her sister, Rachel Wilson, later gained an international reputation as a minister, traveling extensively in the American colonies.[63]

While visiting this serious religious family, Morris produced two remarkable manuscripts within a letter written to another set of cousins, Dr. John Fell of Ulverstone in Lancashire and his wife, Sarah Birkbeck Fell. Two slightly different versions of this letter are preserved among the manuscripts in the London Library of the Religious Society of Friends. One, running to six large pages, seems to be fair copied and includes full names and place references.[64] The other, perhaps an earlier version, uses abbreviations for names and places, and includes some information not found in the fair copy.[65]

The letter opens on a satiric note as Morris dryly observed, "I cannot help taking notice that my Aunt has been writing a Panegyric upon Debby Wilson, and entirely overlooks me," adding, "this I think not quite civil."[66] Eighteenth-century Quakers continued their earlier practice of writing accounts and testimonials in praise of outstanding Friends, so Mary's aunt, Deborah Wilson Birkbeck, may have been writing a tribute to her mother. Yet Morris slyly subverted this religious practice by suggesting that attention to her guest might have been a more polite occupation for her hostess.

"I propose therefore," Morris continued, with the same satiric edge, "undertaking a slight sketch of myself in order to spare her or them the trouble."[67] Morris again used humor to subvert Quaker tradition. Rather than writing a spiritual autobiography, she claimed no religious purpose and eschewed the distinctive language of Quaker spirituality, presenting a secular alternative to religious journal writing.

Protesting that she did not want to "incur the censure of vanity," Morris observed, "that if I am my own Biographer, tis no more than these several Heroes, Philosophers, Statesmen and Bards have been before me."[68] By claiming the power to write her life story as great men had done before, Morris raised the issue of women's place in history. Contemporaries were just beginning to question the view of history as written by, for, and about men. The first volume of Catherine Sawbridge Macaulay's study of the English Civil Wars had appeared two years before, breaking new ground for women writing history.[69] By proposing to write her autobiography, Morris satirically but seriously affirmed a place for herself in the traditionally male preserve of history.

"As they wisely thought," Morris continued, referring to her male predecessors, "so think I, that it's ... much more honest, than to employ a parasite or an hireling to do it for us."[70] By using the words *parasite* and *hireling*, Morris evoked the oppositional language of Grub Street, recalling the civil unrest and radical politics of the late seventeenth and early eighteenth centuries. Her satiric tone also mirrored much of the anti-Court political writing of that era. As the well-educated Morris may have known, some earlier Quaker women participated in Grub Street writing and publishing.[71]

Continuing her satiric tone, Morris introduced a contemporary Quaker leader, saying, "in this case I refer myself to Friend Kendal, a good judge in these matters."[72] John Kendal, about ten years older than her, sold books and worked as a translator. He also served as a "minister and disciplinarian" among Friends, according to James Jenkins. This meant that Kendal played an active role in advising or admonishing wayward Friends.[73]

Leaving Kendal for now, Morris questioned the value of historical and current biographies, sardonically suggesting that autobiographies would be more useful. She asked, "whether it would have been of greater endowment to the present times, had many illustrious personages who adorn both ancient and modern history been constrained ... to have drawn their own portraits." If such personages "proclaimed all their transactions and their motives," she suggested with mock reverence, "what unspeakable benefit would there have arisen to Church and State."

Following this pronouncement, Morris turned to particular comments about two leading radicals of her day. "Delighted with the thought of making such a regulation among the great Folks," Morris proposed, "if my friends approve ... to countermand Wilk's [sic] any eulogiums upon Churchill, cordially leaving him to stand or fall on his own works."[74] John Wilkes and Charles Churchill, as vociferous opponents of the young George III and his minister, Lord Bute, combined criticism of court power with licentious behavior. Wilkes, for example, had recently been acquitted of seditious libel against the king, but he had then been forced to flee the country to avoid prosecution for libeling a bishop in his highly salacious "Essay on Woman." Churchill joined Wilkes in France but became ill and died there. Wilkes had declared his intention of writing a history of England, which might presumably include a eulogy on his friend.[75]

Morris also feigned to warn Wilkes against portraying William Pitt, the Elder. She proposed to advise Wilkes "that instead of his drawing the Patriot, to put the pen into the hand of the glorious Pitt himself immediately upon hearing the gout attacks his vital parts."[76] Although the definition of the word *patriot* continued to be contested, radicals often used the word in mid-eighteenth-century political terminology to evoke devotion to the public good over political gain.[77] Catharine Sawbridge Macaulay, for example, defined a patriot as someone who loved her country (*patria*) more than the ruling monarchy or the governing institutions.[78] Morris seemed to be displaying some ambivalence, if not irreverence, toward Pitt. He had recently lost favor among some radicals, like Macaulay, by accepting a government pension and a peerage for his wife.[79]

The other version of Morris's manuscript contains an additional sentence, evincing her detailed knowledge of John Wilkes and his activities. She seemed willing to allow him to write his autobiography, but she suggested "absolutely prohibiting him drawing a single line of his own portrait till the day before his journey from the T–w–r to Ly–n."[80] Whiles Wilkes defiance of George III made him the leading radical of his day, his indulgence in pornographic writing in the "Essay on Woman" forced him into exile. Morris's satiric statement seemed to question Wilkes's judgment about his writings.

Morris's satire, combined with Macaulay's disapproval of Pitt, suggests the possibility of an alternative female critique of these radical male leaders. Historian Amanda Vickery suggested that "political performance" became "bound up with different constructions of manliness" in the eighteenth century.[81] While Pitt could be seen as a manly wartime leader, for example, Morris, as a pacifist, might have objected to that aspect of his leadership. While Wilkes represented the triumph of liberty over court control, Morris might have questioned his notoriously licentious sexual behavior and the blatant pornography of his "Essay on Woman." Morris's satire indicates that she, and perhaps other female political observers like Macaulay, questioned the construct of manly behavior represented by these leaders even while honoring their radical accomplishments.

Returning to her theme of banning biography in favor of autobiography, Morris boldly proclaimed her own life story to be as important as that of Frederick the Great. Alluding to Voltaire's controversial biography, she called for "an edict to confine Voltaire, and deprive him entirely of the use of pen, ink and paper on the first notice of his intention to write the history of the King of Prussia." Combining satire and seriousness, Morris asserted a strong sense of her self-worth. "Closing with so great a man it may seem ridiculous now to mention myself," she wrote with mock modesty, "but I have the vanity to imagine I am of as much consequence to some as the King of Prussia and much more so to myself."

Having established her claim to write her autobiography, Morris cited the example of "Pope and Swift [who] were of the same opinion" as demonstrated by "giving so distinguished a place in their works to the renowned Memories of P. P. clerk of this parish."[82] The *Memoirs of P. P. Clerk of this Parish* appeared in 1741 among the collected prose of Alexander Pope and had been reissued in 1764. The *Memoirs* satirized Tory High Church politics of the early eighteenth century by portraying an ignorant self-promoting clerk and his corrupt parish priest.[83]

"In emulation of this eminent character," Morris announced, "I introduce the Memoirs of M. M., spinster of this parish." She further underscored the gender issues implicit in her title by claiming to be none other than the younger sister of "the celebrated Martinus Scriblerus."[84] Martinus Scriblerus represented the combined efforts of John Arbuthnot, Alexander Pope, Jonathan Swift, John Gay, Thomas Parnell, and Robert Harley, the Earl of Oxford, collectively known as "Scriblerians." Their *Memoirs of the Extraordinary Life, Works, and Discoveries of Martinus Scriblerus* appeared in 1742, filled with densely packed political allusions, appealing primarily to the most avid of readers.[85] By presenting herself as Martinus's sister, Morris grafted the issue of female self-representation onto the male-dominated political satires of Pope and his friends.

Morris began her "Memoirs of M. M., spinster of this parish" by describing herself. She presented a satiric but not unpleasant view of her physical appearance as "a damsel of a middle stature, and ruddy complexion." Despite her reputation for beauty, she humorously likened herself to a milkmaid, "who looketh not more blue on a frosty morning." She continued this comparison while hinting at her own strong self-will by saying, nor "hath she a pleasanter countenance when Colin meets her in the eventide, then I have when all things go well with me."

Continuing her self-description, Morris announced that "my employment is working in divers colours, and fine-twined woolen, and it is work of curious devices, and of exquisite cunning in the art of the needle."[86] Needlework remained an important skill taught to most girls, especially of the middling sort, throughout the eighteenth century. Girls with leisure and financial means also often received additional instruction in advanced forms of sewing.[87] While needlework remained a staple of practical female education, Morris referred to her work as art and showed obvious pride in her talent.

Morris demonstrated her knowledge of the classics by comparing herself to "Penelope of old," but she also satirically subverted this classical prototype of the patient and devoted wife, and challenged conventions of unmarried women as passive and asexual. "Peradventure, should a young man, well-favoured and of goodly aspect draw near," she declared, "I have not formed a positive resolution upon Penelope's plan" of refusing to entertain any suitors until she completed her weaving while awaiting Ulysses' return. "For tho it becometh us virgins to deport ourselves soberly, and seem as it were contented in this state of celibacy," she declared, "yet it is not unlawful to suffer our eye in a stated degree to glance over an elegant form." With this observation, Morris playfully but seriously challenged the constraints on proper conduct for single women and acknowledged female sexual desire.

Morris again demonstrated a strong sense of self by satirizing the importance of marriage and indicating she had recently declined a suitor. Since it is "incumbent upon us Damsels to provide ... proper partners" for men, she said she intended "to bestow the treasure of my inestimable *Self*, on some lucky, happy individual, as a very proper and suitable help meet." Yet, she continued, "It has been concluded by the learned that I am fallen away of late ... for I have said *No* in the wrong place; sure is it not ominous!" She mockingly wondered if it would be better "to avoid a second mistake, [to] be rash enough to say *Yes* to the first man that asked."[88]

If Morris had before been forbidden to marry outside the Quaker faith, as the Anglican cleric implied in his verses to her, she now asserted her right to choose her own marriage partner. While contemporaries viewed marriage to a suitable spouse as a high priority for all women, some clever and strong willed females of the prosperous provincial classes succeeded in determining their own choice of a mate.[89] Among Quakers, women ministers could also sometimes exercise independence in matters of marriage.[90] Yet, Morris asserted her freedom of choice even though she was not a minister.

This action had evidently brought her into conflict with the before-mentioned Quaker disciplinarian, John Kendal. "It seems he scandalizes me with the name of a Wit," Morris complained, "and says even to my face ... that were he single, he would not have me, that I should make a sad wife, disputing against self-evident propositions." Continuing her grievances, she portrayed Kendal describing her as "wrangling upon every new hypothesis with holes in my stockings, like Jenny Bickerstaff of old."[91]

Morris knew *The Tatler* well enough to understand the insult. In it, the fictitious astrologer and writer, Isaac Bickerstaff, described his sister, Jenny, as a spinster known for her needlework and fine skin. Morris may have resembled her in these ways. Yet Isaac complained that he could not find a husband for Jenny because, "she is so very a Wit, that she understands no ordinary Thing in the World."[92]

Continuing her grievances against Kendal, Morris wondered if he thought that she would "sit, rocking the cradle with one hand, and reading Epictatius [sic] with the other." Here, Morris likely referred to the well-known 1758 English translation of the writings of the Stoic philosopher Epictetus by the leading female intellectual, Elizabeth Carter. Following Kendal's hypothetical description of her as a distracted philosophy-reading mother, in one manuscript version Morris added the emphatic gendered exclamation, *"Foolish Man!"*[93]

Although both were devout Quakers, Morris and Kendal strongly disagreed about the proper education for women. His characterization of her as a wit showed that, as an educated female Quaker, she faced the same negative attitudes as other women intellectuals.[94] In her defense, Morris questioned whether Kendal would rather women live, as she said, "not once considering how necessary it is for each sex and station to qualify and ornament the mind with philosophical lessons ...

thereby dispelling the dark cloud and thick mists of passion, ignorance, and superstition?"

Morris transformed Kendal's criticisms into an argument in favor of teaching women science and philosophy along with cookery. She questioned the gender expectations applied to women by asking, "What pray is the very exalted character of a Pudding-Making Mortal, which men of these superficial times so much revere?" She answered by declaring, "I'll endeavour to prove beyond a possibility of dispute, that Philosophy is not incompatible with cooking."

Morris then launched into the second part of the double manuscript contained in her letter, with a short essay entitled, "The Pudding Making Mortal." In it, she argued that since "accidents may happen to the best puddings in the world," every housewife should be taught science. "What," she asked, "but a mind aided by the light of Philosophy, supported by the cordial of Ethics, and soothed by the anodyne of Metaphysics, could bear such an event?"

To prove her point, Morris first explained how she would react to a bursting pudding bag. Speaking for "all my sisterhood (pardon the seeming vanity for justice belongs to us as well as to others) on this trying circumstance," she described what she and her well-educated sisters would do. "Endowed with physical, reflective, and moral reasoning, [I] should probably then and there, calmly descant on the ... invariable laws of nature," she maintained, "faithfully exerting their influence according to the will and purpose of their author." As a scientifically educated Pudding Making Mortal, she would take the opportunity to teach her servants, "the wondering Betty and the astonished sculleries," the reasons why particles expand.

Morris portrayed herself, "sweetly smiling," demonstrating her grasp of not one but two current scientific explanations of fire and their concomitant Latin phrases. As a scientific housewife, she would note that one theory involved a collision between "the ignited particle" of fire and "the component heterogeneous particles of the pudding, so as to extend their bulk, causing the contents *qua data poster* [to] revert or ... rush out." She would further explain how "some philosophers" argue, "that fire is material *sui generis*" and not composed of particles. Morris concluded this description of herself by observing, "whichever hypothesis we adopt (tho' for my part I incline to the latter), all culinary processes are solved with equal ease *mutatis mutandis.*"

Morris then presented a portrait of the second kind of Pudding Making Mortal. "And now observe your other kind of cook," she wrote. "She who is termed an excellent housewife, and has been taught to think it is the highest absurdity to venture out of the domestic province; behold her!" Morris drew a comic character of a woman in a long apron "trotting about the kitchen ... frizzling and frying, hustle, bustle, a ladle in her hand ... frowning, fretting, and fuming."

When this unphilosophical Pudding Making Mortal sees the pudding bag burst, "down drops the ladle, up goes her hands," and she cries out, "there's a hob-goblin in the pot." This supposedly excellent housewife "raves at Betty, boxes the scullion, kicks the dog from the fire." The dog "throws down the dripping pan, scalds himself, he runs away howling, oversets some of the children, they all set a squabbling, and the frightened husband leaves the house and begs a quiet dinner at his neighbors."

Confident she had made her point, Morris mockingly concluded by offering to forgive John Kendal with some conditions. "Tell Friend Kendal, I doubt not of his being a proselyte to my reasoning, and therefore hope he will make it his business by way of atonement to recommend me and my scientific sisterhood to the discerning of his sex," she joked. Assuming the position of one wronged rather than committing a wrong, she added, "and then I'll freely pardon him for his past declarations." With this, Morris suddenly found herself out of time and paper, and brought her "surprising memoirs to a close."[95]

While Morris successfully combined serious Quaker beliefs with high-spirited sociability, the mix could be combustible, especially concerning gender. Her letter indicated how she differed from Kendal concerning the proper education and conduct of women, particularly a woman's freedom to choose her marriage partner and the best preparation for domestic life. Further research is needed to determine whether this is an isolated incident or an indication of patterns of tensions between some male Quaker elders and forceful female Friends.

Like her earlier religious verses to Clericus, Morris's manuscript letter containing her sketches of "Memoirs of M. M., spinster of this parish" and "The Pudding Making Mortal" assumed a larger social significance. As with the ostensibly private verses written to Clericus, the contents of this letter seem designed to be shared. In it, she aired her differences with Kendal and solicited understanding of her point of view. The existence of two manuscript copies indicates that this letter, like her earlier verses, became a social text, read and passed on by the recipients or by the author herself.

Moreover, because she used literary language and secular examples, Morris may have intended her arguments to appeal to readers beyond Quaker circles. Rather than composing a religious statement, she created a shrewd satire with references to the politics of her day that could appeal to a variety of readers. Since Morris's earlier verses had been presented to an Anglican cleric, non-Friends may well have read this letter. She could have shown the letter to her friend, Anna Seward, for example.

Feminist scholar Eileen Janes Yeo pointed to the importance of women's self-representation as a radical act.[96] The two essays contained in Morris's letter stand as significant examples of a strong female self-identity. In her "Memoirs," Morris satirized her own beauty, revealed her strong-willed nature, and presented herself as a needlework artist. In "The Pudding Making Mortal," she advocated for the education of housewives, proclaimed herself a member of a scientific sisterhood, and argued that all women deserved justice.

By placing "The Pudding Making Mortal" within her satirical "Memoirs," Morris indicated that she did not consider female domestic identity as separate from other aspects of her life but rather incorporated within her daily activities. Like the scholarly Elizabeth Carter, Morris believed that the same intellectual rigor could be applied to cooking as to other areas of study. Morris set out to show pudding making as a form of applied science, just as, years earlier, Carter had laughingly described her own "abilities in the science of puddings."[97]

Morris hinted at her radical religious and political views in this as well as in her earlier manuscript verses. In her dispute with the Anglican cleric, she scorned what she described as enslaving religious beliefs. In her "Memoirs," she showed her familiarity with the early eighteenth-century critics of court politics and, like them, used satire as a tool of oppositional rhetoric. Furthermore, she commented, knowledgably, if not always approvingly, on the political careers of Wilkes, Churchill, and Pitt.

In this context, the "Memoirs of M.M. spinster of this parish" can be seen as a form of radical female self-representation. Although a sincere Quaker, in her memoirs, Morris defied the authority of Kendal as a religious disciplinarian and his pronouncement on her as a wit. In the process, she commented on history, politics, and current scientific theories. She alluded to her sexual interest in men and indicated that she intended to exercise her own judgment in marriage. For Mary Morris in 1765, as for Mary Wollstonecraft writing 25 years later, intellectual self-assertion constituted a form of social, religious, and political action.[98]

As her religious verses and her letter written in 1765 show, Morris, now in her thirties, resisted family and religious authorities and struggled to define her own identity. As a deeply religious but strongly independent woman, she valued spiritual fulfillment for herself and sought to fashion acceptable roles for women both within the Quaker collectivity and in the changing culture of the British provinces. By interacting with Anglicans like Anna Seward and her clerical adversary, Morris tested the boundaries of religious toleration. By actively constructing her own identity, she demonstrated how she, as a woman, could be a needlework artist, political commentator, religious disputant, and social change agent. But she had only just begun.

Notes

1 London, Library of Religious Society of Friends. Portfolio MSS, 11, No. 6, "Some Account of the Life of Esther Morris by her husband Richard Morris, 1709/10." Temporary MSS 403 [Braithwaite Papers], Box 7, Packet 15, File 4, No. 3, "A Short Account of the Life and Departure of Esther Morris, Copied from a manuscript of Joseph Cluton Dated 18th of 1 mo 1724." This more legible fair copy is cited below.
2 *George Fox: The Journal*, ed. Nigel Smith (London, 1998), pp. 33, 11. Moore, *The Light in Their Consciences*, pp. 3–34. Larson, *Daughters of Light,* pp. 16–26.
3 Braithwaite Papers, 7, 15, 4, 3, "Short Account."
4 Ibid.

5 Moore, *Light in Their Consciences*, pp. 214–28. Davies, *The Quakers in English Society*. Richard L. Greaves, "Seditious Sectaries or 'Sober and Useful Inhabitants?'"
6 *Barclay's Apology in Modern English*, ed. Dean Freiday (Newberg, OR, 1991), pp. 40, 91.
7 Moore. *Light in Their Consciences*, pp. 133–8.
8 Larson, *Daughters of Light*, pp. 30–34
9 *George Fox: The Journal*, pp. 35, 129.
10 *Barclay's Apology*, pp. 405, 392.
11 Braithwaite Papers, 7, 15, 4, 3, "Short Account." Details of the earlier life of Richard Morris remain obscure.
12 Walter N. Landor, "An Account of the Manor and Ancient Paris of Rugeley from the Days of the Saxons," Typescript, Rugeley Public Library, p. 152.
13 Barbara Donaldson, "The Registration of Dissenting Chapels and Meeting Houses in Staffordshire, 1689–1852," in Staffordshire Record Society (eds.), *Collections for a History of Staffordshire*, 4th series, vol. 3 (Kendal, 1960), pp. xxii–iv.
14 Braithwaite Papers, 7,15, 4, 3, "Short Account."
15 Later published as *Some Animadversions on the Supposition of the Scriptures Being the Only Principal and Perfect Rule to Salvation* (London, 1798).
16 Braithwaite Papers, 7,15, 4, 3, "Short Account."
17 His birth record has not been located. His death is recorded in London, Public Record Office, RG 6, 1460, Staffordshire Register of Marriages, Births, Burials.
18 "Notes and Queries [C. D. Sturge, Birmingham, 1741]," *Journal of the Friends Historical Society*, 4/3 (1907): 85.
19 Their marriage certificate has not been located, but their three children married at Wigginshill meeting, near Birmingham, indicating a family connection there. Public Record Office, RG 6, 1461, Wigginshill Meeting from 1699.
20 Library of the Religious Society of Friends, "Cheshire and Staffordshire Quarterly Meeting Digest Register of Births," 1730–37.
21 *Voltaire: Candide and Philosophical Letters* (New York, 1992), p. 135.
22 Emma Jones Lapsansky and Anne A. Verplanck, eds, *Quaker Aesthetics: Reflections on a Quaker Ethic in American Design and Consumption* (Philadelphia, 2002), pp. 6–7.
23 Public Record Office, RG 6, 1460, lists his death between 1739 and 1741. Library of the Religious Society of Friends, "Cheshire and Staffordshire Quarterly Meeting Digest Register of Burials" assigns the date to 1739.
24 Landor, "Rugeley."
25 *The Lady's Monthly Museum*, November 1803: 290.
26 Braithwaite Papers, 7, 15, 4, 3, "Short Account."
27 Mary Chorley, as described in Amanda Vickery, *The Gentleman's Daughter: Women's Lives in Georgian England* (New Haven, 1998), pp. 7, 343n.
28 Donald F. Bond, ed. *The Tatler* (Oxford, 1987), pp. 99–100.
29 Davies, *Quakers in English Society*, p. 223.
30 John Brewer, *The Pleasures of the Imagination: English Culture in the Eighteenth Century* (New York, 1997), pp. 573–612.
31 *Letters of Anna Seward, written between the years 1784 and 1807* (6 vols, Edinburgh, 1811), vol. 2, p. 109.
32 Ibid.

33 Rev. Hill Wickham, ed., *Journals and Correspondence of Thomas Sedgewick Whalley* (2 vols, London, 1863) vol. 1, p. 388.
34 Fox as quoted by Moore, *Light in Their Consciences*, p. 121. *Barclay's Apology*, p. 411.
35 Taylor, *Mary Wollstonecraft and the Feminist Imagination*, p. 2.
36 *Letters of Anna Seward*, vol. 1, p. 46.
37 *Barclay's Apology*, p. 407.
38 Samuel Lloyd, *The Lloyds of Birmingham* (3rd edn, Birmingham, 1908), p. 103.
39 Ibid., p. 34.
40 *Barclay's Apology*, p. 411.
41 See, for example, Christopher C. Booth, "The Correspondence of Dr. John Fothergill with Sir Joseph Banks," *The Journal of the Friends Historical Society*, 59/3 (2004): 215–30.
42 Ann Shteir, *Cultivating Women, Cultivating Science: Flora's Daughters and Botany in England, 1760–1860* (Baltimore, 1996).
43 Moore, *Light in Their Consciences*, p. 181.
44 William White, *Friends in Warwickshire in the 17th and 18th Centuries* (3rd edn, London, 1894), pp. 74–8.
45 Library of the Religious Society of Friends, Temporary MSS 1, 35, "Verses to Mary Morris and her reply, 1762." Temporary MSS 5, 30, "Verses: The clergyman's address to Mary Morris and her answer."
46 MSS note in British Library copy, *Compendium of a Controversy on Water Baptism*, (London, 1805).
47 Moore, *Light in Their Consciences*, p. 186.
48 *The Irish Friend: A Monthly Periodical Devoted Chiefly to the Interests of Friends*, 2/9 (September 2, 1839): 71.
49 James Thomson, *The Seasons* (Dublin, 1767), pp. 140–41.
50 Temp. MSS 1, 35, "Verses."
51 Ibid.
52 *Fox: Journal*, p. 19.
53 Temp. MSS 1, 35, "Verses."
54 Ibid.
55 Moore, *Light in Their Consciences*, p. 205.
56 Larson, *Daughters of Light*, p. 179.
57 Margaret J. M. Ezell, *Social Authorship and the Advent of Print* (Baltimore, 1999), pp. 25–45.
58 George L. Justice and Nathan Tinker, eds, *Women's Writing and the Circulation of Ideas: Manuscript Publication in England, 1550–1800* (New York, 2002).
59 Vickery, *Gentleman's Daughter*, pp. 260–76.
60 *Records and Recollections of James Jenkins* ed. J. William Frost (New York, 1984), p. 453.
61 Ibid.
62 Ibid., pp. 453–4.
63 Larson, *Daughters of Light*, p. 318.
64 Braithwaite Papers, 7, 15, 3, 43, "The Pudding Making Mortal."
65 Library of the Religious Society of Friends, Temporary MSS 28, File 7, "Copy of an epistle to Dr. F. dated Jany 1765."
66 Braithwaite Papers, 7, 15, 3, 43, "The Pudding Making Mortal."

67 Ibid.
68 Ibid.
69 Philip Hicks, "Catharine Macaulay's Civil War: Gender, History, and Republicanism in Georgian Britain," *Journal of British Studies*, 41/2 (2002): 170–98.
70 Braithwaite Papers, 7, 15, 3, 43, "The Pudding Making Mortal."
71 Paula McDowell, *The Women of Grub Street: Press, Politics and Gender in the London Literary Marketplace, 16778–1730* (Oxford, 1998), pp. 10, 18–53.
72 Braithwaite Papers, 7, 15, 3, 43, "The Pudding Making Mortal."
73 *Records and Recollections of James Jenkins*, pp. 537–8.
74 Braithwaite Papers, 7, 15, 3, 43, "The Pudding Making Mortal."
75 Peter D. G. Thomas, *John Wilkes: A Friend to Liberty* (Oxford, 1996).
76 Braithwaite Papers, 7, 15, 3, 43, "The Pudding Making Mortal."
77 Linda Colley, "Radical Patriotism in Eighteenth-Century England," in Raphael Samuel, (ed.), *Patriotism: The Making and Unmaking of British National Identity*, vol. 1, *History and Politics* (London: 1989), p. 170.
78 J. G. A. Pocock, "Catharine Macaulay: patriot historian," in Hilda L. Smith, (ed.), *Women Writers and the Early Modern British Political Tradition* (Cambridge, 1998), p. 246.
79 Hicks, "Catharine Macaulay's Civil War."
80 Temporary MSS 28, 7, "Copy of an epistle."
81 Vickery, *Women, Privilege, and Power*, p. 53.
82 Braithwaite Papers, 7, 15, 3, 43, "The Pudding Making Mortal."
83 *The Works of Alexander Pope, Esquire*, vol. 4, *Containing His Miscellaneous Pieces in Verse and Prose* (London, 1764), pp. 211–21.
84 Braithwaite Papers, 7, 15, 3, 43, "The Pudding Making Mortal."
85 *Memoirs of the Extraordinary Life, Works, and Discoveries of Martinus Scriblerus*, ed. Charles Kerby-Miller (New York, 1966), p. vii.
86 Braithwaite Papers, 7, 15, 3, 43, "The Pudding Making Mortal."
87 Margaret Hunt, *The Middling Sort: Commerce, Gender and Family in England, 1680–1780* (Berkeley, 1996), p. 86. Lenore Davidoff and Catherine Hall, *Family Fortunes: Men and Women of the English Middle Class, 1780–1850* (Chicago, 1987), p. 309.
88 Braithwaite Papers, 7, 15, 3, 43, "The Pudding Making Mortal."
89 Vickery, *Gentleman's Daughter*, p. 86.
90 Larson, *Daughters of Light*, p. 135.
91 Braithwaite Papers, 7, 15, 3, 43, "The Pudding Making Mortal."
92 Bond, *The Tatler*, pp. 512–7.
93 Temporary MSS 28, 7, "Copy of an epistle."
94 Sylvia Harcstack Myers, *The Bluestocking Circle: Women, Friendship, and the Life of the Mind in Eighteenth-Century England* (Oxford, 1990).
95 Braithwaite Papers, 7, 15, 3, 43, "The Pudding Making Mortal."
96 Yeo, *Radical Femininity*, pp. 1–10.
97 Carolyn D. Williams, "Poetry, Pudding, and Epictetus: The Consistency of Elizabeth Carter," in Alvaro Ribeiro and James G. Basker (eds), *Tradition in Transition: Women Writers, Marginal Texts, and the Eighteenth-Century Canon* (Oxford, 1996), pp. 3–40.
98 Taylor, *Wollstonecraft and the Feminist Imagination*, p. 51.

Chapter 2

Matrimony, Monarchy, and Fame

Guided by Quaker concepts of unity and love, Mary Morris developed deep friendships with both males and females. Despite her earlier resistance to marriage, she wed happily. Determined not to become a passive wife, she fashioned her own forms of domesticity. She experienced a difficult childbirth, and, unlike other provincial women, recorded her fears and sufferings. She and her husband moved to Birmingham, where she changed their lives through an artistic accomplishment. Gaining fame, fortune, and access to royalty, she negotiated a request for patronage but struggled to maintain her independence. Her financial gains enabled her husband to study at Leyden, and the couple traveled through Europe, conversing with royals there. Returning to England, Mary formed important new connections through her fame, polite Quakerliness, and thoughtful religious discourse.

While visiting Settle in 1764–65, Mary Morris became close friends with John Coakley Lettsom, a young Quaker from the West Indies. Lettsom was born in Tortola, where his family owned several large plantations and as many as 50 slaves. Lettsom came to England as a young boy to be educated. After completing school, he moved to Settle to apprentice with a Quaker surgeon.

Although a long time resident of England, Lettsom retained his identity as a West Indian. He later referred to himself as "a volatile Creole, in his nature and essence changeable." A close associate agreed about his volatility, remembering him as "astonishingly active." His friend also commented on Lettsom's skin color, remarking that his "skin was of a dark yellow tint."[1]

Warm-hearted and voluble, Lettsom "loved the conversation of enlightened women." The Quaker concept of unity among Friends provided a Christian context for cross-gender relationships, but his memoirist described his female friendships in more secular terms. According to his biographer, Lettsom was "devotedly, not to say enthusiastically, attached to the company of the fair sex."[2]

While living in Settle, Lettsom, according to his memoirist, "enjoyed an intimate friendship" with Mary Morris. They expressed their friendship in polite social forms and "occasionally interchanged pieces of poetry, in the construction of which, she was much the superior." Like James Jenkins, Lettsom esteemed her abilities. His memoirist noted, "She excelled also in epistolary correspondence." His memoirs also record that, "in her conversation there was a sprightliness and poignancy which riveted and gratified the attention of every hearer."[3]

Yet, Lettsom also commented unfavorably on Morris's dress, a criticism later reinforced by Jenkins. Evidently repeating a remark made by Lettsom, his memoirist wrote that, "She was very careless in her dress, sometimes to an unpleasant degree." Writing years later, Jenkins agreed, reporting that, "all through life, she was noted, and blamed for a slatternly inattention with respect to dress."[4]

While Morris may have been lax in her dress, contemporaries often associated women intellectuals with untidy clothes and even sexual laxity.[5] In *The Tatler*, Isaac Bickerstaff described his sister, Jenny, by saying, "Her Wit she thinks her Distinction therefore knows nothing of the skill of Dress, or making her Person agreeable."[6] Morris had before been likened to Jenny Bickerstaff, and the comments of Lettsom and Jenkins show that these Quakers, too, may have shared some unfavorable popular perceptions about learned women.

Given such mixed assessments and her own previous comments, it may have surprised some when, on 9 July 1767, Mary Morris married Thomas Knowles, the son of a brewer from Knaresborough, Yorkshire. At age 34, Morris was ten years older than the mean age of first marriage for women of her time, and eight years older than the average marital age for English Quaker women.[7] Knowles, one year younger than his bride, worked as an apothecary. He lived, as did his two sisters, in Mildenhall, near Bury St. Edmunds.[8]

Recalling the wedding years later, Jenkins described the bride as "(even then) the celebrated Mary Morris." His use of the term "celebrated" implied a socially acceptable degree of public status for her as an exceptionally talented woman. Even though criticized for their dress, learned women were also often celebrated for their achievements. Contemporaries described the radical writer and historian Catharine Sawbridge Macaulay as the "celebrated Mrs. Macaulay," for example. By using this term to describe Morris, Jenkins indicated that, despite some criticisms, she enjoyed a positive public reputation at the time of her marriage.[9]

Jenkins, perhaps with a twinge of jealousy, described Thomas Knowles, in sharp contrast to his bride's beauty, as "about the middle size, of a thin habit of body, and of an aspect, dark and unpleasing." Moreover, while Mary was a well-known talker, Jenkins termed Thomas "saturnine" and "deficient both in quickness of conception and fluency of expression." Jenkins further stated that, "there was an imbecility of utterance that rendered his powers of conversation, to be rather below, than above, mediocrity."[10]

Although Jenkins's description suggests a mismatch, Morris seems to have found a mate that satisfied both her and her family. Since she and her mother had previously contested what each had considered an unsuitable alliance, they presumably both approved this one. The fact that the marriage took place at Wigginshilll Meeting House, outside Birmingham, where her sister and brother also wed,[11] was another indication of her family's blessing.

Affection and companionship had been important factors in Quaker marriages since the days of Fox and Barclay. The late marriage of George Fox to Margaret Fell demonstrated the importance of spiritual union independent of procreation.[12] Robert Barclay explained divine love in his *Apology* by comparing it to the love of a husband for his wife. When a man is in love, wrote Barclay, "if it has taken a deep enough possession of his heart and mind, it is hard for him to forget it." Furthermore, he explained, the man "will avoid like death itself the things which might offend the beloved."[13]

Yet, one eighteenth-century Quaker female weighed matrimonial affection against the loss of liberty and bemoaned the unequal status of a wife. Preparing for her wedding, a young Quaker contemporary acknowledged her growing affection for her fiancé. Yet she observed, "So this I suppose is the case with other poor women who are cajoled by degrees to lose their liberty, and then they have nothing to do but quietly submit … men and women's lots are so unequal!"[14] These reflections combined with Morris's earlier resistance to matrimony suggest an internal critique of marriage among some Quaker women who cherished liberty.

After her marriage, Mary Morris Knowles jokingly described how her husband's affection counteracted her independent spirit. The newlyweds set up housekeeping in Mildenhall, where "the Doctor," as she called him, traveled frequently in his work as an apothecary. "The Dr. has not been at home one single day since I came here," she complained to a friend soon after her wedding. She confessed in a "sheepish strain" that she craved his company, "to tell thee truth as it were in a whisper, I begin to mutter at the Doctor's busy work schedule." Employing a scientific metaphor, she jokingly confided, "I begin to suspect him of a design, (permit the chemical allegory) of insensibly reducing, that violent acid quality called my own *Will*, to a perfect *neutral* by the fine alkaline of his love."[15]

Mary wryly observed that Thomas's affection for her threatened to overturn some of her earlier opinions about wives. "I must allow thee to smile at my weakness," she wrote her female friend, "because I have formerly said so much about prerogative, fond wives, etc." She mockingly pledged to beware of his affection. "In future I'll endeavour properly to guard against his insinuating tenderness," she wrote. "I'll keep an eye on him," she told her friend, "for if this transmutation happen, what a poor passive machine after all—what a mere smiling *Wife* shall I descend into."[16]

Although Knowles employed humor, her criticism of passive wives evinced the same kind of ambivalent attitude toward some women that feminist historian Barbara Taylor described in the later writing of Mary Wollstonecraft. Like Wollstonecraft, Knowles believed in the possibility of human perfectibility and set high standards for herself as a woman. Yet, at the same time, like Wollstonecraft, Knowles set herself apart from women whom she considered too submissive.[17]

Although Knowles criticized some women, she developed a deep and lasting friendship with Mary Farmer, the only daughter of wealthy Quakers living in Bingley, near Birmingham. Farmer, 18 years her junior, served as one of her bridesmaids. Accompanying the couple to their new home, Farmer evidently teased Knowles about her marriage. "How I miss my two Bride Maids," Knowles wrote Farmer in August 1767, "my household is so still and quiet (no reflexion observed on your innocent raillery and harmless satire on my newly assumed Character)." After Farmer left, Knowles told her, "How gloomy was the remainder of our parting afternoon." Knowles described how "silent and sad, retiring to her chamber, she viewed with her mind's eye ... those dear friends who have laid such a strong hold of my esteem and affections."[18]

Knowles spoke of their friendship in spiritual terms. Referring to Farmer's "observations on the strength of virtuous friendship," Knowles wrote, "for as that divine love from whence it springs, never had a beginning, so neither can it ever cease to Be!" Using her friend's family name, she urged, "Let us then my Polly, in this deathless energy be mutually dear; indulging toward each other the tenderest charity, and remaining one another's beloved in the unchangeable Truth!"[19]

Yet Knowles also discussed current secular ideas of virtue with Farmer. When Farmer told her about a proposed visit to Carlisle, Knowles responded, "O lonely regions of the North how favouring are you to pensive sublime contemplation!" This comment referenced the theory of the sublime and beautiful made popular by Edmund Burke. Like Burke, Knowles linked contemplation of natural beauty to civic virtue and moral behavior. "From this grand school of Nature," she observed, "what champions of the cause of Virtue are ever and anon appearing!"[20]

Now a matron, Knowles struggled, not always successfully, to balance polite sociability and serious-minded spirituality. In April 1768, Knowles wrote Farmer about a visiting Friend who had been "snatched ... out of the torrent of jovial extravagance and festivity to which his lively intellects had nearly overwhelmed him." Yet, immediately after hearing his remarks, Knowles turned her attention to social invitations. She urged two of Farmer's relatives "to come home with us" but "cou'd not prevail on them." She gently mocked the polite excuses they offered. With "one thing or other," Knowles reported somewhat sardonically, "all the etceteras of apologetic particulars were made pleas" in declining her invitation.[21]

Given her sociability, Knowles experienced loneliness as the wife of a busy provincial professional, and she found rural domesticity limiting. "What have I to dwell upon but the domestic round," she confided, "periodical returns of the Dr ... a ceremonious visit, and a solitary walk?" She wondered that, "I whose family consists of only four persons, and totally free from all matters commercial can be so long depriv'd of a sequester'd hour for this pleasing employment" of writing to Farmer. Moreover, living in a small town, she pointed out, "I had not that fund of facts to go upon, which supplies the ready pens of citizens and residents in the busy scenes of populous life and society."[22]

Knowles used her letters to Farmer and her books to keep in touch with the world outside Mildenhall. "Thou canst not tell what a pretty study, I have converted that little bedroom into," she wrote. "Everything was taken out, and I have filled it up with shelves for books, [and a] writing desk under the window." Like other educated provincial women, Knowles's letters linked her to relatives and acquaintances far from her new home. Like them, she read widely and exchanged news and views through her correspondence.[23]

Knowles also maintained her close ties with her brother Joe. In December 1767, she described "the sudden joy and surprise in the sight of an only Brother, and the commotions in my quiet house consequent on such a tart and syllabub visitor." Joe encouraged her independence. As she told Farmer, he "prevail'd on me to accompany him to London." Knowles went but regretted that, "I did not during my short stay there, pay so many visits as I ought to have done." By continuing to travel with her brother after her marriage, she enjoyed greater mobility than some other provincial wives.[24]

Knowles remained close to her younger sister, too, although she knew Etty regarded her as unusual and not quite a model housewife. "She will perhaps with great fluency tell thee," Knowles wrote Farmer, referring to Etty, "she doubts not the oddity of her Sister's contrivances, ... interlarding her oration with many a word and many a wonder how the poor creature is ever able to go on." Knowles anticipated with gentle humor that Etty might also "display a few intermingledoms of pity for poor Tommy," indicating her family's affectionate name for her husband. Knowles anticipated that Farmer might share Etty's views, adding, "poor Tommy! too, perhaps thy little slyness may smilingly re-echo."[25]

Talented and independent-minded, Knowles did not want to become a passive wife, yet her husband's happiness and Farmer's approbation seemed important to her. She told Farmer, for example, how she had been engaged in "pudding make-ing, with the all the rest of the *–ings* proper to be included in the employment of a most notable Housewife!"[26] She invited her friend to "come here and observe the honest man's content and comfortableness." She insisted Farmer would see that for Thomas there could be no rival to "his wonderful, his notable Dame Mary."[27]

By April 1768, Knowles was six months pregnant. She approached having her first child at age 35 with the same good humor that she bestowed on her correspondence and friendships. She feigned to complain to Farmer that her pregnancy made letter writing difficult. She mockingly listed "my excuses now to my Master," evoking the childish complaints a girl might offer an instructor. First on her list was "the disagreeableness of hanging my head so intently over the table and the wearisome steadiness of posture necessary to such ardent work as fine writing."[28]

Yet her mood turned serious as her delivery date drew near, and she honestly committed her thoughts and fears to writing. Two nearly identical manuscript versions survive of a poem she composed in 20 lines of heroic couplets. As with her earlier writings, the carefully preserved copies suggest that she and her friends valued, circulated, and saved her compositions as social texts. One copy is simply labeled, "Wrote by MK a little before the birth of her first child." The other is more dramatically, but perhaps more accurately, entitled, "Written in the Terrors of Approaching Child Birth."[29]

Knowles began her poem by questioning the most fundamental Old Testament female image and asking God if she must suffer for Eve's sin. The two surviving versions of her poem pose the question in slightly, but significantly, different ways. One version reads, "Say thou Almighty Power that rulest above / Must I the pangs unutterable prove / How great the Sin of our First Mother's fall / Whose dire presumption overwhelmed us all?"[30]

The other version gives more emphasis to the goodness of God and the error of Eve. "Say thou all gracious power that Rulest above / Must I the pangs unutterable prove! / How great the sin of our first Mother's Fall / Whose black ingratitude overwhelm'd us all!"[31] These changes indicate that Knowles, as a deeply religious woman, continued to struggle with the Old Testament female image of Eve.

In both versions, Knowles answered dutifully, seeking submission to the Divine Will. "Oh yes I ought! Be contrite then my Soul," she reminded herself, "Let no impatient wish thy faith controul." Finding comfort in her belief in a gracious God, she steeled herself to take courage. "In pious trust of Mercy be thou Strong," she wrote, "Nor let one Murmur 'scape thy faltering Tongue."

In the remainder of the brief verse, she further strengthened herself by remembering the birth and sufferings of Jesus. "Think of those pains and of that place Forlorn," she wrote, "Where Bethlehem's sweet blessed Babe was born." She found comfort in thinking that her pains would produce a child who would follow Jesus. "Pray, then that thine, with whom thou sorrowest now / May all the states of holy Jesus know," she wrote. She imagined the child's salvation, "Till with his holy Lord he mounts on high / Where Morning Stars together sing and Angels shout for joy."[32]

While Knowles sought comfort in writing, the terror expressed in the title of her poem proved justified. On 27 July 1768, Esther Morris wrote Mary Farmer to say that her sister had lost her baby the week before and almost died in a difficult delivery. Esther attended her sister, reporting, "It would require an abler pen than mine to set forth her sufferings." She added, "her early disappointment in losing her lovely Boy, has greatly retarded the return of her spirits." She closed by observing, "had I not seen it, I cou'd not have believed the maternal ties so strong at so early a period."[33]

On 23 August, Knowles wrote Farmer, addressing her in anguish, "O my Polly! I told thee of *Cares* in the matrimonial Life ... but I told thee not of *Pains*." Her worst apprehensions had not prepared her for the pain she experienced. She told Farmer, "I knew not that an immortal spirit could in abide in a body so tortured!" She described "*spasms*, ... every ten minutes, five minutes, two minutes, *for 14 hours together*" that spoke "in the agonizing language of strong convulsion."

Knowles described how, in the midst of her suffering, two friends experienced intimations that she would survive. She told Farmer that as she was being wracked with pain, Rachel Knowles, her sister-in-law, sought help from a neighbor. The "pious widow" told Rachel not to fear for "it hath now arisen in my mind ... that we shall hear your sister is alive and delivered." At the same time, Mary said her brother-in-law "honest John Foote ... was riding to Bury for the Doctor," presumably referring to Thomas who may have been conducting business there. Then, "as near as we can guess about the time of my release," Knowles wrote,

Foote's "grief and prayers for my happiness [were] so taken from him that he wonder'd at the serenity of his mind."

Knowles reported these intimations to Farmer as comforting proof of God's protecting power. "These things I tell thee my very young friend," she wrote, "that thou mayst join with me in delivering praises to that God that underneath—unseen—supported and safely carried me through the valley of the shadow of death." Knowles's near death experience seemed to strengthen her certainty of salvation. Confident in her capacity for goodness, she "thought I was spared to become more pure, to head the heavenly courts with my redeemer."

Knowles told Farmer she wanted to "spare thy sympathizing bosom a circumstantial recital" of all that she had suffered, yet, she also wanted her to appreciate "the transcendent mercy, of my Saviour in that hour." Summoning a powerful New Testament female figure, she recalled that in her suffering, "methought I had fast hold of my Saviour's feet, ... methought like Magdalene I folded my arms around them; and while the Surgeon's cruellest force was exerted, I cried, 'I *will* not let thee go.'" Knowles described how, at that moment, "I *think*, I verily think, I felt the unction of mercy and peace," but "the favor I supposed I felt, is as yet too much for my shattered strength and spirits." Knowles offered this painful account to her young friend as a religious duty. She told her, "This much I have labor'd to say to thee to glorify his Name!"[34]

As Esther indicated, Knowles deeply mourned the death of her son, named Morris, who lived one day.[35] A month later, Knowles still remembered the baby's cries. "Great, unexpectedly great, have been my conflict respecting the beautiful Babe that wise providence has seen meet to resume to himself," she wrote Farmer. "But oh his little plaintive notes from unavoidable and inward injured received during birth are ever in my ears," she sorrowed, asking, "how my Polly shall I get clear of them?" She found some comfort in her conviction that "he is gone hence into happiness ... had he lived to maturity, in spite of all parental care, it might not have been so."[36]

In describing her experience of childbirth, Knowles differed from other contemporary provincial women. In *The Gentleman's Daughter,* Amanda Vickery found that, "Women rarely appear to have committed the details of their labor to paper. At any rate, no detailed accounts of childbirth have survived in the northern records."[37] Perhaps, as Knowles told Farmer, women wanted to spare the sympathies of their female friends. Yet by focusing on the spiritual significance of her pain and loss, Knowles sought to transcend her sufferings and present them to her younger friend as a lesson in religious faith.

In Mildenhall, as in Rugeley, Knowles found friends among non-Quakers, and a local landed family offered her comfort during her recuperation. Knowles told Farmer that she had taken "this morning an airing in a Gentleman's chariot for several miles, sent to me for that purpose by a most agreeable family who spend a few summer months at their country seat here."[38] As the sociable wife of a successful country apothecary, Knowles interacted with this genteel family, not exclusively with Quakers.

When Knowles recovered her health, she faced increasingly demanding family duties. In Mildenhall, she helped care for Rachel Knowles, "a sensible young woman of exemplary piety," in the final stages of consumption.[39] Meanwhile, her sister, Esther Morris, married Samuel Lythall and moved to Hartshill.[40] Soon afterwards, Mary and Thomas Knowles moved to Birmingham, where they shared their home with her mother, Alice Morris.

Birmingham not only offered closer proximity to her mother but also an expanding array of economic, social, and cultural opportunities. A contemporary observed that, "It would be difficult to enumerate the great variety of trades practiced in Birmingham." A new canal contributed to an "amazing augmentation" of the city, including the addition of 71 streets, 4,172 houses, and more than 25,000 inhabitants in less than 40 years. The religiously diverse population encompassed "Church of England, Baptists, Quakers, Methodists, Catholics and Jewish."[41]

In January 1769, Knowles wrote Farmer from Birmingham, saying her household, and along with it, her domestic concerns had greatly increased. "I steal this busy hour from domestic claims, less pleasing *far* than this employ," she told Farmer. Referring first to "my late and present situation of settling a large family etc. etc." and then to "my present confined domestic sphere," Knowles checked herself. "This, in recollection, is the second time I have introduced my busy self in the domestic character," she noted, "but out of the abundance of the heart, the mouth speaketh, says the proverb."

With wry humor, she confided that her mother "and a few ancients like her ... have somehow taken a fancy to suppose I am not so sharp a looker about me in family matters as they were, in their young days etc." That very morning, Knowles continued, "under some imagined omission, in she comes with the words of a satirical Husband, 'Give me a Woman of common sense!' Is this not very hard, Polly?"[42] Although she made light of it, Knowles acknowledged that her mother questioned her abilities as a housewife, and that she, herself, resented the demands of domesticity.

Yet Knowles insisted that she and "the Doctor" enjoyed their life together in Birmingham, describing their affectionate relationship to Farmer. Knowles opened and closed one letter with cheerful sketches of domestic scenes. She began, "At our evening table—retir'd serene and comfortable, sits the Dr and his grave dame." In closing, she wrote, "Tommy insists on having his love sent, tho' I tell him I'm full late for the post and have scarce any paper left, but it does not avail, he will have it, adieu."[43] As this letter indicates, she and her husband enjoyed a comfortable home life and mutual affection whatever her domestic oddities.

Two deaths in her immediate family, however, must have disturbed her domestic life. In October 1769, her sister, Esther Morris Lythall, died at age 32, leaving her husband and a young son, named Morris Lythall. In September 1770, her mother died at age 71.[44] Alice Morris had raised her three children alone since the death of her husband, Moses Morris, 30 years before. She nurtured Mary's independence through education but sometimes questioned her daughter's unconventional ways. Despite their differences, Knowles evinced a genuine affection for her mother.

Thomas and Mary Knowles continued to live in Birmingham after her mother's death, although little evidence has been located for this period of their lives. As in Mildenhall, Mary wrote neoclassic poetry and entertained visitors. An undated manuscript verse attributed to her, comparing rural beauty to life in Birmingham, may have been written during this time.

Entitled "To T. and I. D. on their intended Visit to Warwickshire," Knowles described the countryside to prospective visitors in heroic couplets in a formal and somewhat stilted style. "Warwick's fair land will then delight your Eye," she wrote, "Whose Hills and Dales in richest prospect lie." Knowles contrasted this idealized scene with the realities of life in Birmingham. She depicted the city as "The gloomy Birmingham involved in smoke / Sounds with her hammers loud incessant stroke." Yet, she recognized the benefits of urban life, writing, "Genius and art upon her labors smile / And golden affluence reward her Toil."

Knowles combined her appreciation of the rural landscape and her understanding of urban economic reality into a meditation on the importance of religious faith. She asked, "Yet what is Earthly Beauty, Wealth or pow'r?" In answer, she concluded, "Let mortal man to heav'n his views extend / Where wrongs, disease and Sorrow have an end! / To joys which tongues of Angels fail to tell / Where just Men's souls made perfect ever dwell."[45] In this verse, as with much of her social behavior, Knowles combined Quaker faith with popular practices to fashion new forms of polite Quakerliness.

Knowles also continued to practice her needlework at a time when British arts in many forms flourished under the patronage of King George III and Queen Charlotte. The king favored the high-minded historical paintings of the American-born artist, Benjamin West. The queen took a special interest in art made by women. In 1768, for example, she helped establish a needlework school for women at Ampthill in Buckinghamshire.[46]

Highly skilled needlework artists, like Knowles, practiced specialized forms such as "printwork." According to expert Margaret Swain, printwork consisted of "Pictures drawn on to a silk or fine linen background ... worked in lines of fine black silk to suggest engravings."[47] An early twentieth-century historian described needlework by Knowles as "exact copies of line engraving done with black silk on white satin. Until one examined them closely," wrote this historian, "one thought they were engravings."[48] Despite this testimony to her talents, no surviving pieces of printwork by Knowles have been located.

Perhaps inspired by printwork, talented embroidery artists in the late 1760s and early 1770s began developing a new art form known as needle painting. Needle painting replicated the appearance of a painted subject through crewel embroidery, using worsted wool stitches to represent brush strokes. In this kind of embroidery, as in other forms of needlework demanding a very high level of skill, the artist aspired to outstanding achievement through the execution of her stitches rather than by the originality of her design.[49]

Needle painting changed the course of Knowles's life when she undertook such a project for the king and queen. Benjamin West may have been her link with the royal family. Although probably not a Quaker himself, West came from a Pennsylvania family with Quaker connections. After studying in Europe, West settled permanently in England, where he had many Quaker associates.[50]

In 1771, according to two secondary sources, West showed Queen Charlotte some fine needlework done by Knowles.[51] According to a later publication, Knowles's "perfection" in needlework "procured an introduction to the Queen."[52] Another writer said that the queen, after seeing Knowles's work, asked if she could render a needle painting of a recent portrait of the king. Confident in her own abilities, Knowles agreed, "though she had never seen anything of the kind."[53]

By agreeing to produce a needle painting of the king, Knowles revealed differences in Quaker attitudes concerning portraiture. Although early Quaker leaders like Fox and William Penn refused to have their portraits made, the Quaker organization did not prohibit portraiture. In colonial America, wealthy Friends in Philadelphia commissioned and sat for portraits throughout the eighteenth century.[54] Noted art scholar Marcia Pointon, however, found no evidence of an English equivalent to American Quaker portraiture.[55] Since portraiture remained problematic for English Quakers, Knowles's ready acceptance of the queen's request indicates not only her artistic self-confidence but also her expanded view of acceptable Quaker participation in the visual arts.

Knowles agreed to replicate a portrait by the German-born court painter, Johann Zoffany. As described by royal curator Oliver Millar, Zoffany's three-quarter length figure of George III showed the king "seated, in a General officer's coat with the ribbons and star of the Garter, wearing the Garter round his leg; his hat and sword" resting on a nearby table. The painting, completed in 1771, portrayed the king, at age 33, with a steady serious gaze, a ruddy healthy face, and a calm assured demeanor.[56]

To accomplish her needlework copy, Knowles would first have had to transfer the design of the painting onto material, either by creating some sort of grid or sketching it directly onto the cloth. Then, she could set to work using a frame, employed by only the most expert needle women because of the difficulty of preparing or "dressing" it.[57] Working on the same scale as Zoffany, Knowles used worsted wool, making large stitches for the background and smaller ones of flesh-colored tones for the face and hands

When she completed her needle painting, Knowles stitched her initials, "MK," and the date, "1771," in one corner (Illustration One). According to a contemporary, the king and queen pronounced the work to be to their "entire satisfaction." The royal family placed the needle painting on display at Kew Palace where it remained for more than 200 years.[58]

Illustration 1 Mary Morris Knowles, *George III* [after Zoffany], 82.6 in x 66.1 in, embroidery, 1771, The Royal Collection.

Whatever celebrity Knowles might have known previously, her fame now quickly multiplied. The *Birmingham Gazette* published news of the needle painting, although not mentioning her by name. "There is lately finished," the *Gazette* reported, "by a Lady of this Town, a Portrait of his Majesty in Needlework." According to the report, her work was "allowed by the Connoisseurs to be the greatest curiosity ever seen of the kind, being the closest likeness to his Majesty, and so highly finished, that it has all the softness and effect of Painting."[59]

Reflecting this increasing public recognition, a London printer published her poetic exchange as "Lavinia" with "Clericus." In 1771, J. Fry and Company in Queen Street, near Upper Moorfields, produced the verses in a three-column broadside under the title, *A Compendium of a Controversy on Water-Baptism*. This publication, like the *Birmingham Gazette*, did not name her. It identified the protagonists only as "A Clergyman" and "A Quaker."[60] Still, her manuscript defense of Quaker beliefs entered the public sphere.

Even more importantly, in the course of completing her needle painting, Knowles gained the friendship of the king and queen. As a polite and well-educated Quaker, Knowles shared many of the values cultivated by the royal family. The serious-minded George III often allied himself socially with members of the middle classes, like her, rather than more worldly aristocrats. The queen, according to a later publication, "was no less pleased with the beauty of her performances, than with the justness and solidity of her remarks."[61]

With her access to royalty came the ability to seek political favors, and a cousin asked Knowles to petition the king on behalf of a friend. Dr. John Fell of Ulverstone, to whom she addressed her "Memoirs of M. M., spinster of this parish," requested her assistance. Because of her close bond with him and his wife, Knowles approached the king and queen, although reluctantly.

"Cautious as I wd ever be of asking favors; for yr sakes, my kind relations, I put the letter in my pocket, and took it with me to court one even'g," she wrote Fell. "I ventur'd to read what seem'd proper and necessary for your friend," she continued, "for which freedom I had no ungracious inattention." While they listened carefully, the royal family referred her to a government department. She "soon found the Admiralty Office was the place where such applications were to be made," she explained to her cousin.

By then, Knowles had become familiar with the ways of the court and received many such petitions. "My cousin w'd smile," she told him, "did he know what abundance of requests I have had from people on behalf of themselves and their friends." The first question always posed by the king and queen, she informed him, inquired whether those asking for favors had "personal knowledge" of the petitioner. If not, they likely concluded that, "one thinks it is a light matter to ask their favours." Knowles confided she had already "refus'd to more than I chuse to mention," observing that, "Those who tread in Courts tread in slippery places."[62]

Knowles's letter provides a written example of the usually verbal requests for patronage and indicates that, like elite females, Knowles, as a well-placed middling woman, engaged in seeking a royal favor. Well-connected aristocratic females, like their male counterparts, used their social access to make requests, usually oral, for places, pensions, preferments, and other forms of patronage.[63] Like them, Knowles used her social access to seek a political favor and exercise real, although in this case unsuccessful, political power.

In her letter to Dr. Fell, Knowles also indicated that she, herself, would receive a payment from court, and she struggled with the idea of becoming a dependent. Using long-standing radical language equating a state payment with government control, she announced, "I am to depart from a state of independence." She assured her cousin of her devotion to liberty, however, by saying, "I hope, through divine assistance, never to be a slave, so that my connexion there shall be not to make a mean use of the favor of that smiling countenance they wear towards me."[64]

In this statement, Knowles combined her religious beliefs and her commitment to political liberty. To her, a slave represented both political and religious servitude. In her earlier verses to Clericus, she presented Quakers as unenslaved by theocracy. Now she expressed her personal determination never to be a slave to the power of the Crown. By cherishing liberty and equating court patronage with dependence, Knowles shared the views of contemporary radicals like Catharine Sawbridge Macaulay. In her recently published *Observations on a Pamphlet Entitled Thoughts on the Cause of the Present Discontents*, for example, Macaulay condemned the "profligate junto of courtiers, supported by the mere authority of the crown, against the liberties of the constitution."[65] Knowles's letter to Dr. Fell showed her reluctance to follow the example of such courtiers.

While Mary Knowles weighed her financial gain against the loss of independence, the payment she received transformed the life of her husband. By the end of 1771, Thomas Knowles left his apothecary business in Birmingham to study medicine at the University of Edinburgh. Quakers could study at the university, then becoming "the premier medical school for English speaking students," but they could not take a degree there.[66]

On 1 November 1771, Jonathan Binns, a Quaker studying at Edinburgh, wrote his brother about the arrival of Thomas. "If you have not heard you may wonder that he is come to study physic," Binns wrote. Binns continued, "he is come to graduate, & this we suppose is occasioned by his wife having executed such a royal performance as the King's picture in needlework."[67]

Binns further reported that Mary remained in England to visit the queen. "Thou'l remember he married Mally Morris," Binns reminded his brother, using a form of her family name. Thomas "would have brot her along with him but that she is to go to wait upon the Queen in the latter end of winter," Binns continued, "and after that we are to expect her."[68]

When Mary went to London to await her audience with the queen, she socialized with Edward Dilly, publisher, bookseller, Dissenter, and radical Whig. The second son of a solid Bedfordshire family, Edward moved to London and become "a bookseller of great eminence 'particularly in the line of American exportation.'"[69] His home, located above his shop at Number 22 in the Poultry, served, according to a later historian, as "a gathering place for leaders of the radical City of London."[70] Edward especially relished the company of the radical writer, Catharine Sawbridge Macaulay. According to a rather pointed remark by an unnamed contemporary, Edward greatly admired the "politics (if not the personal charms) of Catharine Macaulay."[71]

Known as "an ardent Whig," Edward impressed a young female visitor as "one of the greatest talkers I ever met." She described Edward's "tongue, hands, and head all moving at a time with so much rapidity that I wonder how his lungs sustain it." "Politics," she concluded, constituted his "constant theme."[72]

Edward shared his business and his home with his younger brother, Charles Dilly, who visited the American colonies before becoming a partner in the thriving bookshop. Although successful business partners, the bachelor brothers differed significantly in temperament and politics. In sharp contrast to the vivid portrait of the effusive Edward, their country visitor termed Charles "a modest, genteel behaved man."[73] Charles expressed fondness for his brother but deplored his politics. "My brother is really a good natured and well disposed man," he wrote a friend, "but he is dreadfully contaminated with false ideas in politics.[74]

On 19 March 1772, Knowles accompanied Edward Dilly to his home, where she first encountered James Boswell, just arrived from Scotland. The brothers published Boswell's highly successful *Account of Corsica*, and they maintained a close relationship with him. Combining business and hospitality, they frequently provided lodging for Boswell as well as other literary visitors.

Boswell noted in his journal that he dined with Charles, and "in a little, in came my friend, Mr. Edward Dilly," adding, "along with him was Mrs. Knowles, famous for her needlework." Aware of her fame, Boswell recorded further details about her. He noted that she "did a head of the King for which the Queen made her a *present* of £800 but said her work was invaluable."[75]

Boswell indicated that the queen presented this payment as a gift, not a commission, stressing her personal, rather than financial, relationship with Knowles. Although no official record of payment to Knowles has been found, the king and queen often paid artists liberally. The amount mentioned by Boswell corresponds with the sums received by two other female artists. Queen Charlotte, described as having "boundless generosity," paid Mary Moser "upwards of 900L" for her painted flowers. Mary Granville Delaney, who made magnificent cutout flowers, received a house at Windsor and £300 per year from the royal couple.[76]

With a well-practiced eye for female features, Boswell further described, Knowles, now nearing 40, and her husband Thomas. He noted that, "upon his wife's getting this kind of interest at Court," Thomas "bethought himself of commencing physician" and was "now actually studying at Edinburgh to take his degrees." Attentive to her appearance and social charms although seven years her junior, Boswell added, "She was formerly a distinguished beauty and still looked very well, and was a clever agreeable woman."[77]

A few weeks later, Knowles left London to join her husband in Edinburgh. Soon after her arrival, she wrote her cousin, John Fell, but had little to say about the Scottish capital. "I arrived here about 2 weeks ago," she reported briefly, "you have heard too many descriptions of Edin. for me to enter upon it."[78] Knowles might have shared some of the negative views expressed by contemporaries about the northern kingdom. In an earlier letter, she referred unfavorably to "bleak Caledonia."[79] Since Thomas studied in Scotland for less than a year, Mary probably spent only a few months in Edinburgh in early 1772.

In June, Thomas and Mary set out for the University at Leyden where he could take his degree. Joined by Thomas's fellow student Jonathan Binns, the three crossed the Channel, stopping briefly to see The Hague. Arriving in Leyden, Thomas, like all students, submitted a thesis in Latin. His *Tentamen medicum inaugurale de vita sedentaria* was published later that year. In July, Binns wrote his brother, "At Leyden we have had the pleasure of putting frd Knowles a feather in his cap, viz. To make him a lawful Doctor of Physic."[80]

Degree in hand, Thomas and Mary set off on what was later described as "a scientific tour through Holland, Germany, and France."[81] On 12 August 1772, the two jointly wrote a lively letter to Thomas's sister, Tabitha, and her husband, John Foote. Thomas reported that they visited the "fam'd Spa," a popular destination for wealthy British travelers, and then traveled through the Austrian Netherlands to Paris. Delighting in French recipes, Mary wrote in mock pity to her brother and sister-in-laws, "poor *English* things ... can you make a pie of grapes, artichokes, and whole crawfish?" She would share this recipe, she teased, and "many others I may communicate if I find you are sufficiently thankful for these." She added that Thomas was already treating English patients in France.[82]

Since Mary had been presented at the British court, according to a later publication, she and her husband "obtained introductions to the most distinguished personages, such as the Prince and Princess of Orange, [and] at Versailles, the Messieurs and Mesdames of the Royal Family." According to the same publication, Mary "was admitted to the toilette" of Queen Marie Antoinette "by her own desire." The queen "was politely earnest for information" concerning Quaker principles. Impressed with the answers given by Knowles, the French queen "acknowledged these heretics to be philosophers at least."[83]

Returning to England, Mary and Thomas Knowles relocated to London, where two Quaker colleagues had already established highly successful medical careers. John Fothergill, also educated at Edinburgh and Leyden, had become one of the most respected and well-paid physicians in the city. Fothergill acquired a country estate with a large botanical garden and a fortune later estimated at £80,000.[84] John Coakley Lettsom, too, Mary's old friend from Settle, studied at Edinburgh and Leyden and moved to London. The energetic Lettsom became a close friend of Fothergill and quickly acquired many patients and projects.[85]

Mary and Thomas Knowles moved to Great Tower Street, parish of Saint Dunstan's in the east, where, on 5 March 1773, she gave birth to a boy. This time, the delivery seemed untroubled.[86] The couple named the boy George in honor of the king.[87]

A month later, on 7 April 1773, Thomas and Mary joined the nearby Devonshire House Meeting, which numbered 200 Quaker families at mid-century.[88] They produced a certificate of removal from Edinburgh stating that, "the said Thos Knowles and his wife Mary during their residence here conducted themselves commendably, are free from debt, and we are in full unity with them." The Devonshire House Monthly Meeting accepted the certificate, meaning the couple could participate fully in gatherings for worship and in the separate meetings for business for men and women Friends.[89]

On 26 May 1773, Thomas Knowles became a member of the newly established Medical Society in London.[90] John Coakley Lettsom had recently founded the Medical Society to bring together physicians, surgeons and apothecaries into one professional association for the first time. According to a modern expert, "The Medical Society redefined professional relationships in ways which saw cooperation as the first step towards improvement."[91]

Within another year, Thomas Knowles became a Licentiate of the Royal College of Physicians. Fellows of the Royal College had to be graduates of an English university, but the college admitted a limited number of licentiates trained elsewhere. Doctors Fothergill and Lettsom had earlier become licentiates, but the college had recently tightened its rules. Licentiates were now required to study at a university and be examined on Galen, Hippocrates, and other classical texts. At the same time, the college excluded midwives and apothecaries.[92] By joining the Royal College, Thomas entered the highest ranks of the English medical profession.

Meanwhile, Mary practiced her sociability with Quakers living near London. On 7 October 1773, her kinsman, William Forster, a Quaker schoolmaster in Tottenham, wrote his sister Elizabeth in Birmingham about meeting Knowles. "She far exceeds my Expectations in a chearful easy Behavior and in her many Great Qualifications," he told his sister, "which made her Co. truly agreeable." As for the baby, "we think him an extra fine Boy." Forster added, "They proposed taking a House here early in the Spring," suggesting that the family would acquire a second home in Tottenham, a popular retreat for prosperous London Quakers.[93]

In addition to these social activities, Mary Knowles continued to read and think deeply about religion, commenting on a highly charged theological controversy within the Church of England. In 1772, more than 200 Anglican clergy petitioned Parliament to excuse them from subscribing to the required Thirty-Nine Articles of Faith because of its language concerning the divinity of Christ. When members of the House of Commons soundly rejected the petition, Theophilus Lindsay, a leader of the Anglican dissidents, resigned his living, forfeiting his guaranteed income. Lindsay later became a Rational Dissenter and founded the Essex Street Chapel in London, where he developed a liturgy stressing the unitarian nature of God.

Dr. John Calder, the overseer of Dr. Williams's Library in London, a major collection for Dissenters' publications, indicated his respect for Mary as a serious thinker by seeking her opinion concerning Lindsay and his liturgy. In April 1775, Knowles returned a book lent her by Calder and answered his inquiry about Lindsay and his new form of worship. In a formal letter referring to herself in the third person, Knowles wrote, "She thinks Lindsay's sacrifice an ample testimony of his *honesty* at least," alluding to his forfeiture of income when he no longer supported the doctrines of the established church.

Yet Knowles questioned whether Lindsay addressed the form or the substance of religion with his new liturgy. She asked Calder, "Does he do more than substitute one outward body of worship, or form of *words*, for another?" Knowles argued, as Barclay had done in his *Apology*, that the true nature of incarnate divinity could not be known through human reason. "It appears to me the truest wisdom to steer our course between the extremes of Athanasius and Arius," she observed, referring to the conflicting theories advanced by these early churchmen regarding the divinity of Christ. "To take upon us to ascertain this high, sacred, and mysterious distinction is a work we are utterly incapable of," she explained.

Knowles expressed sympathy for Lindsay but maintained her belief in the spiritual presence of Christ within. She told Calder, "May this honest well-intending man bring his flock nearer to the substance and *vital* part—to the gift of grace, or spirit of Jesus Christ in their hearts ... is my anxious wish." For her, Christians should live by this divine spirit, "thereby to regulate their lives in more purity and holiness." This was, as she told Calder, "(all Theology is good for), or at least all the Christian Religion is good for." She ended her letter by stating, "Were the *substance* more known in the world, we should soon get to great unity and simplicity in *form*."[94]

Writing to Calder in the polite language of social formality, Knowles stressed the spiritual content rather than the form of Christianity. By addressing substance over form, she effectively presented her views to someone who did not share her Quaker beliefs. By presenting her views in nonsectarian language rather than using the distinctive Quaker language, such as *thee* and *thou*, she furthered serious religious discourse among Dissenters.

While Mary found her place among religious intellectuals, her family settled in a new home. By 1775, Mary, Thomas, and George Knowles lived at Number Four, Fenchurch Street, where the doctor combined his office with their home. He continued to develop his practice and actively participate in the medical reform movement as a member of the London Medical Society.[95]

As Mary Morris Knowles approached 43, she proved to be remarkably mobile, both geographically and socially, moving from Rugeley to royalty in less than ten years. She became a successful wife and mother while creating her own forms of domesticity. As a polite Quaker, she participated in popular social and cultural practices but maintained her deep spiritual convictions. Having changed her life through her talents and connections, she continued to redefine roles for women within what she called the confined domestic sphere.

Through her art, Knowles also gained fame and public recognition. With it came access to power, and she sought royal patronage even as she struggled to protect her independence. Moving to the capital, she expanded her connections to include influential men like the radical Whig bookseller, Edward Dilly, and religious scholar, Dr. John Calder. Through influential friendships and social interactions like these, she entered into the cultural transformations changing public life in late eighteenth-century London.

Notes

1 Thomas Joseph Pettigrew, ed., *Memoirs of the Life and Writings of the late John Coakley Lettsom* (3 vols, London, 1817), vol. 1, p. 172.
2 Ibid., p. 39.
3 Ibid., pp.154–5, 17.
4 Ibid., p.19. *Records and Recollections of James Jenkins*, p. 454.
5 Myers, *Bluestocking Circle*, p. 4.
6 Bond, *The Tatler*, p. 515.
7 Vickery, *Gentleman's Daughter*, pp. 307–8. Larson, *Daughters of Light*, p. 135.
8 Public Record Office, RG 6, 1091, "Knaresborough Monthly Meeting." Library of the Religious Society of Friends, "Quarterly Meeting of Warwickshire, Leicestershire and Rutland, Digest of Marriages."
9 *Records and Recollections of James Jenkins*, p. 201. Harriet Guest, *Small Change: Women, Learning, Patriotism, 1750–1810* (Chicago, 2000), p. 101. Bridget Hill, *The Republican Virago: The Life and Times of Catharine Macaulay, Historian* (Oxford, 1992), p. 16.
10 *Records and Recollections of James Jenkins*, pp. 201–02.
11 Public Record Office, RG 6, 1461, "Wigginshill Meeting from 1699."
12 Larson, *Daughters of Light*, p. 138.
13 *Barclay's Apology*, p. 411.
14 Betty Fothergill (1752–1809) in John Fothergill Crosfield, *The Crosfield Family* (privately printed, 1980), p. 61.
15 Library of the Religious Society of Friends, Temporary MSS 403 [Braithwaite Papers], Box 7, Packet 15, File 3, Number 35, "To James Farmer, Birmingham, for M. F. 8th 28 1767."
16 Ibid.
17 Taylor, *Wollstonecraft*, pp.17–19.
18 Library of the Religious Society of Friends, Dictionary of Quaker Biography, "Mary Farmer Lloyd (1751? – 1821)." Braithwaite Papers, 7, 15, 3, 35, "8th 28, 1767."
19 Ibid.
20 Braithwaite Papers, 7, 15, 3, 36, "To James Farmer, Birmingham, For M. Farmer, Mildenhall, 12th mo 7 1767."
21 Braithwaite Papers, 7, 15, 3, 39, "To James Farmer, Nr Birmingham, For M. Farmer, p. London, Mildenhall, 4th 5th /68."
22 Ibid.
23 Braithwaite Papers, 7, 15, 3, 35, "8th 28 1767." Vickery, *Gentleman's Daughter*, p. 287.

24 Braithwaite Papers, 7, 15, 3, 36, "12th mo 7 1767." Vickery, *Gentleman's Daughter*, p. 266.
25 Braithwaite Papers, 7, 15, 3, 39, "4th 5th /68."
26 Braithwaite Papers, 7, 15, 3, 35, "8th 281767."
27 Braithwaite Papers, 7, 15, 3, 39, "4th 5th /68."
28 Ibid.
29 Braithwaite Papers, 7, 15, 3, 33, "Wrote by MK a little before the birth of her first Child." Library of the Religious Society of Friends, Portfolio MSS 6, No. 58, "Written in the Terrors of Approaching Childbirth 1768 by Mary Knowles."
30 Portfolio MSS 6, 58, "Written in Terrors."
31 Braithwaite Papers, 7, 15, 3, 33, "Wrote by MK."
32 Ibid.
33 Braithwaite Papers, 7, 15, 3, 30, "James Farmer / Birmingham P. London / For M. Farmer E. Morris / Mildenhall 7mo 27 68."
34 Braithwaite Papers, 7, 15, 3, 37, "Mildenhall 8mo 23d 68."
35 Library of the Religious Society of Friends, "Suffolk Quarterly Meeting Digest Register of Burials," 7th mo 21 1768.
36 Braithwaite Papers, 7, 15, 3, 37, "Mildenhall 8mo 23d 68."
37 Vickery, *Gentleman's Daughter*, p. 102.
38 Braithwaite Papers, 7, 15, 3, 37, "Mildenhall 8mo 23d 68."
39 *Records and Recollections of James Jenkins*, p. 202. "Suffolk Quarterly Meeting Digest Register of Burials," 11 10th 1770.
40 Library of the Religious Society of Friends, "Quarterly Meeting of Warwickshire, Leicestershire and Rutland Digest Register of Marriages, 11 mo 10 day 1768."
41 W. Hutton, *An History of Birmingham to the End of the Year 1780* (Birmingham, 1781), pp. 45, 73. *The Birmingham Directory* (Birmingham, 1777), p. xxxv.
42 Braithwaite Papers, 7, 15, 3, 40, "David Barclay jun. Mercht, London, for M. Farmer, Birmingham, 1st mo 31 1769."
43 Ibid.
44 Library of the Religious Society of Friends, "Quarterly Meeting for Warwickshire, Leicestershire and Rutland, Digest Register of Burials," 10 mo 7 day, 1769, 9 mo 16 day 1770.
45 Braithwaite Papers, 7, 15, 3, 29, "To T and I D on their intended Visit into Warwickshire. MK."
46 Oliver Millar, *The Later Georgian Pictures in the Collection of Her Majesty the Queen* (2 vols, London, 1969), vol. 1, pp. 86–8. Pamela Warner, *Embroidery: A History* (London, 1991), pp. 127–39.
47 Margaret Swain, *Embroidered Georgian Pictures* (Princes Risborough, Buckinghamshire, 1994), pp. 4–5.
48 James Johnston, Abraham, *Lettsom: His Life, Times, Friends and Descendants* (London, 1933), p. 69.
49 Swain, *Embroidered Georgian Pictures*, pp. 18–21. Warner, *Embroidery*, pp. 127–39. Margaret Swain, *Figures on Fabric: Embroidery design sources and their application*, (London, 1980), p. 11.
50 Charles Henry Hart, "Benjamin West's Family: The American President of the Royal Academy of Arts Not A Quaker," *Pennsylvania Magazine of History and Biography*, (1908): 1–25.

51 Bernard and Therle Hughes, "An Artist in Needlework." Swain, *Embroidered Georgian Pictures*, pp. 19–20.
52 *Lady's Monthly Museum*, November 1803: 289.
53 Mrs. [Mary] Pilkington, *Memoirs of Celebrated female Characters Who Have Distinguished Themselves By Their Talents and Virtues in Every Age and Nation* (London, 1804), pp. 218–9.
54 Dianne C. Johnson, "Living in the Light: Quakerism and Colonial Portraiture," in Lapsansky and Verplanck (eds), *Quaker Aesthetics*, pp. 122–46.
55 Marcia Pointon, "Quakerism and Visual Culture, 1650-1800," *Art History*, 20/3 (1997): 142.
56 Millar, *Georgian Pictures*, p. 148.
57 Swain, *Figures on Fabric*, p. 11.
58 Swain, *Embroidered Georgian Pictures*, pp. 19–20. *Lady's Monthly Museum*, November, 1803: 289.
59 John Alford Langford, ed., *A Century of Birmingham Life* (2 vols, Birmingham, 1868), vol. 1, p. 151.
60 Library of the Religious Society of Friends, *A Compendium of a Controversy on Water-Baptism, Between a Clergyman and a Quaker* in Tracts, Vol. C, number 48.
61 Pilkington, *Memoirs of Celebrated Female Characters*, pp. 218–19.
62 Temporary MSS 28, 7, 4, "Cousin M. Knowles / Dr. Fell, Ulverstone near Lanc."
63 Elaine Chalus, "'To Serve My Friends': Women and Political Patronage in Eighteenth-Century England."
64 Temporary MSS 28, 7, 4, "Cousin M. Knowles."
65 Catharine Macaulay, *Observations on a Pamphlet Entitled Thoughts on the Cause of the Present Discontents* (London, 1770), p. 7.
66 Adrian Wilson, "The Politics of Medical Improvement in early Hanoverian London," in Andrew Cunningham and Roger French, (eds), *The Medical Enlightenment of the Eighteenth Century* (Cambridge, 1990), pp. 40–57.
67 George Jonathan Binns, "A Short Account of the Life of Jonathan Binns, M. D." Typescript, Liverpool City Library, p. 42.
68 Ibid.
69 *Gentleman's Magazine*, May 1807: 478–80.
70 Lyman Butterfield, "The American Interests in the Firm of E. and C. Dilly, with their letters to Benjamin Rush, 1770–1795," *The Papers of the Bibliographical Society of America*, vol. 45 (1951), pp. 285–6, 292.
71 *Gentleman's Magazine*, May 1807: 478–80.
72 Crosfield, *Crosfield Family*, p. 63.
73 Ibid.
74 Butterfield, "The American Interests in the Firm of E. and C. Dilly," p. 292.
75 William Wimsatt, Jr. and Frederick A. Pottle, eds, *Boswell for the Defense, 1769–1774* (New York, 1959), p. 36.
76 Olwen Hedley, *Queen Charlotte* (London, 1975), pp. 95, 132. Frank Prochaska, *Royal Bounty: The Making of a Welfare Monarchy* (New Haven, 1995), pp. 17, 37.
77 *Boswell for the Defense*, p. 36
78 Temporary MSS 28, 7, 4, "Cousin M. Knowles."
79 Braithwaite Papers, 7, 15, 3, 36, "12thmo 7 1767."
80 Binns, "Short Account," p. 46.

81 *Lady's Monthly Museum*, November 1803: 289–90.
82 Haverford, Pa, Haverford College Library, Quaker Collection, "Thos and Mary Knowles to J. Foote, Mildenhall, 1772."
83 *Lady's Monthly Museum*, November 1803: 289–90
84 R. Hingston Fox, *Dr. John Fothergill and His Friends: Chapters in Eighteenth-Century Life* (London, 1919), p. 21. *Gentleman's Magazine*, April 1781: 165–7.
85 Pettigrew, *Memoirs of John Coakley Lettsom*. Abraham, *Lettsom*, pp. 70, 78–95.
86 Public Record Office, RG 6, 329, "Births of the People of God called Quakers in and about the City of London and Westminster, the County of Middlesex and the Borough of Southwark," vol. 3, 1773.
87 Wilson Armistead, *Select Miscellanies* (6 vols, London, 1851), vol. 4, p. 169.
88 William Beck and T. Frederick Ball, *The London Friends' Meetings* (London, 1869), pp. 169–72.
89 Library of the Religious Society of Friends, "Devonshire House Monthly Meeting Book of Certificates," vol. 1, p. 131. "Minutes of the Devonshire House Monthly Meeting," vol. 9, "7th 4th 1773."
90 Thomas Hunt, ed., *The Medical Society of London, 1773-1973* (London, 1972), pp.1–6.
91 Robert Kilpatrick, "Dispensaries, Philanthropy, and Reform," in Cunningham and French, (eds), *The Medical Enlightenment of the Eighteenth Century*, p. 271.
92 Sir George Clark, *A History of the Royal College of Physicians of London* (3 vols, Oxford, 1966), vol. 2, pp. 554–72.
93 *Journal of the Friends Historical Society* (1924): 72. Dictionary of Quaker Biography, "William Forster (1747 – 1824)." Theodore Compton, *Recollections of Tottenham Friends and the Forster Family* (London, 1893).
94 John Nichols, *Illustrations of the Literary History of Eighteenth-Century London* (8 vols, London, 1822), vol. 4, pp. 830–31.
95 Katharine Backhouse, ed., "A Memoir of Mary Capper," in William Evans and Thomas Evans, eds, *The Friends' Library* (14 vols, Philadelphia, 1848) vol. 12, pp. 5–6. *The New Complete Guide to All Persons Who Have Any Trade or Concern with the City of London and Parts Adjacent* 14th edn, 1775.

Chapter 3

Confronting Samuel Johnson

On 15 May 1776, Mary Knowles met Samuel Johnson at a dinner party at the home of Edward and Charles Dilly. By then, the brothers' dining room had become the gathering place for one of the most influential literary coteries in London.[1] On this occasion, a surprising combination of guests included several leading radicals. As a polite and well-connected Quaker, Knowles discussed religion and other subjects with Johnson and with men and women of various faiths in this and other social settings. She enjoyed a wide circle of acquaintances and befriended Jane Harry, a young Jamaican-born woman, whose origins and upbringing reflected "the politics of complexion."[2] The two very different women shared a talent for art, and Harry confided her religious doubts to Knowles. At another dinner at Dillys' in April 1778, Boswell noted that Knowles disputed with Johnson about women's liberty and defended Harry's decision to leave the Church of England. Afterwards, Knowles claimed that Boswell did not fully record her dialogue with Johnson. She insisted that she had confronted Johnson concerning his attitudes toward Quakers and defended Harry's moral agency to choose her religion. Moreover, Knowles cited another participant as saying that she had chafed the mighty literary lion.

According to a contemporary, Edward and Charles Dilly were "zealous in cultivating the friendship of the literati," probably for both social and commercial reasons. The same contemporary later recalled that their "parties were not large, but they were frequent; and in general so judiciously grouped, as to create a pleasantry of intercourse not often to be found in mixed companies."[3] By mixed companies, the observer seems to mean that the bachelor brothers invited women and men of varied religious and political views. As later chronicled by James Boswell, the guests often discussed recent publications, political events, and social news.

Literary scholar Robert DeMaria, Jr., described Dillys' dining room as the scene of an influential literary coterie because the guests who gathered there helped shape the taste and set the tone for the increasingly important production and consumption of print.[4] While only invited guests could participate, the opinions expressed by the influential participants could assume a larger public significance. Neither entirely private nor wholly public and sometimes including both women and men, Dillys' dining room can be considered an associative social space, an adaptation of a term suggested by historian Lawrence Klein.[5]

In the spring of 1776, as Boswell wrote in his account published later, Edward Dilly invited him to join "some of what he calls his patriotick friends" for dinner.

The meaning of the word *patriot* changed over the course of the long eighteenth century, as has been noted. Judging by the guest list, Edward Dilly seems to have applied the term to supporters of the American colonies at a time when tensions with Britain reached the breaking point. John Wilkes, chief among the guests, had returned to London, where he remained a radical leader and upheld the claims of the colonists to determine their own taxation. Arthur Lee, another expected visitor, was an American and a strong ally of Wilkes. Lee "studied physick at Edinburgh" and linked English radicals with those demanding liberty in America.[6]

Dr. John Coakley Lettsom, Mary Knowles's longtime friend and her husband's medical colleague, was another invited guest. Although the Quaker organization advised Friends to eschew partisan politics, Lettsom seems to have been allied with the radical Whigs. As his memoirist later explained, Lettsom "appeared strongly attached to what are usually denominated Whig principles." Writing decades later, after the French Revolution, the memoirist added, "He was a Whig of the old school ... a Friend of Reform but respectful of Monarchy and Aristocracy."[7]

Boswell, on an extended visit in England, was also invited to attend. Distracted by the pleasures of London, he neglected his journal keeping from mid-April through mid-June 1776,[8] but, years later, he revealed that he persuaded Dilly to include Johnson in this dinner. Boswell wanted to invite Johnson so that he could observe his reaction to meeting Wilkes. As Boswell later aptly observed, "Two men more different could perhaps not be selected out of all mankind."[9]

Johnson's responses to politics were highly complex and shaped much more by his moral and religious beliefs than by partisanship. Yet, in his later years, according to one biographer, he evinced "a strengthening of his conservative tendency to emphasize the importance of social institutions in government at the expense of individual rights." Johnson vehemently denied American claims for liberty and reluctantly supported the use of force against the rebellious colonists.[10]

Sensitive to Johnson's views, Edward Dilly at first declined to invite him. According to Boswell, Edward demurred, saying, "'What with Mr. Wilkes? Not for the world.'" Boswell pressed him, promising to "be answerable that all shall go well." Dilly then agreed, and the planned dinner was set for the 15th of May.[11]

As Boswell later reported, Knowles joined the all-male gathering after dinner in company with William Lee, a London Alderman and radical politician. The elder brother of Arthur Lee, William also strongly supported Wilkes and the American cause. While Boswell's account noted Knowles's entry, he did not explain her presence on this occasion.[12]

Previously discussed evidence indicates that Knowles shared the patriot views of several of the male guests. She had long been interested in Wilkes's career, as demonstrated in her "Memoirs of M. M." She formed close friendships with John Coakley Lettsom and Edward Dilly, both acknowledged Whigs. She scorned slavery and defended liberty in her earlier writings. Now, she entered the dinner in company with the radical William Lee.

If Boswell had persuaded Dilly to invite Johnson to witness his reaction to Wilkes, then Dilly might have invited Knowles to see Johnson's reaction to her. On an earlier occasion, Edward invited Catharine Sawbridge Macaulay as a surprise after-dinner guest to elicit a reaction from someone who did not share her views. "We were chattering around the Fire," a visiting American had written a few years before, "and I had no more idea that Mrs. Macaulay was to favour us with her Presence, than I had of seeing a Ghost." Knowing that the visitor disapproved of American independence, Dilly invited Macaulay to see how "A t'other-Side-of-the-Question-Man" might react to a "Revolutioner."[13]

Dilly could have been curious about Johnson's reaction to Knowles because Johnson had recently displayed angry behavior towards Quakers. According to Boswell's journal, two months before, on 22 March 1776, Johnson had exploded in anger while visiting the home of Mary's cousin, Sampson Lloyd III, in Birmingham. Calling on Lloyd and his wife, Rachel, Boswell said Johnson saw a copy of Barclay's *Apology* in their library and became enraged at what he considered its unorthodox sentiments.[14]

A later member of the Lloyd family added that Johnson "flung the volume to the floor and stamped on it." During dinner, according to the family story, Johnson spoke so loudly against what he mistakenly thought Barclay had written that he frightened the children.[15] Given Knowles's close relationship with the Lloyds and Boswell's close relationship with the Dilly brothers, this story could easily have reached London by the time the dinner party was scheduled to take place.

Scholars still debate Johnson's attitudes toward women, with special attention often given to his demeaning comparison, as reported by Boswell, of Quaker women preachers to dancing dogs.[16] Yet Kathleen Nutton Kemmerer provided examples from Johnson's writings to demonstrate his sympathy and support for some women.[17] Irma Lustig and Norma Clarke also pointed to Johnson's many female friendships as indications of his supportive attitudes toward women.[18] Johnson's attitudes toward women, like his political views, appear to have been complex and sometimes contradictory. Given his unpredictability and reports of his recent angry behavior toward Knowles's relatives, her meeting with him could have promised as much diversion to Dilly as Johnson's meeting with Wilkes did to Boswell.

Knowles's entry after dinner corresponded with Quaker practice and reflected changing customs in this important associative social space. Quakers, believing in the divine spirit within all, did not differentiate between appropriate settings and conversational topics for men and women, so they did not follow the custom, common in some circles, of women withdrawing from male company after dinner.[19] The Dilly brothers did not always adhere to the custom of separating women and men after dinner, as demonstrated by the previous anecdote concerning Catharine Macaulay. Some historians have argued that the late eighteenth century marked a new "Age of Informality," as social customs such as this became more relaxed.[20]

When Knowles joined the male guests after dinner, changing standards of polite behavior in this influential literary coterie converged with Quaker social practice.

Knowles impressed Johnson favorably at their first meeting, as he wrote his friend, Hester Thrale, the next day. Johnson wondered at himself, "breaking jokes with Jack Wilkes upon the Scots," and then added, "And there was Mrs. Knowles, the Quaker, that works the sutile pictures." In earlier writings elsewhere, Johnson had referred to "sutile pictures which imitate tapestry." He now used the rare word to describe the needle painting and other embroidery work done by Knowles.

Johnson told Thrale that Knowles "is a great admirer of your conversation," reporting, "She saw you at Mr. Shaw's, at the election time."[21] Historian Judith S. Lewis argued that elite women often participated in elections in the late eighteenth century, and female participation in electoral politics was accepted and even expected.[22] Johnson's remark indicates no surprise or disapproval that Knowles mentioned seeing Thrale, both middling women, in connection with an election.

Hester's husband, Henry Thrale, stood for election in the Borough of Southwark in 1774. Henry Thrale supported Lord North and the king against the opposition, which included Whigs and radicals. Hester, even though pregnant and disdainful of politics, took an active part in her husband's campaign. "Now for this filthy Election!," she wrote a friend, complaining about leaving her infant daughter at home, "While I go fight the Opposition in the Borough."[23]

Although she mentioned seeing Hester at the election, given Knowles's patriot views and association with radicals, her sympathies more likely lay with the opposition. Knowles later socialized with Mary Wilkes Hayley, the sister of John Wilkes, who campaigned for her brother in the election of 1774. John Wilkes's biographer later described how, "From an open window in a neighbouring house" overlooking the hustings, Mary Wilkes Hayley "smiled approval upon the freeholders" as they returned her brother as a Member for Middlesex.[24] The participation of Hester Thrale and Mary Hayley, as middling women, on different sides of the election of 1774 confirms the need for more research on eighteenth-century election activities by females below the level of the greater gentry.[25]

Knowles may have tactfully refrained from mentioning her political sympathies to Johnson at their first meeting, and she may also have chosen not to discuss their religious differences, concentrating instead on their common roots in the country. Johnson described Knowles to Thrale as "a Staffordshire woman," drawing a playful parallel between his move to the city and hers. "Staffordshire is the nursery of art," he observed, "here they grow them up till they are transplanted to London." Confirming his positive impression of Knowles, Johnson ended his report by telling Thrale, "I am to go and see her."[26]

Whether or not Johnson visited Knowles after their meeting, her literary fame increased. A broadside edition of her *Compendium on Water Baptism* appeared in Dublin, identifying her by birth name as the author. Thomas Harding in Meath Street printed her verses in three columns on large paper like the 1771 edition.

Significantly different, however, the 1776 edition revealed her birth name by bearing the full title, *A Compendium of a Controversy on Water-Baptism, In a Letter from a Clergyman to M. Morris, one of the People called Quakers*.

The same publisher also issued a smaller version printed in two columns, but without a date. The smaller version carried a condensed title but still included her birth name, appearing as *A Letter from a Clergyman, to M. Morris, one of the People called Quakers*.[27] These publications, available in two popular formats with her birth name attached to both, made her religious views widely available to the reading public.

Mary Deverell, an Anglican from Gloucestershire, also wrote about religion, and Knowles and other leading figures supported the publication of her sermons. A second edition of Deverell's *Sermons on Various Subjects* appeared in London in 1776, sold by Edward and Charles Dilly among others. In a revised dedication to this edition, Deverell apologized for using the word *sermons* but defended her decision by stating, "though the Salique Law in some countries prevails in regard to political government, it no where extends to intellectual endowments." She also added a concluding sermon, drawing heavily on female religious figures. The second edition of Deverell's *Sermons* thus made a strong statement in support of both female content and authorship in religious writing.

"Mrs. Knowles, Ingram Court, Fenchurch Street, London" helped finance the publication of the second edition by an advance subscription as did the mother and sister of John Wilkes. The subscription list included in the second edition named "Mrs. Wilks Sr. Old Palace Yard" who bought "two copies." Her daughter, "Mary Wilkes Hayley, Goodman's Fields, London," too, purchased an advance copy.[28]

Anglicans, like Samuel Johnson and the Bluestocking Queen, Elizabeth Robinson Montagu, for example, also subscribed to Deverell's *Sermons*.[29] Their support indicates that Deverell's writing appealed to men and women from a spectrum of religious, political, and social views. More research is needed to identify who supported, purchased, and read works by eighteenth-century women religious writers to assess their influence more fully.

Knowles also participated in serious religious discussions by serving as a mentor to two young Anglicans from Rugeley. Visiting London, Jasper Capper told Knowles that his older brother intended to become an Anglican priest. In response, she drew up "a description of the qualifications which she deemed essential to a true minister of the gospel." Deeply moved by what she wrote, Jasper Capper eventually became a Quaker and remained a lifelong associate of Knowles.[30]

In October 1776, Jasper's younger sister, Mary Capper, joined him in London, where she also enjoyed the company and religious advice of Mary and Thomas Knowles. She "spent a rational, agreeable evening" with the couple, describing Thomas as "a man of learning and affability, polite without ceremony, perfectly good humoured." She soon returned to spend an afternoon at their home. "We had much serious conversation," she recalled, "and the doctor and his wife explained the benefit arising from silent meetings," an enduring characteristic of Quaker worship.

Mary Knowles made a strong impact on Mary Capper, just as she had on Jasper. The young woman later said, "It is impossible to be otherwise than happy" in her company. She recalled how, when she felt poorly, "M. Knowles was so obliging as to read in the *Life of William Penn*." Mary Capper left London in January 1777 to study at a French convent. While there, she "received a pleasing epistle from M. Knowles, containing a few serious directions on the most important object of our lives!" Mary Capper, like her brother Jasper, later joined the Friends, and she became a leading minister.[31]

Knowles's selection of the recently published *Life of William Penn* indicates her support for the Americans at a time when the revolution tested the loyalties of English radicals and the pacifist principles of Quakers on both sides of the Atlantic. Edmund Rack, an ecumenical Quaker, wrote *A Brief Account of the Life of William Penn, Esq.* after Britain and her colonies went to war. Rack lived in Bath where he associated with the pro-American Catharine Macaulay. Although not overtly pro-American himself, Rack indicated his sentiments with such statements as, Pennsylvania "has added much commerce, riches and stability to the *British* empire."[32] By focusing on the achievements of Penn and the virtues of Pennsylvania, pacifist Quakers like Rack and Knowles expressed their sympathies for the Americans without supporting their war for independence.

During this time, too, Knowles became a close friend and advisor to Jane Harry, the young woman from Jamaica whose life reflected the social complexities of British colonialism, best summed up as "the politics of complexion." Jane, or "Jenny" as friends called her, was the natural daughter of Thomas Hibbert, an English plantation owner, and a Jamaican woman now known only as "Mrs. Harry." As a young man, Hibbert left Manchester for Jamaica where he prospered greatly. He acquired three estates and became a Judge of the Grand Court and a member of the local governing assembly.[33] English males, especially those of the landowning class, far outnumbered English females in Jamaica. Hibbert, like other resident plantation owners, developed a long-term relationship with a Jamaican woman.[34]

Very little is known about Mrs. Harry. A contemporary later described her as a "mulatto," suggesting a mixed heritage.[35] Evidence discussed later indicates she could read and was or became free. Her union with Hibbert may or may not have been consensual, and it certainly involved the unequal status of colonizer and colonized. Hibbert and Harry never married but had two daughters, Jane, born about 1756, and Margaret, named for his mother, born nine years later. Jane and Margaret Harry were baptized in an Anglican church in Kingston and, when they grew older, went to England to be educated, like other children of affluent planter fathers and Jamaican mothers.[36]

Jane's father placed her under the care of Nathaniel Sprigg in Barnes, Surrey, while her sister went to boarding school in London. With Sprigg and his wife as guardians, Harry enjoyed a life of material comfort at Barn Elms, an ancient manor house with a colorful history. The background of Sprigg's wife, described as the former Miss Benfield of Cheltenham and Lombard Street, London, suggests the melding of prosperous provincials and wealthy commercial families taking place elsewhere in England. At Barn Elms, the Sprigg family frequently entertained distinguished visitors from London, including Samuel Johnson and Mary Knowles.[37]

Available evidence does not reveal whether, living in England, Jane Harry considered herself, or was considered by others, as a woman of color. While a nineteenth-century publication described her as a "quadroon," no such contemporary racialized references to her have been found.[38] Unlike John Coakley Lettsom, there is no record of Harry identifying herself as a West Indian or comments about her skin color. Her future husband once described her as "that West Indian girl."[39] Yet place of birth, social status, and color were often conflated in the eighteenth-century lexicon, so that while a West Indian might be considered *black*, so might persons from Ireland or coal miners and other manual laborers. As literary scholar Vincent Carretta observed, "Social status could supersede race as a defining category" in Georgian England.[40] While Harry's social position as a member of the middling sorts has been documented, her identity in terms of race or color has not. This absence suggests the fluidity of metropolitan, as opposed to colonial, racial categories in the late eighteenth century.[41]

Ambivalence about color combined with attitudes toward gender contributed to what literary scholar Felicity Nussbaum described as "the politics of complexion." Nussbaum showed how various eighteenth-century white women writers negotiated the unstable and elusive constructs of gender, *blood*, and social privilege. Yet she recognized "the seemingly insurmountable difficulty" of studying women of color because of "the scant testimony from the women themselves."[42] In the absence of evidence from Harry, herself, she, like women who later migrated to England from the British colonies, seems to have been "classified as neither Black nor White."[43]

Mary Knowles met Jane Harry at a time when the younger woman experienced loss and spiritual soul searching. The two women became close friends, and each had a profound impact on the life of the other. Because information about Caribbean-born women living in eighteenth-century England is scarce and this friendship became so significant to both women, the origins of their relationship are presented here in detail.

Jane Harry's sister, Margaret, died while at boarding school, and Jane grieved deeply, saying she felt as though she had "lost a part of myself." Sorely troubled, she turned to the study of the Bible, especially the New Testament. During this time, as Harry later wrote her father, "there came a Quaker Lady, a Mrs. Knowles" on a social visit to Barn Elms.[44]

Knowles seems to have been connected to Sprigg through his wife's family, the Benfields. Since the Benfields had a home in Lombard Street, Knowles might have met them in London. Yet Harry also told her father, "I have been told she has seen you," adding "It was at the time she was working the celebrated picture of the King." This remark indicates the fame Knowles attained through her needle painting and the range of her social networks before she moved to London.

Harry, who studied drawing and painting, found that Knowles also "had a genius for painting, which she doubtless would have pursued more, had she not been restrained by her religious principles."[45] While Knowles gained fame through her embroidered needle painting, she evidently did not feel equally free to display her talents with the brush. Harry indicated, however, that Knowles privately provided her with artistic advice. "As I was engaged in painting while she was at Barnes, she was so obliging to favor me with many useful hints in this Art, and with much of her conversation on other subjects," Harry recalled.

Harry later visited Knowles in London, and she reported that the two spent much time painting. Her comments indicate that Knowles practiced painting privately even though she did not exhibit her artwork publicly. This duality confirms art expert Marcia Pointon's observation that many Georgian Quakers "negotiated their way between prohibition and acceptance in some kind of compromise" concerning participation in the visual arts.[46]

Knowles demonstrated her sociability to Anglicans by inviting Harry to visit, and, like other young people, Harry found much to admire in Knowles. "She is a Woman of a fine understanding, highly cultivated; of an amiable disposition, condescending to converse familiarly with any, however inferior to herself in her various accomplishments," Harry told her father. She also described Thomas Knowles as "a very sensible and agreeable man."

While visiting Knowles, Harry met other Quakers who impressed her favorably. She later recalled that she "was much surprised when I discovered a genuine politeness, an amiable simplicity of manners, benevolence and integrity of heart" among the Quakers she encountered. Harry evidently expected Quakers to be unschooled in good manners, and, perhaps, somewhat suspect in their behavior, but she now wanted to explore their beliefs.

Still disturbed by the death of her sister, Harry turned to Knowles for guidance. "As my mind was much unsettled," she explained later, "I thought it my duty to enquire into their principles." She told her father, "I therefore disclosed my mind to Mrs. Knowles, telling her that I admired the Quakers much and that I wanted to know something of their principles." Disillusioned with Anglican rituals, Harry added, "for ... I had no faith in the ceremonies of the Church of England."

When the young woman made known her feelings to Knowles, "She seemed rather thoughtful and doubtful what answer to make me," Harry later told her father. "After careful consideration," Harry continued, "at length she said these or nearly these words: 'Jenny, there are good people of all denominations; it is not the name, or the outward profession of any religion that can make us good, but a steady adherence to that which is right in our own consciences.'" Knowles assured Harry that, "'Thou mayst be a very good Girl professing the religion of thy Education, as long as thou Canst be satisfied with it.'" Knowles added, "'But if thou cans't not, I would advise thee to have recourse to that inward light, which will guide thee into all truth.'"[47]

In her interaction with Harry, Knowles expressed a tolerant view of other denominations, an ecumenical faith in divine guidance from within, and a belief in the liberty and responsibility of Harry to choose her religion. Here, as in her earlier letter concerning the nonsubscribing clergy, described in Chapter Two, Knowles placed her faith in inner convictions rather than membership in a particular religious group or the practice of a certain form of worship. She further advised Harry to read the scriptures closely and think carefully about her decision.

After returning to Barn Elms, Harry obtained a copy of Barclay's *Apology* to learn more about Quaker beliefs. She did not see Knowles for several months, but when Knowles visited the Sprigg family again, Harry sought her out. "I informed her I had read Barclay's *Apology* and was convinced of the principles it contained," Harry recalled. "She advised me by all means to make my sentiments known to my Friends, and particularly to Mr. Sprigg." Harry "dreaded the thought of such a discovery," as she later told her father, "but, as I intended to make it, I gave her reason to believe I should, and she was satisfied."

After some delay, Harry reluctantly revealed her thoughts to her guardians. Mr. Sprigg responded with anger and an ultimatum. He gave her two weeks to decide whether she would return to her Anglican beliefs and remain under his protection or pursue her newfound religion and leave his home. His reaction, as described by Harry to her father, indicates the deep ambivalence of some members of the polite middle classes toward Quakers. On one hand, Sprigg welcomed Knowles, as a prosperous and sociable colleague, into his home. On the other, he deeply disapproved of the idea that his ward might become an adherent of the Quaker faith.

The Sprigg and Hibbert families urgently tried to persuade Harry to abandon her Quaker interests. The Spriggs' sent her to meet with "Mrs. Hibbert," perhaps the mother or sister of her father, and two Anglican clergymen. Mrs. Sprigg and Mrs. Hibbert both urged her to write Sprigg and beg his forgiveness. Intimidated, Harry agreed. "I thought I could reconcile myself to a conformity," she later explained.

But soon, she told her father, "I began to feel deep remorse for my late temporizing conduct." In this disturbed state of mind, she went to London to stay with a friend. There, she unexpectedly met "Mrs. Knowles, whom I had not seen in a long time." Harry later carefully explained their chance meeting to her father.

"Her coming there was then accidental," she told him, "to deliver a message to me from Sir Joshua Reynolds about a Picture he had lent me."[48] This remark represents the only indication found to date of a connection among Harry, Knowles, and Reynolds. Reynolds worked through the Royal Academy of Art to raise the standards and pay of trained artists, and he also befriended promising young painters, often lending his pictures to aspiring students.[49] Harry's scant reference shows that she and Knowles both knew Reynolds and participated in his practice of lending his paintings. While Knowles may have been restrained by her religion from publicly exhibiting her paintings, she, along with Harry, may have privately studied Reynolds's work.

Yet Harry had more than painting on her troubled mind, and she confided her worries to Knowles. She took this opportunity to tell her "what had happened to me, and of the displeasure of my Friends." By now, Harry had determined that she could no longer remain an Anglican. She told Knowles "that though I had once flattered myself with the hopes of returning again to the Established Church, that I then found I could not."

Knowles again advised Harry to follow her conscience, but she also tried to preserve her good relationship with the Sprigg family. According to Harry, Knowles "went to Barnes the next day and told them she had seen me." After that, Harry did not see Knowles again for some time.

Torn between the fear of offending her guardian or offending God, Harry adopted a desperate plan. "When I went to Town to attend my drawing Master," she later reported, "I went to the house of a Quaker, where I had been once before with Mrs. Knowles." Summoning her courage and "without telling the person any particulars," she continued, "I wrote an account of myself to Mr. Sprigg." Her worst fears were realized when, as she told her father, Sprigg "much upbraided me with ingratitude, and I find still continues to do so."

Harry worried most of all because "it was first imagined by my Friends that the Dr. and Mrs. Knowles were privy to my departure and necessary to it; but they were entirely ignorant and innocent of both." She earnestly assured her father of the honorable behavior of the Quaker couple. "That matter," she said, "has been so indubitably proved that Mrs. Sprigg has acknowledged to me they now believe them both totally clear of any knowledge of it." Even so, Harry remained "extremely concerned that this worthy couple should have been so unjustly censured." She told her father that, "The family at Barnes, without an injury done to them or me, still continue their unreasonable resentment" against Thomas and Mary Knowles.

When Sprigg realized that Harry would not change her mind and return to her Anglican beliefs, he declared she could no longer live with his family. His wife's relatives found her "a lodging at a Grocer's near London Bridge." From there, Harry wrote her father a 28-page letter detailing the events leading to her spiritual change of heart. Now alone, Harry pleaded for her father's support. Will "you ... pity your poor Child," she entreated, "I have much need of your parental Love, and who have I else in this World to look unto?"[50]

Thomas Hibbert evidently declined to provide further financial or emotional support to his only surviving child, so Mary and Thomas Knowles became her protectors. While she remained in London, Harry boarded at their home.[51] Furthermore, based on evidence discussed later, the Quaker couple apparently acted in the place of her parents.

The story of the Sprigg family's reaction to Harry's rejection of her Anglican beliefs highlights the social limitations of religious toleration in the Georgian Age. Although the law recognized the rights of Quakers to practice their religion, Harry's guardians applied social sanctions when she expressed interest in Quaker beliefs. Knowles, too, negotiated the social limits of toleration by first explaining her actions to the Sprigg family and then taking Harry into her home when her guardians refused to accept her change of beliefs.

While becoming closely associated with Harry, Knowles continued to socialize with Anna Seward, her old friend from Lichfield, as well as with Edward Dilly and Boswell. On Sunday, 12 April 1778, Boswell noted in his journal that he "Went and called on Dr. and Mrs. Knowles." There, he found "Miss Seward of Lichfield," and "Mr. Edward Dilly was just leaving." The ever sociable Edward prolonged his visit, as Boswell wrote, "till I came away," and the two men left together.[52]

Seward still lived with her father, but she sometimes visited London. Although an aspiring writer, she disliked what she considered the increasingly commercialized literary life of the capital.[53] She seemed to enjoy meeting Knowles's acquaintances, however. As Seward's biographer later observed, "Mrs. Knowles, who was a brilliant woman, could introduce her to a circle of eminent friends."[54]

Through her friendship with Knowles, Seward became acquainted with Harry or at least with her story. Seward later wrote that Harry "often observed" to Knowles that "Dr. Johnson's displeasure (whom she had frequently seen at her guardian's house and who had always been fond of her) was amongst the greatest mortifications of her then situation." Furthermore, Seward said Harry "once came home in tears," telling Knowles "she had met Dr. Johnson in the street and ventured to ask him how he did; but he would not deign to answer her." According to Seward, Harry asked Knowles "to plead for me," knowing she would soon dine with Johnson at the home of Edward and Charles Dilly."[55]

On 15 April 1778, according to Boswell, Knowles and Seward dined at Dillys' with him, Johnson, "Rev. Dr. Mayo," a Dissenting minister, and "Rev. Mr. Beresford tutor to Duke of Bedford." A day or two later, Boswell made lengthy notes in his journal about the free-flowing conversation.[56] These notes, unvarnished and sometimes disjointed, represent Boswell's attempt to capture the conversation and also include some of his private thoughts.

Boswell said the conversation began with Knowles making a telling comment about Johnson's reading habits, revealing her understanding of reading as critical analysis. Immediately upon arriving, according to Boswell, Johnson "seized" a copy of the recently published *Account of the late Revolution in Sweden* by Charles Francis Sheridan and "read ravenously." Observing Johnson, "Mrs. Knowles said well," Boswell noted, "'He reads better than anyone, gets at substance of a book directly, tears out the heart of it.'"[57] Subsequent scholars have often quoted this apt observation, preserved by Boswell, although not always attributing it to her.[58]

Amidst discussions of cookbooks and literary business, Knowles, perhaps thinking of Harry, introduced the subject of women's liberty. In Boswell's words, "Mrs. Knowles complained that men had much more liberty allowed them women." Johnson, noted Boswell, disagreed, saying, "'Madam, women have all the liberty they should wish to have.'" Speaking on behalf of men, Johnson continued, "'We have all the labour and all the danger, and the women the advantage. We go to sea, we build houses, all to pay our court to the women.'"

Boswell noted that Knowles, undeterred, challenged Johnson directly. He said she countered, "'The Doctor reasons very wittingly, but not convincingly.'" Johnson had mentioned building houses, so she gave an example of unequal social standards applied to a mason and his wife. "'The mason's wife, if she's in liquor, is ruined,'" Knowles pointed out, but the mason "'may get himself drunk as often as he pleases, and let his wife and children starve.'"

Johnson again disagreed, according to Boswell's notes, underscoring the legal and physical differences between the sexes. "'Madam,'" he argued, "'in the first place, if the mason does get himself drunk and let wife and children starve, the parish will oblige him to find security for their maintenance.'" Equating gender differences with the separation of humans from animals, he continued, "'We have different modes of restraining evil: stocks for the men, ducking stool for the women, and pound for beasts.'"

Defending different social standards for women and men, Johnson asserted, according to Boswell, "'If we require more perfection from women than from ourselves, tis doing them honour.'" Johnson added that, "'women have not the same temptations we have.'" Women, he continued, "'may always live in good company. Men must mix indiscriminately.'" So, he concluded, "'If a woman has no inclination to do ill, there is no restraint in being hindered.'" Johnson ended by linking excessive liberty with madness. "'I have liberty to walk in to the Thames,'" he declared, "'But if I were to try it, my friends would restrain me in Bedlam.'"[59]

Boswell indicated that Knowles remained unpersuaded, noting that she "still insisted as a hardship that less *indulgence* was given to women than to men." He later remembered Johnson answering her, "'One or t'other must have the superiority.'" Edward Dilly joked that Knowles would have a man and woman ride a horse "'in panniers, one on each side.'" This prompted Johnson to pronounce, according to Boswell, "'Then, Sir, the horse would throw them both.'"[60]

This exchange has not been thoroughly analyzed in the scholarly debates concerning Johnson's attitudes toward women. While literary scholar Irma Lustig, for example, cited the exchange and observed that Johnson argued against the equality of the sexes, she did not link his statements to her larger exploration of "the myth of Johnson's misogyny."[61] Johnson's exchange with Knowles deserves deeper consideration because it provides important insights into the thinking of both of them, indicating her continuing commitment to women's liberty and his views supporting gender-based social differences.

According to Boswell's journal, when Johnson and Edward Dilly rebuffed her social arguments in support of women's liberty, Knowles turned to a religious one. She "hoped in another world sexes [will be] equal," noted Boswell. While this scriptural reference reflected her Quaker beliefs in women's spiritual equality, Knowles applied it ecumenically to all.

Boswell said he joined the conversation, replying, "'You are too ambitious. We may as well desire to be angels.'" He "insisted that in Heaven a carman and Sir Isaac Newton equally good would still have different degrees of happiness." Boswell added later reflections to this journal entry concerning gender differences, noting, "David Hume's saying little Miss as happy as great orator" in heaven. Boswell indicated that he later "tried Johnson" about an argument by a Dutch divine refuting Hume, and "*after a little thought* [sic]," Johnson "came over to the parson."

Returning to the conversation at hand, Boswell noted, "I talked with horror of death," reflecting his long-standing fears. He portrayed Knowles as again expressing her religious beliefs in nonsectarian terms by quoting the New Testament. "'No,'" he said Knowles replied, "'tis gate of life.'"

The subject of death also disturbed Johnson, who, according to Boswell, observed that, "no rational man could die without apprehension." Knowles responded by quoting Proverbs, summarized by Boswell, as "'Righteous shall have *hope* in his death.'" Johnson worried that, "'No man can be sure that his obedience and repentance will obtain salvation.'" Knowles again answered readily, "'But divine intimation may be made to the soul.'"

During this intense conversation, Boswell noted that, "Mrs. Knowles seemed to enjoy a pleasing serenity in the persuasion of divine light to the soul." Drawing a contrast with his own fears, he wrote, "I stood in suspense and uneasy to think of the subject ... though I inclined to think and hope with Mrs. Knowles." When Dr. Mayo pointed out "there was danger of *presumption* in [the] *assurance*" of salvation, Knowles remained unperturbed, quoting "St. Paul: 'I have fought the good fight.'"[62]

According to Boswell, Knowles further impressed both him and Johnson with her comments on *A View of the Internal Evidence of the Christian Religion* by Soame Jenyns. When the subject of this book was introduced, Boswell indicated that he directed the conversation to her. "I said," he wrote, "'Mrs. Knowles should like his principle of courage not being Christian.'" Perhaps Boswell thought this principle accorded with Quaker ideas about pacifism.

Her reply seemed to surprise him because, "She talked of his saying friendship not Christian, and was against him."[63] Knowles had read closely to recall that under "Proposition III," Jenyns argued that friendship cannot be considered a religious virtue "because it is too narrow, and confined, and appropriates ... benevolence to a single object."[64] According to Boswell, Johnson remarked, "'Surely, Madam, you must approve of this. For you call *all* men *friends*.'"

Rather than referring to her Quaker beliefs, Knowles replied as a Christian, quoting the New Testament that, "'We are commanded to do good to all men, but especially household of faith.'" Johnson seemed unimpressed, answering, according to Boswell's notes, "'Well, Madam. Household of faith [is] wide enough.'" Yet Knowles persisted, "'But, Sir,'" she continued, "'our Saviour had twelve apostles, yet one whom he loved. John was the disciple whom Jesus loved.'"

This response pleased Johnson and Boswell. Boswell noted that, "with eyes sparking," Johnson said, "'Very well, indeed Madam. You have said very well.'" Boswell deemed it, "'A fine application.'" He asked Johnson "if he had thought of it" before, and Johnson said he had not.[65] By making what they considered an original application of New Testament scripture, Knowles not only demonstrated her familiarity with the Bible but also her skill in presenting her beliefs in ecumenical terms to win acceptance from Christians of other denominations.

Johnson's mood suddenly changed, however, and he abruptly announced, according to Boswell, "'I am willing to love all mankind, *except an American*.'" This remark prompted Seward to reveal her pro-American sympathies. Seward knew Johnson from Lichfield and did not fear challenging him. Boswell noted that, "Miss Seward said very well to him, 'Sir this is an instance that we are always most violent against those whom we have injured.'"

As Seward must have anticipated, her reply angered Johnson more. Boswell wrote that Johnson "roared again, till he was absolutely hoarse ... the noise was grating and shocking." Boswell eventually succeeded in turning Johnson's attention to other subjects. Commenting on Johnson's shifting moods, Boswell compared his conversation to "a warm summer climate" that produces "luxuriant foliage, luscious fruits," but also "violent thunder and lightening or a terrible earthquake."[66]

After the earthquake subsided, Boswell said Knowles introduced the subject of her young friend. He noted that, "Mrs. Knowles wished to vindicate herself from the suspicion of having made a proselyte of Miss [Harry], a young lady whom Dr. Johnson knew." Although Harry had told her father that Knowles had not abetted her departure from the Sprigg household, Boswell's comment indicates that he, and perhaps others, believed that Knowles had inspired Harry's change of faith. These suspicions seem justified given the influence Knowles had on the conversions of both Jasper and Mary Capper, as previously described.

Boswell said that Johnson responded to Knowles by calling Harry "an odious wench" and arguing that she was incapable of choosing her own religion. According to Boswell, Johnson stated, "'She could not have any proper conviction that she should change her religion.'" Furthermore, Johnson insisted that, "'she knew [no] more of the church she left than the difference between the Copernican and Ptolemaic systems.'"

As noted by Boswell, Knowles answered that Harry "'had the New Testament,'" but Johnson insisted that Harry could not comprehend its meaning. "'Madam,'" Boswell said Johnson replied, "'she could not understand the New Testament, the most difficult book in the world, for which the study of a life is required.'"

Undeterred, Knowles "said twas clear as to essentials." Johnson countered, "'But not as to controversial points.'"

In the exchange that followed, Boswell quoted Johnson's comments but paraphrased the responses given by Knowles. According to Boswell, Johnson warned about the danger "'if you err when you choose a religion for yourself.'" Boswell said Knowles asked, "were we to go by implicit faith?" Boswell indicated that Johnson ended the conversation by answering decisively, "'Why, the greatest part of our knowledge [is] implicit faith. Have we heard all that a disciple of Confucius, all that a Mahometan can say for himself?'"[67]

At the end of his paragraph describing this serious religious exchange, Boswell wrote in his journal, "I *loved* the mildness of Mrs. Knowles." He indicated that, "I said I should like to be married to a rich Quaker, to have her in my arms like a *lamb*." Boswell did not note whether he said these words aloud or whispered them as an aside. Nor did he record what response, if any, Knowles or others made to his incongruous statement.

Continuing to muse about his Quaker lamb, Boswell wrote in his journal, "But it should be a rich one, I'd have a *lamb* with golden fleece."[68] Given that Boswell had noted on their first meeting that Knowles looked well and that she had received £800 pounds from the queen, he could have been thinking of her as the rich Quaker lamb with the golden fleece. Whomever the object of his thoughts, his journal indicates that he had matters other than religion on his mind at this time.

Returning to his notes on the conversation, Boswell described how Johnson "was enticed to stay supper." Following the meal, Boswell indicated that Johnson said "(To Mrs. Knowles.) 'You have been flattering me all this night. I wish you'd now give Bozzy a little.'" By reporting this remark, Boswell revealed that Knowles focused her attention on Johnson rather than on him. "'If you knew his merit as I do,'" Johnson continued, according to Boswell, "'you'd say a great deal. He is the best traveling companion in the world.'" If Knowles answered Johnson's pointed remark to her, Boswell did not note it in his journal.

Boswell said the conversation that night ended with a joke. He said Johnson signified his disapproval of a man bringing a literary lawsuit by calling him "'a *Whig*.'" "'What!' said one of the ladies," whom Boswell later identified as Knowles, "'a *prig*?'" "'Worse,' said he, 'Madam, a Whig. But he's both.'" Boswell transformed this joke into a comic rhyme "in the Doctor's own style" and concluded with evident satisfaction, "Thus ended this excellent interview."[69]

Boswell's journal entry for this dinner presents Knowles in a mixed but mostly favorable light. He portrayed her as speaking strongly about women's lack of liberty, but he also subsequently commented on her serenity, careful reading, and original Biblical analysis. Even when she pursued the difficult subject of Jane Harry, Boswell said he loved her mildness.

Yet Knowles later charged Boswell with omitting the most important part of her conversation with Johnson that night. She maintained that her reference to Harry sparked a much longer confrontation between them. She subsequently published her version of their dialogue in *Gentleman's Magazine*.[70] In it, she indicated that she addressed Johnson using the distinctive Quaker forms of *thee* and *thou*, in the words of George Fox, "without respect to rich or poor, great or small."[71]

According to her account, Knowles said she began the conversation by saying, "'Thy friend Jenny H – desires her kind respects to thee, Doctor.'" This corresponds to Seward's report, noted earlier, that Harry asked Knowles to attempt reconciliation between her and Johnson. Like Boswell, Knowles said Johnson immediately answered, "'I hate the odious wench.'" Knowles added that Johnson continued, "'for her apostasy.'"[72]

From this point on, however, Knowles's account differs significantly from Boswell's notes in his journal. According to Knowles, Johnson turned his wrath on her, charging, "'it is you, Madam, who have seduced her from the Christian Religion.'" Johnson seemed to be repeating the view, suggested by Boswell, that Knowles had convinced the young woman to change her religion. Moreover, Johnson's angry reply indicated that he did not consider Quakers to be Christians.

"'This is a heavy charge indeed,'" Knowles said she protested, countering, "'I must beg leave to be heard in my own defense.'" Addressing the assembled guests, she said she continued, "'I entreat the attention of the present learned and candid company, desiring they should judge how far I am able to clear myself of so cruel an accusation.'" Knowles said Johnson became "much disturbed at this unexpected challenge" and tried to avoid a debate, citing her gender. "'You are a woman, and I give you quarter,'" Johnson retorted, according to Knowles.

Knowles said she refused his offer and confronted him instead, saying, "'I will not take quarter.'" Citing the spiritual equality of women, as Boswell had noted she had done earlier, she declared, "'There is no sex in souls, and in the present case I fear not even Dr. Johnson himself.'" According to Knowles, "'Bravo!' was repeated by the company, and silence ensued."

Knowles said that Johnson repeated his charge "that 'you have seduced Miss H[arry] from the Christian Religion.'" Ignoring his claim that she had convinced Harry to become a Quaker, she calmly replied, "'If thou really knewest what were the principles of Friends, thou would'st not say she had departed from Christianity.'" Yet Knowles said she declined to argue that point further.

Instead, Knowles focused on Harry's moral agency as the central issue at stake. Harry, she told Johnson, "'had an undoubted right to examine and to change her educational tenets whenever she had found them erroneous; as an accountable creature, it was her *duty* to do so.'"[73] The language concerning individual moral accountability corresponds to what Harry told her father Knowles had said, as described earlier.[74] Moreover, in his journal entry, quoted above, Boswell noted that Johnson referred to giving up "'a religion in which one has been educated'" and warned of the danger "'if you err when you choose a religion for yourself.'"[75] These statements by Johnson, reported by Boswell, can be seen as a reply to the arguments Knowles said she presented about Harry changing her educational tenets.

According to Knowles, Johnson scoffed at the idea of the young girl being morally accountable. She said he exclaimed, "'Pshaw! Pshaw! – an accountable creature! – girls accountable creatures!'" She further said that Johnson asserted that Harry did not have the right to choose her own religion. "'It was her duty to remain with the Church wherein she was educated,'" Knowles reported him as saying, "'she had no business to leave it.'"[76] This statement, as reported by Knowles, accords with Boswell's notes concerning Johnson's views on the limited liberty of women.[77]

Knowles said she chose to debate Johnson's point that no one—female or male—should change her or his religion. By this logic, she told him, turning his argument on him, "'hadst thou been born in Turkey, it would have been thy duty to have remained a Mahometan, notwithstanding Christian *evidence* might have wrought in thy mind the clearest conviction.'" Knowles asked, "'how would thy *conscience* have answered for such obstinacy at the great and last tribunal?'"

According to Knowles, Johnson responded that his "'conscience would not have been answerable,'" because, "'In adhering to the Religion of the State as by law established, our implicit obedience therein becomes our *duty*.'" This prompted her to ask those present if they had ever encountered "'a State, composed of millions of people ... stalking forth into the next world, loaded with its mighty conscience, there to be rewarded or punished, for the faith, opinions, and conduct of its constituent *machines* called men?'" She answered her own question by exclaiming, "'Surely the teeming brain of Poetry never held up to fancy so wonderous a personage!'"

Knowles reported that this image amused the company but angered Johnson more. "When the Laugh occasioned by this personification was subsided," according to Knowles, "the Doctor very angrily replied, 'I regard not what you say as to the matter. I hate the arrogance of the wench, in supposing herself a more competent judge of religion that those who educated her.'"

Johnson repeated his charge of Knowles's complicity, saying that, "'She imitated you, no doubt, but she ought not to have presumed to determine for herself in so important an affair.'" Knowles again ignored his charge against her, and instead returned to her central point. "'True, Doctor,'" she said she replied, "'if, as thou seemest to imply, a wench of twenty be not a moral agent.'"

Johnson escalated the debate into an attack on Friends, according to Knowles, by questioning "whether those deserve that character who turn Quakers." Stung by what she termed "'This severe retort,'" she answered strongly that she could only "'charitably ... hope that thou must be totally unacquainted with the principles of the people against whom thou art so exceedingly prejudiced, and that thou supposest us a set of Infidels or Deists.'" Now in full opposition, Knowles said Johnson answered, "'Certainly, I do think you little better than Deists.'"

Underscoring his lack of knowledge concerning Quaker theology, Knowles questioned why "'a man of such universal reading and research had not thought it at least *expedient* to look into the cause of dissent of a society so long established and so conspicuously singular!'" According to Knowles, Johnson responded, "'Not I, indeed! I have not read your Barclay's Apology. I never thought it worth my while.'"[78] This statement corresponds to the incident described earlier by Boswell and the Lloyd family when Johnson denounced Barclay's book without reading it.

Knowles said Johnson continued angrily, "'You are upstart Sectaries, perhaps the best subdued by silent contempt.'" As an experienced defender of the Quaker faith, Knowles said she compared his words "'with the language of the Rabbis of old, when their Hierarchy was alarmed by the increasing influence, force, and simplicity of dawning Truth.'" By equating his attack with the opposition of some Jews to early Christians, she positioned Quakers as true Christians but also participated in the prevailing anti-Semitism.

Knowles maintained that she continued to challenge Johnson. "'The reason thou givest for not having read Barclay's Apology is surely a very improper one for a man whom the world looks up to as a Moral Philosopher of the first rank; a Teacher from whom they think they have a right to expect much information,'" she reported saying. Continuing this line of argument, she asked, "'To this expecting, enquiring world, how can Dr. Johnson acquit himself of remaining unacquainted with a book translated into five or six different languages, and which has been admitted into the libraries of almost every Court and University in Christendom!'"

At this point, Knowles said, "the Doctor grew very angry." According to her, Johnson became enraged not only by her words but "at the space of time the Gentlemen insisted on showing [her as] his antagonist wherein to make her defense." Knowles said Johnson's "impatience excited one of the company, in a whisper, to say, 'I never saw this mighty lion so chafed before!'"[79]

Knowles reported that, "The Doctor *again repeated*, that he did not think the Quakers deserved the name of Christians." Knowles once more sought and received permission to explain her beliefs. "'Give me leave then to endeavour to convince thee of thy error, which I will do by making thee, and this respectable company, a confession of our faith,'" she asked. She pointed out that, "'Creeds, or confessions of faith, are admitted by all to be the standard whereby we judge of every denomination of professors.'" By equating Quaker beliefs with the more formal creeds of some churches, Knowles presented the Quaker religion as similar to, rather than different from, those of other Christians.

Granted permission, she said she began, "'Well then, I take upon me to declare that the people called Quakers do verily believe in the Holy Scriptures, and rejoice with the most full and reverential acceptance of the divine history of facts, as recorded in the New Testament.'" She pointed out that Quakers believed in the Apostles' Creed with only two exceptions, its language referring to "'our Saviour's descent into Hell, and the resurrection of the body.'" She explained that, "'These mysteries we humbly leave just as they stand in the holy text, there being, from that ground, no authority for such assertion as is drawn up in the Creed.'" She ended, "'And now, Doctor, canst thou still deny us the honourable title of Christians?'"

According to Knowles, Johnson allowed, "'I must own I did not at all suppose you had so much to say for yourselves.'" Yet he still could not accept Harry's action, speaking harshly of her. "'I cannot forgive that little slut,'" he stated, said Knowles, "'for presuming to take upon herself as she has done.'"

Seeking reconciliation, Knowles observed, "'I hope, Doctor, thou wilt not remain unforgiving; and that you will renew your friendship and joyfully meet at last in those bright regions where Pride and Prejudice can never enter!'" Johnson parried, "'Meet her! I never desire to meet fools anywhere.'" Knowles concluded, "This sarcastic turn of wit was so pleasantly received that the Doctor joined in the laugh; his spleen was dissipated; he took his coffee, and became the remainder of the evening very cheerful and entertaining."[80]

According to Knowles's account, during her confrontation with Johnson, she successfully negotiated her gender and religious differences in this important literary coterie by behaving politely. By assuming what historian Amanda Vickery described as "the mantle of politeness,"[81] Knowles effectively defended Harry and her own deeply held religious beliefs amidst the mostly male company. She successfully employed courteous conventions to facilitate her participation as a polite Quaker and win acceptance for her views among those present.

Yet her account of her confrontation with Johnson also indicates the limitations, as well as the possibilities, of female participation in this male-dominated literary coterie. While the Dilly brothers invited her and Seward to participate, her account indicates that when the conversation became disputatious its continuation depended on the approval of the mostly male company. Although Knowles obtained permission, her continued discussion angered Johnson and perhaps bored or embarrassed Boswell, causing his thoughts to wander to the rich Quaker lamb with the golden fleece.

Johnson's angry reaction to Harry's decision to change her religion, like that of her guardians, further indicates the social limits of religious toleration in the long eighteenth century. Like Sprigg, Johnson accepted Knowles, a wealthy, mature, and socially skilled Quaker, as a colleague. Yet both men deeply disapproved of the younger woman's action and applied social sanctions to indicate their displeasure. As Johnson well knew, admitting Harry's free choice in religion would subvert the established order and have serious moral consequences for both women and men. He argued the point furiously with Knowles, and he refused to forgive Harry.

If few scholars have made use of Boswell's account of Johnson's conversation with Knowles concerning women's liberty, even fewer have examined her report of her debate with Johnson about Quakerism and Harry's religious liberty. In *Daughters of Light*, Rebecca Larson mentioned Knowles's account in a footnote, citing it to show how "The conversion of an Anglican woman to Quakerism often distressed her immediate relatives and friends."[82] While this is true, the account also reveals important information about the relationship between Knowles and Johnson and his views on Quakers and on female moral agency.

Knowles's published report offers an important resource to scholars interested in more fully examining Johnson's behavior and attitudes toward women. As many scholars, such as James G. Basker and Kathleen Nutton Kemmerer, now recognize, it is crucial to distinguish between Johnson's views on women and Boswell's presentation of Johnson's views. Both Basker and Kemmerer, for example, cited Johnson's writings in *The Rambler* to suggest that he supported the moral agency of women. Yet, neither of them examined Knowles's claim that Johnson argued heatedly against Harry's moral agency.[83] Knowles's account adds the dimension of a woman's view of Johnson, independent of Boswell's portrayal of him, and suggests the complexity of Johnson's views on female moral agency, a key question in the late eighteenth century.

Knowles's account of her dialogue with Johnson also demonstrates the strong friendship between her, as an English matron approaching 45, and Harry, a West Indian woman of about 20. Her account provides a rarely documented example of a close friendship between two women of different ages, marital status, and diverse cultural backgrounds. Knowles's debate with Johnson concerning Harry testifies to the strength of their bond, despite these differences.

Knowles's longtime friendship with Anna Seward also remained important to her. On 21 April 1778, one week after the confrontation with Johnson, James Jenkins, the Quaker chronicler, spotted the two women at the wedding party of Jasper Capper, Knowles's friend from Rugeley. Capper, now a convinced Quaker, married Anne Fry, the daughter of Jonathan and Frances Head Fry of Whitechapel, the old friends of Knowles and guardians of Jenkins. After the wedding, Knowles and Seward joined the large dinner party at the White Hart Tavern.

Jenkins, already well acquainted with Knowles, recognized Seward even though she "had not then acquired that celebrity of literary character which she afterwards sustained." Jenkins expressed disappointment that, "These two accomplished women mixed but little with the rest of the company, but almost exclusively enjoyed each other's conversation."[84] The two women seem to take delight in their friendship, but perhaps they also discussed the heated exchange in Dillys' dining room the week before. The spirited dispute between Knowles and Johnson concerning Harry and witnessed by Seward would have long-lasting implications for all three women.

Notes

1 Robert DeMaria, Jr., *Samuel Johnson and the Life of Reading* (Baltimore, 1997), p. 100.
2 Nussbaum, "Women and race: 'a difference of complexion.'"
3 Brewer, *Pleasures of the Imagination*, pp. 157–8.
4 DeMaria, Jr. *Samuel Johnson and Life of Reading*, p. 100.

5   Lawrence E. Klein, "Gender and the Public/Private Distinction in the Eighteenth Century: Some Question about Evidence and Analytic Procedure," *Eighteenth-Century Studies*, 29/1 (1995): 97–109. Klein used the term "associative public sphere," p. 104.
6   James Boswell, *Life of Samuel Johnson, LL.D.* (2 vols, London, 1791), vol. 2, p. 83. Thomas, *John Wilkes*, pp. 163–9.
7   Pettigrew, *Lettsom*, vol. 2, pp. 80–3.
8   Charles Ryskamp and Frederick Pottle, eds, *Boswell: The Ominous Years, 1774–1776* (New York, 1963), p. 345.
9   Boswell, *Life of Johnson*, vol. 2, p. 83.
10 Robert DeMaria, Jr., *The Life of Samuel Johnson* (Oxford, 1993), pp. 243–53.
11 Boswell, *Life of Johnson*, vol. 2, p. 83.
12 Ibid., p. 89.
13 Butterfield, "The American Interests of the Firm E. and C. Dilly," p. 289.
14 Ryskamp and Pottle, *Boswell: Ominous Years*, p. 287–8.
15 Lloyd, *Lloyds of Birmingham*, p. 108.
16 James G. Basker, "Dancing Dogs, Women Preachers and the Myth of Johnson's Misogyny," *The Age of Johnson*, 3 (1990): 63–90.
17 Kathleen Nutton Kemmerer, *"A neutral being between the sexes:" Samuel Johnson's Sexual Politics* (London, 1998).
18 Irma Lustig, "The Myth of Johnson's Misogyny in the *Life of Johnson*: Another View," in Thomas Crawford (ed.), *Boswell in Scotland and Beyond* (Glasgow, 1997). Norma Clarke, *Dr. Johnson's Women*, (London, 2000).
19 Thomas Clarkson, *A Portraiture of Quakerism* (3 vols, London, 1806), vol. 1, p. 398.
20 Judith S. Lewis citing Mark Girouard in *Sacred to Female Patriotism*, p. 96.
21 R. W. Chapman, ed., *The Letters of Samuel Johnson with Mrs. Thrale's Genuine Letters to Him* (3 vols, Oxford: Clarendon Press, 1952), vol. 2, p. 131.
22 Lewis, *Sacred to Female Patriotism*, p. 40.
23 Mary Hyde, *The Thrales of Streatham Park* (Cambridge, Mass, 1977), pp. 107–08.
24 Horace Bleackley, *Life of John Wilkes* (London, 1917), pp.15, 286.
25 Vickery, *Women, Privilege and Power*, p. 18.
26 Chapman, *Letters of Samuel Johnson*, vol. 2, p. 131.
27 Library of the Religious Society of Friends, *Tracts*, Vol. C, numbers 49 and 47.
28 Mary Deverell, *Sermons on Various Subjects* (2nd edn, London, 1776).
29 Ibid.
30 Backhouse, "A Memoir of Mary Capper," p. 4.
31 Ibid., pp. 7–9.
32 [Edmund Rack, ed.] *Caspipina's Letters ... To which is Added The Life and Character of William Penn, Esq.* (2 vols, Dublin, 1792), vol. 2, pp. 76–7. The dedication is dated "Bath, January 7, 1777."
33 Joseph J. Green, "Jenny Harry, later Thresher (c. 1756-1784)," *Friends Quarterly Examiner* (10th Month 1913): 559–82. Joseph J. Green, "Jenny Harry, later Thresher (c. 1756-1784 (concluded)," *Friends Quarterly Examiner* (1st Month 1914): 43–64. Eric Williams, *Capitalism and Slavery* (New York, 1966), pp. 88, 232.
34 Verne A. Shepherd, "Trade and Exchange in Jamaica in the Period of Slavery," in Hilary McD Beckles and Verne Shepherd, (eds), *Caribbean Slavery in the Atlantic World: A Student Reader* (Princeton, 2000), p. 662.

35 John Wilson Croker, ed., *The Life of Samuel Johnson LL.D., including a Journal of a Tour to the Hebrides by James Boswell* (5 vols, London, 1831), vol. 4, p. 155.
36 Green, "Jenny Harry," (10th month 1913). W. J. Gardner, *A History of Jamaica from its Discovery by Christopher Columbus to the Year 1872* (London, 1971), pp. 165–73. Christine Barrow, *Family in the Caribbean: Themes and Perspective* (Princeton, 1998), p. 245.
37 Green, "Jenny Harry," (10th month 1913). John Eustace Anderson, *A History of the Parish of Barnes in the County of Surrey* (Richmond, 1900).
38 W. Beck, W. F. Wells, H. G. Chakley (compilers), *Biographical Catalogue* (London, 1888), pp. 33–7.
39 Green, "Jenny Harry," (1st month 1914).
40 Vincent Carretta, ed., *Unchained Voices: An Anthology of Black Authors in the English-Speaking World of the Eighteenth-Century* (Lexington, 1996), p. 3.
41 Nicholas Hudson, "From 'Nation' to 'Race:' The Origin of Racial Classification in Eighteenth-Century Thought," *Eighteenth-Century Studies*, 29/3 (1996): 258.
42 Nussbaum, "Women and race."
43 Joyce O. Ifekwunigew, "Diaspora's Daughters, Africa's Orphans?' in Heidi Safia Mirza (ed.), *Black British Feminism: A Reader* (London, 1997), p. 127.
44 Green, "Jenny Harry," (10th month 1913).
45 Ibid.
46 Pointon, "Quakerism and Visual Culture, 1650–1800."
47 Green, "Jenny Harry," (10th month 1913).
48 Ibid.
49 Brewer, *Pleasures of the Imagination*, pp. 288–95.
50 Green, "Jenny Harry," (10th month 1913).
51 Library of the Religious Society of Friends, Portfolio MSS 3, 126, "Notes of a Conversation between Dr. Johnson and Mary Knowles, in a Letter to Boswell."
52 Charles McC. Weis and Frederick Pottle, eds, *Boswell in Extremes, 1776–1778* (New York, 1971), p. 271.
53 Brewer, *Pleasures of the Imagination*, pp. 573–612.
54 Margaret Ashmun, *The Singing Swan: An Account of Anna Seward and Her Acquaintance with Dr. Johnson, Boswell, and Others of Their Time* (New Haven, 1931), p. 107.
55 Portfolio MSS 3, 126, "Notes of a Conversation."
56 *Boswell in Extremes*, p. 285. Boswell included notes on what "Mr. E. Dilly told me next day," indicating this entry was written at least one day later.
57 Ibid., p. 282.
58 For example, DeMaria does not attribute the quote to her in his *Life of Samuel Johnson*, p. 9, but does in *Samuel Johnson and the Life of Reading*, pp. 12, 184.
59 *Boswell in Extremes*, p. 284.
60 Ibid., pp. 284, 290–91.
61 Irma S. Lustig, "*The Myth of Johnson's Misogyny*."
62 *Boswell in Extremes*, pp. 284–6.
63 Ibid., p. 287.
64 [Soame Jenyns] *A View of the Internal Evidence of the Christian Religion* (London, 1776), pp. 52–60.

65 *Boswell in Extremes*, p. 287.
66 Ibid., pp. 287–8.
67 Ibid., pp. 288–9.
68 Ibid., p. 289.
69 Ibid., p. 290. Boswell, *Life of Johnson*, vol. 2, p. 229.
70 *The Gentleman's Magazine*, June 1791: 500–502.
71 *George Fox: The Journal*, p. 36.
72 *The Gentleman's Magazine*, June 1791: 500.
73 Ibid., p. 501.
74 Green, "Jenny Harry," (10th month, 1913).
75 *Boswell in Extremes*, p. 289.
76 *The Gentleman's Magazine*, June 1791: 501.
77 *Boswell in Extremes*, pp. 284–5.
78 *The Gentleman's Magazine*, June 1791: 501.
79 Ibid.
80 Ibid., pp. 501–2.
81 Vickery, *Gentleman's Daughter*, p. 9.
82 Larson, *Daughters of Light*, p. 373.
83 Kemmerer, "A neutral being," pp. 23–7. Basker, *"Dancing Dogs."*
84 *Records and Recollections of James Jenkins*, pp. 107–8.

Chapter 4

Revolutionary Politics and Literary Skirmishes

As the American Revolution continued to test Quaker loyalties and pacifist principles, Knowles used her royal connections to exercise political influence on behalf of Friends. At the same time, she satirized Lord North, the Government leader, in a comic verse and developed ties with the emerging antislavery movement. She created a new form of self-representation, commented on her fame, and developed acquaintances with two well-known radical women. Knowles maintained her close friendship with Jane Harry, who struggled with the politics of complexion within her family. Anna Seward wrote her account of Knowles's confrontation with Johnson concerning Harry, differing somewhat from that of Boswell and of Knowles. As Thomas Knowles became increasingly prosperous, he and Mary embraced new forms of polite Quakerliness, but they also experienced tensions within the Quaker community. In the midst of these accomplishments, Mary faced the unexpected deaths of two dearly loved ones.

According to a later account, Mary Knowles remained "a great favourite with the King and Queen, and had frequent access to the Royal Family."[1] This royal connection became particularly important as the American Revolution presented new challenges to English Quakers. Many English Friends shared strong family ties, spiritual bonds, and economic interests with their co-religionists in the American Colonies, producing painfully divided loyalties. Leading Friends in London, for example, helped collect funds to replace property losses suffered by Quakers in Philadelphia, an action that could be seen as undermining British military efforts.[2]

In this context, the practice of pacifism by English Quakers became even more problematic. Given the close connections and overt sympathy of many of them for American Friends, their pacifism could be interpreted as a lack of national loyalty. Moreover, as in other wars, some men claimed to be Quakers to avoid military impressments, calling into question the authentic beliefs of true pacifists.[3]

In 1778, as British troops faced stiff resistance from Americans, Knowles presented her five-year-old son at court. The king received the boy kindly, asking his name. "When the proud mother answered 'George,'" according to a later account, "the King seemed to feel the compliment and bowed very complacently." Knowles then "proposed," so the story went, "with the King and Queen's permission, that her little boy should recite some lines she had composed, to which they assented." As the royal couple looked on, young George delivered 14 lines of heroic couplets written by his mother.

The poem began by upholding the Quaker principle of peace, but stated in classical language with a broad Christian appeal. "Though with no awful services, I come," the boy recited, "Forbid to follow Mars' dire thund'ring drum; / My faith no warlike liberty hath given, / Since 'peace on earth' sweet angels sing in heaven." As in her earlier writings, Knowles aligned Quakers with true Christians, shown here as following the guidance of angels. Conversely, she linked those who supported war with the pagan followers of Mars. At the same time, she characterized Quaker pacifism as a restraint on "warlike liberty" rather than a sectarian dictum.

Continuing his recitation, her son pledged his loyalty to the king and asked him to maintain royal protection for Quakers. "Yet I will serve my prince as years increase," the boy declared, "And cultivate the finest arts of peace. / As loyal subjects, then, great George, by thee / Let genuine Quakers still protected be." The boy ended by asserting his manhood and his affection for the royal family. "I must, I will assume the man this day / I've seen the King and Queen! Huzza! Huzza!" According to the later writer, "the King and Queen and Royal Family laughed heartily" at the boy's performance.[4]

Knowles had once before requested a royal favor for a friend of her cousin's, and she now took shrewd advantage of this social situation to exercise political influence. She acted as a Quaker leader by defending her faith, even though not a minister, and participated in politics by soliciting royal protection for Friends. Although she could neither hold office nor vote, she, like other well-connected women, exercised political power through her social position. Drawing on her long relationship with the royal family, she articulated a Quaker form of loyal but pacifist Christian citizenship, tied not to military service but to dedication to the person of the king. In this way, she facilitated the social integration of Quakers as loyal Christian Britons even though pacifism precluded them from military service.

While Knowles maintained her royal friendships, she also continued to serve as a friend and protector to Jane Harry. Despite Johnson's angry dismissal of her, Harry won an important public recognition for her painting. Although Harry had left the Church of England, she had not yet joined the Quakers. As a talented female artist, she, unlike Knowles, felt free to display her painting publicly.

In 1778, Harry received a gold medal for painting from the London-based Society for the Encouragement of Arts, Manufactures and Commerce.[5] Founded in 1754, the Society for the Arts, popularly called, encouraged the participation of women, unlike its newer rival, the Royal Academy of Art. Each year, the Society awarded special premiums, including cash payments, to outstanding young female artists aged 20 or younger. The Society also framed and exhibited the selected works. As art expert Charlotte Grant pointed out, "The premiums offered by the Society for young women artists complicate our current model of the relations between women and 'the public spirit' in the practices and discourse of eighteenth-century art."[6] An unnamed contemporary, perhaps Knowles, later recalled Harry's gold medal as an important public honor.[7]

Despite her own scruples about displaying her paintings with a brush, Knowles continued to practice her needle painting. She produced a needlework copy for her portrait of King George III (Illustration 2). Somewhat rougher and less finished, the copy still appears remarkably lifelike and detailed. Knowles kept this copy in her possession and does not seem to have displayed it publicly, although she may have shown it privately to friends and relatives.

Even more remarkably, given the dearth of portraiture by English Quakers, Knowles stitched her own self-portrait in needlework, which she signed and dated 1779 (Illustration 3). She portrayed herself sitting before her embroidery frame, on which her needle painting of the king can be seen. She looks directly out at the viewer with a steady gaze and a slight smile. A cloth cap sits atop her neat and unpowdered brown hair. She wears a plain ribbon around her neck and an undecorated but attractive low-cut gown with a simple scarf. As described by a modern expert, the self-portrait shows her "in demure cap and fichu, with the portrait of George III on the frame."[8]

Although her cap and scarf can be described as "demure," Knowles challenged conventions in both the form and content of this needlework self-portrait. Art experts Bernard and Therle Hughes noted that she used irregular stitches "as if she sought to break free of the limitations imposed by her chosen medium and, as it were, paint with her needle." They pointed out how, by "Stitching in any direction that suited her purpose, she ... achieved effects of fine shading, even of facial expression, where most of her contemporaries lamentably failed."[9] Having privately practiced painting, Knowles applied painterly techniques to needlework to achieve new levels of artistic excellence.

Furthermore, this needlework self-portrait demonstrates that at age 46, as in her youth, Knowles continued the radical practice of female self-representation. This visual self-representation, like her earlier literary memoirs, referenced her facial features, pride in her needlework, and insistence on defining herself. By showing herself with her embroidery frame, she both documented her expertise and commemorated her most important artistic accomplishment. Like her earlier memoirs and the copy of her needle painting of the king, she seems to have created her self-portrait for her personal enjoyment, but she probably showed it to family and friends. Although not publicly displayed until the twentieth century, her self-portrait provides visible evidence of her strong self-image.

While Mary tested Quaker attitudes toward art, Thomas prospered as a physician and tested precepts about plain living. The family acquired property and possessions, marking them as highly successful members of the growing middling classes. Dr. Knowles owned rental property in Whitechapel[10] and additional homes in Edinburgh and Brighthelmstone,[11] a favorite holiday location for wealthy Londoners. A visiting relative reported that the Doctor "at last" acquired "a coach

76   *Gender, Religion, and Radicalism*

Illustration 2 Mary Morris Knowles, *Portrait of George III (after a painting by Zoffany*, 4ft 8.75 in x 4ft 2.34 in, colored worsteds embroidered on canvas ground, 1771–1807, V & A Museum.

Illustration 3 Mary Morris Knowles, *Mary Knowles at her embroidery*, 35.1 in x 33.2 in, late eighteenth century, The Royal Collection.

of his own," an important symbol of polite respectability. The relative described the coach as "elegant, a dark olive with a metal *K* on the door of considerable magnitude." The doctor may have considered the coach a necessity for his medical practice, but, as his relative implied, that did not explain the large letter *K*. The same relative also observed Mary going out "in full dress to pay the Bride visit."[12] By combining serious Quaker beliefs with their prosperous lifestyle, Thomas and Mary Knowles helped fashion new standards of polite Quakerliness.

Mary also continued to test the limits of Quakerliness by exploring new religious ideas. On 4 April 1779, Boswell dined with Johnson, afterwards noting briefly in his journal, "Mrs. Knowles reading Swedenborg."[13] It seems from Boswell's entry that Johnson conveyed this information to him. If so, Knowles continued to interact with Johnson and discuss religion after their confrontation.

Knowles's choice of reading indicates the range of her theological study and her interest in mystical revelations. Emmanuel Swedenborg, a well-born and highly educated Swede, described how God appeared to him, enabling him to visit heaven and hell and speak with spirits and angels.[14] By referring to this mystical treatise, Knowles demonstrated that she studied and discussed non-Quaker texts.

Although Knowles mixed with non-Quakers, she also enjoyed rich platonic friendships with two like-minded Quaker men in Bath. Knowles visited the fashionable spa town, where she socialized with Edmund Rack, described in Chapter Three as the author of the life of William Penn and friend of Catharine Macaulay. Rack also sometimes wrote essays and poems under the name "Eusebius," an early church father who favored religious toleration and moderation.

In December 1779, Knowles spent a literary afternoon in company with Rack and his close friend, William Matthews. Rack and Matthews helped found the Bath Agricultural Society and the Bath and West of England Philosophical Society, among the best known of many similar associations being formed throughout the country.[15] Like Knowles, these two sincere and devout Quakers participated in provincial cultural activities with intellectuals and artists of various backgrounds.

In a poem entitled, "To M. K. on her Departure from Bath, written after conducting her to her Dilligence," Matthews described how he, Rack, and Knowles celebrated their friendship through poetry. Acknowledging her as "my honoured Friend," Matthews characterized their relationship as "a chaste, enlarging sentimental love." Writing in the polished poetics of heroic couplets, Matthews referred to Knowles by her pen name, "Lavinia." He described the three writing poetry together by saying, "Sweet were our lays, we answered line to line / ... Lavinia caught it [inspiration] foremost of the three / Eusebius next, and next it came to *me*." Matthews praised Knowles for her poetic facility and spiritual inspiration. "Come then, Lavinia!" he wrote, "in whose favour'd mind / The gospel day springs from on high hath shined."[16] Judging from this poem, despite their gender differences, Matthews and Rack portrayed Knowles as a respected intellectual, inspired Quaker, talented poet, and cherished companion.

Even with these kinds of cross-gender friendships, long-standing tensions simmered among some Friends in London and throughout the country as a new generation of male leaders, like Thomas Knowles, came into prominence. According to James Jenkins, the Quaker chronicler, these new leaders challenged, "an Aristocracy of Elders [who] ruled with an almost exclusive sway" in Quaker business meetings. Jenkins, who rented lodgings from Thomas in Whitechapel, "rejoiced in observing him (both in Monthly and quarterly meetings) a frequent attacker of the feudal lords." Jenkins did not detail the causes of these differences, but generational tensions seemed to be a factor. When new men, like Thomas Knowles, became recognized leaders, Jenkins hailed it as "the commencement of a great revolution amongst us."[17]

Although tensions developed among some Quakers, Mary Knowles deepened her close relationships with the Lloyds of Birmingham, linking them with her friend, Jane Harry. Sampson Lloyd III, her contemporary, and his wife, Rachel, now lived on the family estate at Farm with a growing brood of children, eventually numbering 17. Knowles arranged for Harry to serve as a governess to the older Lloyd children. Harry moved to Farm where she presumably worked for pay since she no longer had the support of her father or guardian.[18]

Frequent visitors to Farm included Sampson's half-brother, Charles Lloyd and his family. Charles, a classically educated scholar and successful banker, married Mary Farmer, Knowles's one-time bridesmaid and early correspondent. This marriage added another link to Knowles's already strong connections with the Lloyds. Charles and Mary Lloyd also soon had an ever-growing family.[19]

In 1780, Knowles presented the Lloyd children with a beautiful book she created, containing original watercolor sketches and poems. Described by a descendant as a "small square book, bound in red morocco" with gilded letters reading, "M. K. to C. H. LL and Juniors, 1780," it seems to have been intended for Charles, the five-year old son of Charles and Mary Lloyd and his younger siblings. Its twentieth-century owner found the book surprising because of its lighthearted poems and fanciful illustrations.[20] Evidently, Knowles felt free to display her visual art and exercise her imagination in a family context, if not publicly.

The book illustrates Knowles's warm affection for the Lloyd children and for Harry. In one poem, Knowles described Harry in quick moving cadences with sometimes comic rhymes. Addressing herself to the children, Knowles drew their attention to Harry's good nature and devotion to them. "Behold slim Jane's sagacious look," she appealed to the children, "Smiling, 'My pretty dears,' she cries / And twinkles both her jetty eyes; / Her slender form towards you bending, / To all your little wants attending."

With evident affection for both the governess and her charges, Knowles cited Harry as a good example to inspire the youngsters to behave correctly. With gentle admonition, she asked, "And now is Jenny ever seen / Against her own chair back to lean?" In answer, Knowles concluded, "O, no, no I could lay a guinea / You've no such tale to tell of Jenny!" She pointedly added, "And let me hope it is as true /

She's no such tale to tell of you." Knowles ended by adding, "That this dear maid I recommend / As a most faithful bosom friend."[21]

Despite their close ties, Knowles differed with the Lloyds concerning standards of appropriate dress for Quakers. In another comic poem entitled, "The Lamentation of Timothy Tattle on the capricious Fashions and the satirical cast of the present Times," Knowles assumed a male identity, indicating how men, too, followed fashion. Knowles, as Tattle, humorously recalled, "When I was young, and in my prime, / Such were the days of yore. / It n'er was thought a sin or crime / Whatever people wore."

Contrasting those days to the present, Tattle lamented, "But *now*, by tyrant Fashion rule/ (so gen'ral her controul,) / Howe'er absurd – still on the mode / Trots *every* silly soul!"[22] By denouncing fashion as a female "tyrant," Knowles comically applied her commitment to liberty to an individual's choice of dress. In doing so, she provides an example of what historian Margaret Hunt described as the eighteenth-century female domestication of seventeenth-century radical political terminology.[23]

Demonstrating the tyranny of fashion, Tattle told what happened in Birmingham when "A gentlewoman neat, / A place of worship went into / And gravely took her seat." The unnamed woman made all "The Congregation smile" because she wore a gown of Canterbury, an English-made fabric woven with a silk warp and cotton filling, rather than "Rich silks that stand on end!" According to Tattle, "the kind Pair at Farm," evidently referring to Sampson Lloyd III and Rachel, were "in a bustle and a stir / For they are both kin to her, / And shame their cheeks did warm." In the end, Tattle tells the embarrassed congregation "you're too *proud and high* / This Gentlewoman wins the battle / By her Humility" and "still she always charms me most, / In her strip'd Canterbury."[24]

In this light-hearted but serious poem, Knowles grappled with the power of fashion, asserting the primacy of internal virtues over outward appearances. She did not advocate any style or color of dress, even approving of stripes, but she stressed that the best dress need not be the most costly. In this case, for her, inward values rather than outward style defined Quakerliness.

Yet, even as she reinforced serious religious values, Knowles playfully subverted Quaker restrictions on music. She prefaced her rhythmical "Lamentation" by writing that "the reader may *repeat* (not sing) [the words] in the *tone* (not tune) of 'Three Children Sliding on the Ice, All on a Summer's Day.'"[25] Knowles again made it clear that she did not consider sincere Quaker beliefs inimical to the enjoyment of the arts.

Knowles revisited the theme of the tyranny of fashion in another short undated, and perhaps unfinished, manuscript poem, entitled simply, "On Fashion." In it, she again satirized the power of fashion, here personified as a "female Magician." Fashion "forms and transforms and does all but *inform* us," she wrote. She portrayed the tyranny of fashion as it "Turns our world upside down, and our minds inside out / Bids us taste and distaste, bids us do and undo." Determined not to be ruled by fashion, Knowles had no intention, as she concluded, of wearing clothes that made women "look like Dame Cocks ready trimmed for the fight."[26]

Knowles understood fashion first hand not only because of her activities in London, Bath, and Birmingham, but also because she participated in a well-known, if sometimes maligned, provincial literary salon. In 1781, Knowles appeared at the poetic competitions organized by Sir John and Lady Anna Riggs Miller at their villa in Batheaston, outside Bath. Sir John owned land in Ireland and served as a captain in the Seven Years' War. His wife, also from Ireland, authored *Letters from Italy* and aspired to become a serious literary patron.[27]

During the season at Bath, Lady Miller opened her house weekly for public days when visitors participated in poetic competitions. She worked hard at attracting male and female poets, writers, and society figures. She insisted that her motives centered on charity, since she printed and sold the poems, donating the proceeds to a worthy cause.[28] Contemporaries both praised and criticized the poetry, but Knowles's friend Anna Seward, who often visited, pointed out that the competitions first gave her the courage to put her poems before the public.[29]

Knowles visited this literary salon at least once, on 18 February 1781. Eliza Hayley wrote her husband, the popular poet, William Hayley, "I arrived about an hour before the ceremony began," referring to the placing of the poems in a vase to be judged, "during which time I had some pleasant conversation with Mrs. Knowles and others."[30] This casual reference indicates that Knowles already knew the Hayleys and, more than likely, other men and women who conversed there. Eliza Hayley's brief note shows that the Millers welcomed Knowles, as a polite and distinguished Quaker, as their guest. Moreover, Knowles participated in this provincial associative social space, just as she dined at Dillys' in London.

This kind of behavior by Knowles provoked conflicting comments by two Quaker males. On 14 June 1781, Richard Shackleton, a schoolmaster in Ballitoire, Ireland, alluded to her in a letter to his daughter, Mary Shackleton, later Leadbeater. His daughter's letters were subsequently published with personal names deleted. In the published letter, Shackleton wrote, "xxx is a sprightly, sensible woman; but would suit my taste much better, if more of *the* diffident, *the* humble, *the* simple entered into her composition." Drawing a lesson for his daughter, Shackleton added, "And even true genius and literary accomplishments receive a softness and lustre from these qualities highly ornamental."[31]

James Jenkins, as a friend and admirer of Knowles, took umbrage at these comments. "That Mary Knowles was here meant, there cannot (I think) be the smallest doubt," he wrote, explaining how she befriended Shackleton's daughter. Jenkins believed the father should have given "his daughter advice boldly without sinking the character of his friend." Jenkins continued, "Now, the fact is that to his daughter, he feared Mary Knowles was as a Prototype, and lest she (his daughter) should be deficient in *the* diffidence, *the* humility, and *the* simplicity, this *side-wind advice* was given." In Jenkins's opinion, given Knowles's "transcendent abilities, the great admiration they excited, and her wealth considered, she was really a pattern of *the* diffident, *the* humble, and *the* simple."[32]

Although Jenkins defended Knowles, he also expressed concerns about her participation in many popular pastimes. He praised Knowles for her "very first rate abilities" frequently applied to literary subjects, but he regretted to see her so "often stopping to divert herself and others, with the puzzles of letters, and syllables, with the playthings of science, rebusses, riddles, and charades." He further noted that she spent "hour, after hour at the backgammon board."[33] As a married woman in her 40s, Knowles sparked debate about appropriate behavior for Quaker women just as she had done before her marriage.

As Knowles tested the limits of polite Quakerliness, her friend, Jane Harry, confronted the politics of complexion in her own family. In 1780, Harry's father, Judge Thomas Hibbert, died in Jamaica, leaving her £2,000, while bequeathing more than £100,000 to his nephew, named Thomas Hibbert, Junior. When Harry learned of this, she wrote the heir, her cousin, protesting the unequal legacy.

Her cousin answered coldly, "How freely so ever *you* used the Word 'Father,' you will find that in speaking of you, *he* never used the Word 'Daughter.'" Even more cruelly, the heir continued, "So far was my late Uncle from desiring that you should be held up to the world as his child, that no consideration gave him more Uneasiness, than that of you being so publicly known to be so." He added that his uncle had originally determined to leave her only £1,000, but that he had been persuaded to increase the amount to £2,000 by her former guardian, Nathaniel Sprigg, who had also since died.[34]

In this disdainful reply, Thomas Hibbert, Jr., reflected inextricably intertwined attitudes toward gender, colonialism, and condition of birth. He did not explain whether her father's uneasiness grew from the fact that he had not married her mother or because of her mother's Jamaican heritage or both. Whether the heir considered it unnecessary or impolite to be more specific, his thinly veiled prejudices indicate that references to race, ethnicity, and colonial origins remained submerged but potent in the socioeconomics of this successful West Indian trading family. His attitudes may not have been unusual since similar disparate legacies involving children of English planter fathers and West Indian mothers have also been documented in eighteenth-century Bristol.[35]

In her letter to the heir, Harry also expressed concern about what provision Judge Hibbert had made for her mother. "To your dutiful and proper enquiries after your mother, I answered that she was comfortably provided for," he reminded her. The heir told his cousin that her father had left land and slaves to Mrs. Harry, indicating her status as a free person. The heir also told of "another lot of land" near her mother's house, which Harry would inherit at her mother's death.[36]

According to an unnamed contemporary, perhaps Knowles, Harry "formed a design of going to Jamaica, the residence of her mother, with a view to procure the freedom of her mother's Negroes, and to instruct them in the principles of the Christian religion."[37] Harry had, perhaps, felt powerless to persuade her father against slave holding, but, when she learned her mother had inherited his slaves, she resolved to act. Her resolution predated the beginning of the organized movement in Britain against slavery and the slave trade. She may well have been influenced by her Quaker convictions and personal knowledge of Friends like John Coakley Lettsom, who had freed the slaves he inherited. Yet neither the Quaker organization nor any other group in Britain publicly supported emancipation.[38]

Harry could not, however, act on her resolution because of the continuing war with the American Colonies. As the same unnamed contemporary later explained, "The great commotion of public affairs" caused by the war "frustrated her noble design."[39] Yet Harry did not forget her resolution.

Now financially independent, Harry joined the Quakers and became engaged to an English Friend. While serving as a governess, Harry met Joseph Thresher, then beginning his practice as a surgeon in Worcester. After agreeing to marry him, she returned to London, and the two corresponded about their future plans.

Through all these changes, Jane Harry maintained an affectionate regard for her mother. She helped Thresher revise a letter to her mother, requesting her permission for their marriage. Mrs. Harry could read, but significant educational differences existed between mother and daughter. "My alterations may perhaps have render'd it less elegant," Jane told Thresher, referring to his letter, "but I think the form is rather more simple, and may therefore be better understood."[40]

On 26 November 1782, "Jane Harry, late of Kingston in Jamaica, but now of the City of London" married "Joseph Thresher, Junior, of Worcester, surgeon," at the Devonshire House Meeting. Their marriage records list Thomas and Mary Knowles as "relations," in the same manner as the parents of the groom, indicating their status as Harry's guardians or protectors.[41] After their wedding, the Threshers settled into their new home in Worcester.

The continuing war with America not only prevented Harry from returning to Jamaica, but it also caused serious problems for the British government, inspiring Knowles to compose a poem satirizing Lord North, the king's leading minister. To finance the long war, North borrowed funds from private citizens at guaranteed rates of return. Many contemporaries accused North of personally benefiting from this loan program by negotiating favorable agreements with his friends.[42]

Knowles revealed her political sympathies and tensions among Quakers in her satirical poem skewering North along with Thomas Smith, a quirky London Friend. In her poem, Knowles described Smith, a banker, as "A Quaker well-known / In fair London town / For his prim puritanical airs."[43] James Jenkins described him in much stronger language as one of a "trio of the most uncouth, and rude tradesmen that perhaps ever disgraced the character of Friends." While Smith's "talk was sometimes light and silly, his manner uncourteous," Jenkins continued, his actions could be "consequential."[44] Knowles's poem described just such a silly but consequential action taken by Smith.

Knowles portrayed Smith as being offended that he had not been asked to participate in a recent government loan. She described Smith awakening one morning and determining to call on North. "I'll straightway go forth / To the home of Friend North," he resolved, "And tell him, he has not done right."

Knowles criticized North through her portrayal of Smith. She depicted Smith fuming about North, remembering, "What service for him I have done." Through Smith, she implied that political favoritism formed the basis for the government loans. "Yet the ill-natured foe," continued Smith, referring to North, "To his shame and my woe, / Has left me quite out of his loan."

On reaching North's house, Smith demanded entry with a "strange pompous air," leading the servant "to think it was Governor Penn, / Or some such great man / Come in with a plan, / To restore us to peace once again." With this allusion, Knowles probably referred to Thomas Penn, a descendant of William Penn. By referring to a plan for peace, she subtly conveyed her hope of ending a war that ran counter both to her pacifism and her commitment to liberty.

Admitted by the misled servant, Smith traded anti-Semitic remarks with North before being curtly dismissed by him. When Smith threatened never to lend the government money again, North countered, saying, "'All Jews young and old, / Love to put out their gold / Where the highest per cent can be made.'" Smith retorted angrily, "'I never was Jew called before.'" North coolly replied, "'In matters of trade / You know Jew and Gentile are one.'" North further taunted Smith, "'For should I bring you cash / You would say it was trash, / But it's gold, when we treat of the loan.'" Furious, Smith concluded, "'With thee I'll have nothing to do.'" According to Knowles, he "returned to the city, / (And here ends my ditty), / As great and as wise as he went!"[45]

Knowles evinced a shrewd grasp of politics and economics in this verse, but she also employed anti-Semitic humor. The status of Jews in England had been hotly debated ever since Parliament repealed the Jewish Naturalization Act of 1753 by popular demand. According to historian Paul Langford, some Britons strongly believed that making Jews "equal competitors in trade and manufacture was ... in accord both with English tradition and natural rights."[46] Knowles portrayed Smith as narrow minded and comical in taking offense at North's remark about Jews and Gentiles being equal in trade. While she might have intended her humor to have the positive effect of supporting commercial access for Jews, the poem could also have had the negative effect of furthering anti-Semitism by North's references to Jews as preoccupied with gold.

Although not published until the twentieth century, this poem, like many of her earlier verses, seems to have become a social text. Readers copied and circulated two manuscript versions under the titles, "Lord North and the Quaker" and "The Minister and the Quaker."[47] In this way, Knowles effectively protested government corruption and financial mismanagement, longstanding radical issues. By so doing, she expressed her political opinions and expanded female political participation.

As a polite and sociable Quaker, Knowles continued her longtime friendship with Anna Seward of Lichfield, who reinforced her links with other writers and with a rising visual artist. In August 1782, Seward wrote to the popular poet

William Hayley and his wife "from the House of Dr. Knowles." She described Mary and Thomas warmly, saying, "Mrs. Knowles is very well, the same kind and interesting being – as well and as kind is the good Doctor."[48]

Seward told Hayley that the two women visited the studio of George Romney. Hayley served as a patron to Romney, then attaining great success as a portrait painter.[49] If Knowles declined to exhibit her paintings, she did not hesitate to express her opinions about Romney's. Seward praised Romney's work, adding that, "Mrs. Knowles who, if she has less enthusiasm, has much more judgment, asserts the superiority of Romney's power to that of any other painter."[50] Later, when Romney painted Seward's likeness, she told Hayley that Knowles pronounced it "one of the finest portraits she ever saw."[51]

Seward also wrote Thomas Sedgewick Whalley, a well-known English poet living abroad, about Knowles's growing public reputation. Seward recounted Knowles telling her with amusement, that "Settling in London, and her fame reaching from thence" back to her hometown, "the gentry in the little town of Rugeley ... pay every homage to the recollection of her and seem to take pride and consequence to themselves that she was born and educated at Rugeley." Seward also commented on Knowles's reputation in Lichfield. She noted, somewhat sardonically, "that when a literary being descends amongst us, whose fame has gone forth in the world, especially if they are of independent fortune, how lavish these good folks are with their encomiums." Classifying Knowles with two of the most famous male poets of their day, Seward observed that, "Their enthusiasms appear to glow so fervently whenever they talk to me of yourself, Mr. Hayley, and Mrs. Knowles."[52]

Maintaining a wide circle of friends in London, Knowles socialized with Mary Wilkes Hayley, the sister and political supporter of John Wilkes and cousin by marriage to William Hayley. Mary Wilkes Hayley's second husband, George Hayley, became "one of the wealthiest merchants in the city" and served as a Member of Parliament.[53] After he died, she took over his business and became highly successful in the transatlantic trade. She also delighted in acquiring literary acquaintances. According to a contemporary, she dashed around London in a fine carriage, cultivating "with much avidity, the Society of those who were distinguished in the world by their talents and their writings."[54]

On 1 August 1783, William Hayley wrote with obvious relish to his wife Eliza that, "I seize a pen to tell you that I have passed an agreeable and successful morning with those animated geniuses in petticoats, the Ladies Knowles and Hayley."[55] William clearly enjoyed the company of the two women, yet his colorful description captures some of the ambiguities surrounding females in the public gaze. While he praised the women for their intellect, he also evoked the well worn metaphor of the petticoat often linked to females in public as a sexualized reference to their intimate underclothes.[56] While Hayley's terminology appears benign, it adds a complex sexual allusion to his otherwise favorable description of these two talented women.

"The fair Quaker introduced me to our cousin," William told his wife, indicating Knowles's prior acquaintance with Mary Wilkes Hayley. William admired his cousin, although he noted she resembled her notoriously unhandsome brother. "Though she is certainly like her brother John Wilkes in masquerade," he wrote, "I thought her one of the most pleasing women I have met in my travels." Impressed by her business acumen, he observed, "She is still a great merchant." Noting that she would soon send two ships to America, William reported that, "if she prospers in her voyage ... she is going to collect commercial debts to the amount of £98,000."[57]

While Mary Knowles gained fame and a wide circle of friends, Thomas also earned a public reputation and ever greater prosperity as a successful London physician. *Kent's Directory* of London businesses for 1783 listed him as, "Thomas Knowles, M. D., Number 19, Lombard Street."[58] Seward later recalled how she "had been a witness, during some weeks, at different times, to Dr. Knowles's immense practice." She added that he told her about "having realized ten thousand pounds in the year 1783."[59]

The Knowles's family moved to Lombard Street, a busy commercial artery lined with fine buildings, and in 1784 they transferred their membership to the nearby Gracechurch Street Meeting.[60] According to later Quaker historians, the members at Gracechurch Street "were a more influential and prosperous class" than those of other London meetings. Moreover, "a large amount of general hospitality prevailed" among the wealthy Friends of Gracechurch Street Meeting.[61]

According to James Jenkins, Dr. Knowles prospered by focusing on his medical practice. Jenkins noted that while "many of the medical tribe in London" were "tiring the town with incessant publication," Dr. Knowles "went on collecting guineas." Jenkins continued approvingly, "the tangible possession of which, he judiciously preferred to the delusive phantom of literary fame."[62]

Yet Dr. Knowles did receive at least one literary visitor. In May 1783, Boswell noted that he "Called Dr. Knowles's. Saw him a little; she not in."[63]

Increasingly recognized as a Quaker leader, Thomas and eight other men presented a petition to the king in June 1783, as the long struggle between Britain and her colonies at last came to an end. Like the poem Mary had written for their son's royal recitation, the petition linked Quaker pacifism to loyalty to George III. The king's reply, reported in *Gentleman's Magazine*, "assured" Friends of his "constant protection."[64] His answer indicated that these Quakers, like Mary, succeeded in reconciling pacifism and national loyalty to the king's satisfaction.

At the same time, Thomas participated in Quaker efforts to end trading and holding slaves within the British Empire. In June 1783, the British Quaker organization, spurred by the continued urging of American Friends, appointed a 23-member committee, including Thomas, to consider action concerning slavery and the slave trade. In July, he and five other men Friends met in an informal association "to consider what steps could by them be taken for the Relief and

Liberation of the Negro Slaves in the West Indies, and the Discouragement of the slave trade on the coast of Africa."[65]

This smaller committee of six met secretly, perhaps to avoid the oversight of the Quaker organization and to foster ecumenical support. During the summer of 1783, this informal association met frequently at the Lombard Street home of Mary and Thomas Knowles.[66] Jane Harry's struggle with the realities of colonial slave holding could have influenced Thomas and Mary's support for antislavery efforts.

Abolition represented one of many new elements in Britain's highly contested political landscape following the resignation of Lord North and the loss of the American Colonies. In this charged political atmosphere, Dillys' dining room remained an important associative social space even after the early death of the devoted Whig, Edward Dilly. After Edward died at age 47, Charles Dilly took over the bookselling business. Although Charles did not share his brother's radical views, he continued to host brilliant literary dinners.

On 1 May 1784, Charles wrote a friend, "I had the pleasure of the Co. last Tuesday of Dr. Price, Mrs. Macaulay Graham and her Daughter, and the sensible Quaker Mrs. Knowles."[67] While writing her multi-volume history, Catharine Macaulay had outraged public opinion by publicly, and many said excessively, celebrating her 46th birthday in Bath. The next year, 1778, she shocked public opinion again by marrying William Graham, aged 21.[68] Despite these public outcries, she remained a friend of Charles Dilly and other influential men.

Catharine Macaulay Graham and Knowles had many mutual acquaintances, so they may have already met. They both knew Edmund Rack in Bath, for example. Moreover, Graham had once been closely associated with John Wilkes, so it seems likely she knew Mary Wilkes Hayley, also a friend of Knowles. Graham socialized with the radical American brothers, Arthur and William Lee,[69] as did Knowles. These webs of radical connections point to the need for more research on the cross-gender friendships of middling class females whose political activities did not depend on land-owning status and aristocratic loyalties.

Since the company that night included Dr. Richard Price, the conversation probably turned to radical politics despite Charles Dilly's dislike of the subject. Price belonged to the Club of Honest Whigs composed of many Dissenters and London radicals who, like Macaulay Graham, had supported the American Revolution. Before the war, Price wrote *Observations on the Nature of Civil Liberty* urging radicals to look beyond national loyalties and support the natural rights of all men to political freedom.[70] Natural rights ideology came to constitute an important component of the evolving radicalism of the late eighteenth century.

While Knowles may have enjoyed socializing with radicals in London, she must have deeply mourned the unexpected death of her dear friend, Jane Harry Thresher. In May 1784, Thresher gave birth to a boy but became mortally ill. Knowles later wrote to Seward describing Thresher's dying days. Seward's response indicated that Knowles may have been with Thresher during her last illness. Seward told Knowles she had read Knowles's letter to mutual friends who "talked of the dear saint, your Jenny Harry." Seward continued, "They were much impressed by the pathos with which it describes the soft resignation, which, dying in the bloom of her life, drew the sting of death from her bosom."[71] According to Quaker records, "Jane Thresher, wife of Joseph Thresher, Surgeon, died on the 17th of the 8th month called August 1784 ... aged about twenty-eight."[72]

The next month, *Gentleman's Magazine* carried a beautifully written obituary of "Mrs. Thresher," possibly composed by Knowles.[73] In it, the unnamed author described Thresher's "accomplishments of education, amiable manner, and benevolence of heart." The writer knew the young woman well and clearly loved and respected her, recounting, for example, how she won the gold medal from the Society for the Arts. Appearing in the section entitled, "Obituaries of Considerable Persons," the tribute served as a public memorial to the brief life and accomplishments of this young woman.

According to the obituary, Thresher continued her concern for her mother's slaves throughout her final illness. "We are informed," said the writer, "she has requested her husband that, if the said Negroes be liberated at her mother's decease, he will pay the premium to the Island, for such liberation, if any should be required."[74] Jane Harry Thresher's deathbed action points to the need for more research on colonial-born women involved in both slave holding and emancipation. Her obituary served as a public statement against slave holding, just as abolition emerged as an important political issue.

Another death later that year caused a much greater public stir. Samuel Johnson died at age 75 on 13 December following an extended illness. Seward and Knowles compared his tortured final hours to the peaceful passing of Thresher a few months before. "O! Yes, as you observe, dreadful were the horrors which attended poor Johnson's dying state," Seward wrote Knowles, as the two discussed his well-known fears concerning death.[75]

Soon after Johnson's death, Boswell wrote Seward requesting information for his biography. Seward sent what Boswell then described as a "valuable treasure" of anecdotes of Johnson's life in Lichfield. On 15 February 1785, Boswell wrote her again from Edinburgh asking for additional items. He included in this request, "if you can recollect it, his tremendous Commination at Mr. Dilly's when we talked of the 'odious wench' who turned Quaker."[76]

A few weeks later, Boswell stopped in Lichfield to visit Seward. She presented him with most of the information he requested, but she did not include her account of Knowles's confrontation with Johnson. In a letter dated the day Boswell departed, Seward wrote Knowles, saying, "He desires I will send him the minutes I made at that time of that, as he justly calls it, tremendous conversation, at Dilly's between you and him of the subject of Miss Harry's commencing a quaker."[77]

Boswellian scholar Marshall Waingrow argued that in requesting Seward's account, Boswell was "cultivating the informant as much as the information."[78] This could be true, because, as literary scholar Irma Lustig noted, Boswell tried to seduce Seward.[79] Yet whatever interest, sexual or otherwise, Boswell may have had in Seward, it does not fully explain why he specifically requested information concerning this particular conversation. Since the scant paragraph in his journal concerning the dispute does not match his description of it as a "tremendous Commination," it seems reasonable to suppose that Boswell requested the information because he sincerely wanted to fill a gap in his journal.

Seward told Knowles, "I had omitted to send it in the first collection from my hopelessness that Mr. Boswell would insert it in his life of the Colossus." She further explained her "hopelessness" by saying that, "Boswell had so often spoke to me, with regret, over the ferocious, reasonless and unchristian violence of his idol that night." She concluded, "it looks impartial beyond my hopes, that he requests me to arrange it."[80]

Boswell did not, evidently, ask Knowles for her version of the conversation, although he called on her frequently. After his wife's death, Boswell moved to London, and he visited Knowles amidst other diversions. One morning in April 1785, he watched a hanging and then visited "Mrs. Knowles." On 13 May, he began the day with his favorite prostitute, "twice," called on Charles Dilly, "Then breakfasted Molly Knowles, fine," and had "Tea with her." Later that day, Boswell attended Quaker Yearly Meeting, perhaps with Knowles. He listened as "one man and two women preached very well," but then his attention lagged. He read the *Saint James Chronicle* until spotted by "A stiff Quaker" who "rebuked" him.[81]

Knowles continued to receive visits from Boswell often in the spring and summer of 1785. Two weeks after attending the Quaker meeting, he noted, "Tea, Molly Knowles." In July, Boswell "visited Mrs. Knowles" twice in less than two weeks. In August, he called on her again, "After breakfast."[82]

Seward, meanwhile, wrote up her minutes of the confrontation between Knowles and Johnson, as requested, and sent her account to Boswell. Boswell seems to have subsequently burned her letter to him containing this account, along with other information she sent him, as will later be explained. Yet an unknown scribe made a copy of Seward's letter, perhaps based on her original. The copy is preserved in the London Library of the Religious Society of Friends as "Notes of a Conversation between Dr. Johnson and Mary Knowles in a Letter to Boswell."[83] This undated copy, whether made at the time or later, is examined here in detail because it contains information not found in either Boswell's journal or Knowles's published version of her conversation. This account is also compared with those of Knowles and Boswell to pinpoint similarities and differences.

The manuscript copy of Seward's letter begins, "You ask me for the Minutes I once made of a certain Conversation which passed at Mr. Dilly's in a literary party in which Dr. Johnson and Mrs. Knowles disputed so earnestly." This corresponds to Boswell's request to Seward concerning this conversation. "As you seem to have an idea of inserting this dispute in your future meditated work (the life of Johnson)," Seward continued, "it is necessary that something should be known concerning the person who was the subject of it."

Unlike Knowles and Boswell, Seward included a great deal of personal information concerning Knowles, Harry, and the Sprigg family in her account. "Miss Jenny Harry was (for she is no more) the Daughter of a rich Planter in the West Indies," Seward explained. Describing Knowles as "the ingenious Quaker lady," Seward reminded Boswell, "you know with what clear and graceful eloquence she speaks on every subject."

Seward reported that when Knowles visited the Sprigg family, they sometimes questioned her religious beliefs. According to Seward, Knowles "opposed their idle and pointed Raillery to deep and long-studied reasoning in the precepts of Scripture delivered in persuasive accents, and clothed with all the beauty of language." Seward's letter shows how Knowles debated her beliefs in this polite social setting as she had done in Dillys' dining room.

Seward believed that Knowles unintentionally influenced Harry, whom Seward portrayed as immature and undereducated. Given Knowles's superior abilities, Seward wrote, "without any design of making a proselyte, she *gained one*." Harry, said Seward, "at the age of eighteen had received what is called a proper and polite Education, without being much instructed in the nature and grounds of her serious belief." According to Seward, Harry "grew very serious and meditated perpetually on all which had dropt from the lips of her Quaker friend, till it appeared to her, that Quakerism was true Christianity." Seward added, "we all know the force of first impressions in Theology and Mrs. K's arguments were the first she had listened to."

Seward wrote that Harry's father, Judge Hibbert, "made her choose between an hundred thousand pounds and his favour, or two thousand pounds and his renunciation" if she became a Quaker.[84] Although this dramatic scene probably never took place, the amounts Seward cited correspond to the disparate inheritances between Harry and her father's heir. Moreover, other friends also believed that Harry lost her legacy because of her religious change, as will be seen. Finally, since Nathaniel Sprigg forced her to leave his house when she decided to become a Quaker, she forfeited a comfortable life under his protection, if not a large fortune.

Turning to the confrontation between Knowles and Johnson, Seward quoted Knowles as beginning, "'I am to entreat thy indulgence, Doctor, towards a gentle female to whom thou used to be kind, and who is unhappy in the loss of that kindness.'" According to Seward, Knowles added, "'Jenny Harry weeps at the consciousness that thou wilt not speak to her.'" Like Knowles and Boswell, Seward said Johnson called Harry an "odious wench." Like Knowles, Seward said Johnson named the source of his anger as Harry's "apostasy." After this, the three accounts diverge but not always in ways that are necessarily incompatible.

Seward agreed with Knowles that Johnson indicated that he did not consider Quakers to be Christians. Yet Seward greatly abbreviated this part of the conversation, which was a primary focus of Knowles's account. Seward noted Knowles's statement that, "'I hope the name of Christian is not denied to sectaries.'" Seward said Johnson replied, "'If the name is not, the common sense is.'" Seward did not, however, include Knowles's longer defense of her Quaker principles. As the daughter of an Anglican cleric, Seward, perhaps, did not choose to report the details of Knowles's Quaker beliefs.

Like both Knowles and Boswell, Seward said Johnson insisted that Harry should not have changed her religion. Yet Seward quoted Johnson as using stronger words than the other two. She said Johnson argued, "'well therefore may I hate the arrogance of a young Wench, who sets herself up for a Judge in theological points and deserts the Religion in which she was nurtured.'"

While Knowles presented Harry as an accountable moral agent, Seward focused instead on Harry's personal pathos and portrayed Knowles as persistently seeking Johnson's sympathy for her. She said Knowles was willing to "'suppose it granted that in the eyes of a simple girl, the weaker Argument appeared the Strongest.'" According to Seward, Knowles entreated Johnson, "'her want of better judgment demands thy pity, not thy Anger.'" Seward said Johnson, unmoved, replied, "'it has my anger and always will.'"

According to Seward, Knowles asked Johnson to "'consider the fortune she has sacrificed.'" This statement indicates that both women believed that Harry forfeited her inheritance because of her beliefs. Seward said Johnson did not deny the inference but answered unsympathetically that, "'The association of Folly cannot eliminate guilt.'" Seward said Knowles again referred to Harry's financial sacrifice by asking, "'can we suppose the Deity will not pardon a defect in Judgment, if such it should prove ... where the desire of serving him ... has been a preferable consideration to that of Worldly interest.'"

Seward portrayed an increasingly angry Johnson focusing his rage on Harry. She quoted him as saying, "'I hate the odious wench, and shall ever hate her,'" She also indicated that Johnson stressed Harry's gender, saying "'I hate all impudence; but the impudence of a Chit's apostasy, I nauseate.'"

Seward presented Knowles as pleading for Harry, telling Johnson, "'Jenny is the most timid creature breathing, she trembles to have offended her parent, ... she grieves to have offended her Guardian, and perhaps she grieves yet more to have offended Dr. Johnson, whom she loved, admired, and honored.'" Seward said Johnson asked, "'Why, then, Madam, did she not consult the man whom she pretends to have loved, admired, and honoured, upon her newfangled Scruples?'"

Seward said Knowles explained that, "'Jenny thinks Dr. Johnson great and good, but she also thinks the gospel demands a simpler form of worship than the Established Church.'" Seward described Knowles as employing ecumenical terms, telling Johnson that Quakerism "'appears to her [Harry] a plain and regular System [which] asks only the simple obedience and homage of a devoted heart.'"

According to Seward, Johnson warned Knowles not to "'pester me about the ridiculous wench,'" but Knowles again linked Johnson's forgiveness to divine toleration, this time with more success. "'Suppose her ridiculous, she has been religious and sincere,'" Knowles pointed out. She asked, "'Will the gate of Heaven shut to the tender and pious mind, whose first consideration has been that of apprehended duty?'"

Finally seeming to soften, Johnson replied, according to Seward, "'Pho, pho, who says it will, Madam?'" Bent on reconciliation, Knowles asked, "'Then if Heaven do not shut the Gate, shall Man shut his Heart?'" Knowles concluded by directly invoking heavenly toleration. "'If the Deity accept the homage of such as sincerely serve Him, under every form of worship,'" Seward quoted her as saying, "'Dr. Johnson and this humble girl will, it is to be hoped, meet in a blessed eternity whither earthly animosities must not be carried.'"

Knowles's account included a similar closing statement. Both women quoted Johnson's reply in almost the exact same words. Seward said Johnson answered, "'Madam, I am not fond of meeting fools anywhere.'"

Knowles ended her account there, but Seward included two additional statements. Seward said Johnson admonished Knowles, saying, "'and so you may tell the odious wench, whom you have persuaded to believe herself a Saint and whom soon you will convince to be a preacher; but I'll take care she does not preach to me.'" This statement recalls Johnson's disparagement of Quaker women preachers, discussed earlier.

Yet, more importantly, Seward identified Boswell as the speaker of the line, also quoted by Knowles, indicating that Johnson had been bested. In her letter, Seward told Boswell, "I remember you whispered to me, 'I never saw this mighty lion so chafed before.'"[85] Knowles quoted these same words but attributed them only to "one of the Gentlemen."[86]

If Boswell had cultivated Seward, this letter shows Seward cultivating him. She ended with a compliment. She told Boswell, "This loud and angry tone in which he thundered out these replies to his calm, but able, antagonist frightened us all, except yourself, who gently, not sarcastically, smiled at his injustice."[87]

Seward's account, along with Harry's letter to her father concerning her change of beliefs, circulated in oral and written forms as social texts. In December 1785, Seward visited friends in Warwickshire where she met "the favourite friend" of Jane Harry Thresher. In a letter to Knowles, Seward wrote, "Mrs. [Harriet Delebere] Granville shewed me Jenny Harry's apologetic tract on quitting our church in favour of quakerism, at so vast a sacrifice of worldly interest." Here again, Seward linked Harry's conversion to her diminished inheritance, and her wording suggests that Granville also believed the story to be true.

Reading Harry's letter to her father "occasioned us to comment, with fresh indignation, upon the ruffian-asperity of Dr. Johnson on this subject," Seward further reported to Knowles. "I had previously recounted to them the conversation of that tremendous evening, as Mr. Boswell calls it, at Dilly's," she continued. Seward again recalled Boswell's "emphatic whisper, 'I never saw this mighty lion so chafed before.'"[88]

Seward also showed her manuscript to Knowles, as Seward later told Helen Maria Williams, author of the popular anti-slavery poem "Peru." Although here and again later, Seward wrote to Williams about Knowles, no other documentation has currently been found linking these two radical women. Since both Williams and Knowles supported liberty, promoted the abolition of slavery, and shared Seward's friendship, they may have been acquainted. More research is needed about the social networks of these and other middling women radicals.

Seward confided to Williams that, "Mrs. K. is curiously dissatisfied with that tract." Seward seemed puzzled by Knowles's displeasure, but one reason seems to justify Knowles's reaction. Seward acknowledged that her manuscript "does not record a long theologic dispute, which succeeded to what I did put down, and in which she ably defended the Quaker principles from the charge of deism and absurdity, which the doctor brought against them."[89] Seward's reference corresponds with Knowles's account, which quoted Johnson as saying he considered Quakers "little better than Deists."[90] So while Seward referred to Knowles's able defense, she did not include it in her account.

"She fancies that she appears in a poor eclipsed light in this same manuscript, because she there opposed only calm and gentle reasoning to the sophistic wit of her antagonist," Seward further told Williams.[91] Seward's description of Knowles accords with Boswell's statement that he "loved the mildness of Mrs. Knowles."[92] Furthermore, Seward told Williams that Knowles answered Johnson with rational replies, as Boswell had also noted in his journal.

Despite Knowles's dissatisfactions, Seward sent another copy of her account in a letter to "Mrs. Mompessan," later included among Seward's correspondence published after her death.[93] Comparing her published letter with the manuscript copy of her letter to Boswell indicates that Seward changed the next-to-final sentence. In her published letter, printed after her bitter public disputes with Boswell, she deleted her compliment to him, writing that Johnson's angry replies "frightened us all, except Mrs. Knowles, who gently, not sarcastically smiled."[94]

Nineteenth-century Tory critic John Wilson Croker attacked Seward's account in her letter to Mompessan;[95] and, twentieth-century literary scholar James L. Clifford questioned the authenticity of her posthumously published letters in general.[96] Yet other scholars argued that Seward's letters, including her account of Knowles's confrontation with Johnson, offer valid information and provide important first-hand perspectives, if analyzed with care.[97] Literary scholar Helen Pennock South compared Seward's published letter with the published accounts of Boswell and Knowles and concluded that the different foci and interests of the three authors can explain their differences. As South pointed out, Boswell cared most about what Johnson said, while Knowles focused on her Quaker beliefs and Harry's moral agency, and Seward centered on Harry's personal story.[98]

Examining Seward's published letters with care further shows that she and Knowles continued to enjoy a strong friendship despite some serious tensions. They especially disagreed about the role of the military. As a pacifist, Knowles questioned how a soldier could be a Christian. Seward answered. "Surely you are too hard upon the military profession by denying all compatibility between the life of a soldier and the faith of a Christian."[99]

Yet the two women shared an interest in politics. Seward appreciated a humorous political analogy in a letter from Knowles and read it to her friends. On a visit to Warwickshire, she wrote Knowles, "The ingenious comparison of the late intoxicated, and now sick and disordered kingdom, to a tavern company, after a drunken riot, highly pleased the somewhat fastidious taste of my ingenious host." She informed Knowles that her host "called your manner of writing, vivid, strong, and original," adding, "we are perfectly in unison concerning the strength and fertility of imagination in your letters." By sharing her letter, Seward presented Knowles's abilities and opinions to male and female acquaintances in her social network, and both women participated in political discourse.

Seward also delighted in Knowles's humorous accounts of London society. Knowles seemed to be a sought-after guest, selective about accepting social invitations. "What a truly comic scene is formed by your description of Mrs. – in her fine coach," Seward wrote Knowles, "and yourself standing upon your own steps, and hammering out excuses for not having returned her visits!"

As country born-women of the middling classes, Knowles and Seward poked fun at some forms of urban sociability. "How was I diverted by the fine lady's fine lamentation in her fine coach, for the loss of your society," Seward chortled. Yet Knowles must have made fun of herself, too, comparing her appearance to that of a turkey. "When I came to the Turkey-poot passage, I exclaimed, 'O! I see them! I see them!'" Seward exclaimed, "You always stoop and poke out your pretty long neck, when you are nonplussed."[100]

Knowles also entertained Seward with a satire on a self-important doctor. In October 1786, Knowles visited Lichfield, and Seward wrote William Hayley that, "Mrs. Knowles brought hither her admirable stage coach manuscript." In it, Knowles seems to have lampooned Dr. Richard Brocklesby, a well-known physician who attended Johnson in his last illness. Seward delighted in Knowles's irreverent portrait, exclaiming, "What admirable fun she made of his epicurism, his spleen, and his culpability!"[101]

As the wife of a prominent physician, Knowles also seemed to be acquainted with Dr. John Wolcot, better known as Peter Pindar. After taking his medical degree at Aberdeen, Wolcot moved to London where he gained fame for his poetical satires of leading public figures, including artists, politicians, and, most notably, the king. A cousin of Knowles later recalled being "in company with Dr. Woolcot" at her home sometime in 1786.[102]

That same year, a listing for "Thomas Knowles, M.D., 19 Lombard Street" again appeared in *Kent's Directory* of "persons in public business, merchants, and other eminent traders in the cities of London, Westminster and the Borough of Southwark." Dr. Knowles seems to have procured separate establishments for his medical practice and his home. Local records for that year list Knowles as also paying a tax assessment of £11 pounds 12 pence on Number 58 Lombard Street.[103]

Thomas Knowles joined other public-minded medical practitioners in supporting dispensaries, begun by Dr. John Coakley Lettsom, for treating poor patients. Financed by subscriptions, dispensaries combined medical reform and philanthropy by providing care for poor people in clinics rather than hospitals, which often harbored fevers and other contagious diseases.[104] The Eastern Dispensary in Alie Street, Whitechapel, became the seventh dispensary in London in 1782. Not long afterwards, Dr. Knowles joined the staff.[105]

Thomas Knowles "was renowned for the exercise of successful skill" in the treatment of fevers, according to James Jenkins. Yet fever proved fatal to the Doctor. On 16 November 1786, Thomas Knowles, age 52, "died of a fever caught from one of his patients."[106]

Anna Seward much "regretted the death of my excellent friend, Dr. K." She described him as "Humane and gentle, tender and attentive to all that could affect my peace." To another friend, she wrote, his "soothing benevolence was salubrious to the spirits, as was his medical skill to the frame." Seward described the doctor as quiet and deeply religious, rather than quick witted and demonstrative. "Without the lustres of genius, or that *ignus-fatuus* wit, his intellects had strength and clearness," she told her friend. Moreover, "his strict piety [had] no shade of moroseness, and the kindness of his heart tempered a very inflexible sincerity."[107]

Joseph Woods, a fellow member of the antislavery association, attended Thomas's funeral at the Quaker cemetery at Bunhill Fields. "Poor Dr. Knowles is gone before us into the world of spirits," Woods wrote. He noted that four Friends spoke before the interment.[108]

Now, at age 53, Mary Morris Knowles faced life as a widow.

Notes

1 Armistead, *Select Miscellanies*, vol. 4, pp. 168–70.
2 *Records and Recollections of James Jenkins*, pp. 98–9. Kenneth L. Carroll, "The Mary and Charlotte Fiasco: A Look at 1778 British Quaker Relief for Philadelphia," *Pennsylvania Magazine of History and Biography*, 52/2 (1978): 212–23.
3 For a later example, see *Gentleman's Magazine*, February 1797: 128.
4 Armistead, *Select Miscellanies*, vol. 4, pp. 168–70
5 *Gentleman's Magazine*, September 1784: 716.
6 Charlotte Grant, "The Choice of Hercules: the polite arts and 'female excellence' in eighteenth-century London," in *Women, Writing and the Public Sphere*, pp. 98–9.
7 *Gentleman's Magazine*, September 1784: 716.
8 Swain, *Embroidered Georgian Pictures*, p. 20.
9 Bernard and Therle Hughes, "An Artist in Needlework."
10 *Records and Recollections of James Jenkins*, p. 129.
11 Public Record Office, Prob 11/1147, quire 573, Will of Thomas Knowles.
12 "Letters of William Forster of Tottenham," *Journal of Friends Historical Society*, 26 (1929): 25–6.

13 Joseph Reed and Frederick Pottle, eds, *Boswell: Laird of Auchinleck, 1778–1782* (New York, 1977), p. 65.
14 Emmanuel Swedenborg, *A Treatise Concerning Heaven and Hell, Containing a Relation of many Wonderful Things therein, as heard and seen by the Author* (London, 1778).
15 Langford, *Polite and Commercial People*, p. 104.
16 Library of the Religious Society of Friends, MSS Vol 347, "William Matthews to M. K. on her Departure from Bath."
17 *Records and Recollections of James Jenkins*, pp. 128–9, 133.
18 Samuel Lloyd, *Some Account of Jenny Harry* (privately printed, 1912), pp. 1–6.
19 Braithwaite Papers, Introduction
20 E. F. Howard, "Mary Knowles and the Lloyds of Birmingham," *Friends Quarterly Examiner*, (1934): 91–2.
21 Ibid.
22 Library of the Religious Society of Friends, Temporary MSS 28, File 7, Number 5, "The Lamentation of Timothy Tattle."
23 Hunt, *The Middling Sort*, pp. 194–6.
24 Temporary MSS 28, 7, 5, "Lamentation.
25 Ibid.
26 Braithwaite Papers, Box 7, Packet 15, File 3, Number 43, "On Fashion by Mary Knowles."
27 Ruth Avaline Hesselgrave, *Lady Miller and the Batheaston Literary Circle* (New Haven, 1927). [Anna Riggs Miller]. *Letters from Italy* (3 vols, London, 1776).
28 See, for example, [Lady Anna Miller], *Poetical Amusements at a Villa near Bath* (2nd edn, London, 1776).
29 Brewer, *Pleasures of the Imagination*, pp. 601, 603–04.
30 John Johnson, *Memoirs of the Life and Writings of William Hayley, Esq*, (2 vols, London, 1831), vol. 1, p. 228.
31 *The Leadbeater Papers: A Selection from the Manuscripts and Correspondence of Mary [Shackleton] Leadbeater* (2nd edn, 2 vols, London, 1862), vol. 2, p. 112.
32 *Records and Recollections of James Jenkins*, p. 455.
33 Ibid., p. 454.
34 Green, "Jenny Harry," (1914).
35 Margaret Dresser, *Slavery Obscured: The Social History of the Slave Trade in an English Provincial Port* (London, 2001), pp. 73–7.
36 Green, "Jenny Harry" (1914).
37 *Gentleman's Magazine*, September 1784: 716.
38 Pettigrew, *Memoirs of Lettsom*, vol. 1, p. 28. J. Jennings, *The Business of Abolishing the British Slave Trade, 1783–1807* (London, 1997).
39 *Gentleman's Magazine*, September 1784: 716.
40 Green, "Jenny Harry" (1914).
41 Public Record Office RG 6, 510, "A Register of the Marriage Certificates of the People Called Quakers belonging to the Monthly Meeting of Devonshire House London in the County of Middlesex," 1782.
42 Lewis, *Sacred to Female Patriotism*, p. 91.
43 Library of the Religious Society of Friends, Temporary MSS 28, File 7, Number 3, "The Minister and the Quaker."

44	*Records and Recollections of James Jenkins*, pp. 293–4.
45	Temporary MSS 28, 7, 3, "The Minister and the Quaker."
46	Langford, *Polite and Commercial People*, p. 177.
47	Temporary MSS 28, 7, 3, "The Minister and the Quaker" and "Lord North and the Quaker," *Journal of the Friends Historical Society*, 17/3 (1920): 77–9.
48	Johnson, *Memoirs of William Hayley*, vol. 1, p. 281.
49	David A. Cross, *"A Striking Likeness": The Life of George Romney* (Brookefield, Vermont, 2000).
50	Johnson, *Memoirs of William Hayley*, vol. 1, p. 281–2.
51	*Letters of Anna Seward*, vol. 2, p. 194.
52	Wicham, ed, *Journals and Correspondence of Thomas Sedgewick Whalley*, vol. 3, pp. 387–8.
53	John Brooke and Sir Lewis Namier, *The History of Parliament: The House of Commons, 1754 – 1790* (London, 1964), pp. 602–3.
54	Rev. William Beloe, *The Sexagenarian: Or the Recollections of a Literary Life* (2 vols, London, 1817), vol. 1, p. 325.
55	Johnson, *Memoirs of William Hayley*, vol. 1, pp. 308–9.
56	Gleadle and Richardson, eds. *Women in British Politics*, pp. 1–8.
57	Johnson, *Memoirs of William Hayley*, vol. 1, pp. 308–9.
58	*Kent's Directory for the Year 1783* (51st ed., London, 1783).
59	*Letters of Anna Seward*, vol. 1, p. 347.
60	Library of the Religious Society of Friends, "Devonshire House Monthly Meeting," Vol. 10, "3rd of 2nd mo 1784."
61	Beck and Ball, eds, *The London Friends' Meetings*, pp. 145–7.
62	*Records and Recollections of James Jenkins*, pp. 201–2.
63	Irma S. Lustig and Frederick A. Pottle, eds, *Boswell: The Applause of the Jury, 1782–1785* (New York, 1981), p. 138.
64	*Gentleman's Magazine*, June 1783: 535.
65	Jennings, *Business*, p. 23.
66	Library of the Religious Society of Friends, Thompson-Clarkson MSS, vol. 2, p. 9, "Minute Book."
67	Butterfield, "The American Interests of the Firm of E. and C. Dilly," p. 317.
68	Hill, *Republican Virago*, pp. 94–8, 107–10.
69	Ibid., pp. 17–9, 192–6.
70	Ibid., pp. 188, 224.
71	*Letters of Anna Seward*, vol. 1, pp. 104–8.
72	Public Record Office RG 6, 808, "Monthly Meetings of Worcestershire," Burials, 1665–1793, p. 360.
73	Green, "Jenny Harry" (1914).
74	*Gentleman's Magazine*, September 1784: 716.
75	*Letters of Anna Seward*, vol. 1, pp. 104–8.
76	Marshall Waingrow, ed.. *The Correspondence and Other Papers of James Boswell Relating to the Making of the Life of Johnson* (2nd. edn, Edinburgh, New Haven and London, 2001), p. 47.
77	*Letters of Anna Seward*, vol. 1, p. 48.
78	Waingrow, *Correspondence and Other Papers of James Boswell*, p. 48.
79	Lustig, "The Myth of Johnson's Misogyny."

80   *Letters of Anna Seward*, vol. 1, p. 48.
81   *Boswell: Applause of the Jury*, p. 293. Adam Sisman, *Boswell's Presumptuous Task: The Making of the Life of Johnson* (New York, 2001), p. 88.
82   *Boswell: Applause of the Jury*, pp. 302, 326, 327, 331.
83   Library of the Religious Society of Friends, Portfolio MSS 3, 126, "Notes of a Conversation between Dr. Johnson and Mary Knowles in a Letter to Boswell."
84   Ibid.
85   Ibid.
86   [Knowles], *Gentleman's Magazine*, June 1791: 502.
87   Portfolio MSS 3, 126, "Notes of a Conversation."
88   *Letters of Anna Seward*, vol. 1, pp. 104–8.
89   Ibid., vol. 2, pp. 79–80.
90   [Knowles]. *Gentleman's Magazine*, June 1791: 501.
91   *Letters of Anna Seward*, vol. 2, 79–80.
92   *Boswell in Extremes*, p. 289.
93   *Letters of Anna Seward*, vol. 1, pp. 97–104.
94   Ibid., vol. 1, p. 103. This letter also mistakenly identifies Harry's father as being from the East Indies instead of the West Indies.
95   Croker, *Life of Samuel Johnson, LL.D.*, Vol. 4, p. 157.
96   James L. Clifford, "The Authenticity of Anna Seward's Published Correspondence," *Modern Philology*, 34/2 (1941): 113–22.
97   James D. Woolley, "Johnson as Despot: Anna Seward's Rejected Contribution to Boswell's Life," *Modern Philology*, 70/2 (1972): 140–45. Brewer, *Pleasures of the Imagination*, pp. 604–05.
98   Helen Pennock South, "Dr. Johnson and the Quakers," *The Bulletin of the Friends Historical Association* (Spring 1955): 19–42.
99   *Letters of Anna Seward*, vol. 1, pp. 104–8.
100 Ibid.
101 Ibid., vol. 1, p. 181.
102 Library of the Religious Society of Friends, MSS Vol. 150 [Luke Howard Collection], number 29, "Letter from Morris Birkbeck to Anna Seward, 5. 15. 90."
103 *Kent's Directory for the Year, 1786*, p. 101. London, Guildhall Library, Land Tax Assessment Books, 1786–87, Number 11, 316, 263, "An Assessment upon the Inhabitants and Premises in the Precinct of Burchin lane and All Hallows, 1786."
104 Robert Kilpatrick,"'Living in the Light:' Dispensaries, Philanthropy and Medical Reform in late Eighteenth-Century London," in Cunningham and French, *Medical Enlightenment*, pp. 256–75.
105 *Gentleman's Magazine*, December 1786: 1003.
106 *Records and Recollections of James Jenkins*, p. 202.
107 *Letters of Anna Seward*, vol. 1, pp. 209, 247.
108 Matthews MSS, "Joseph Woods to William Matthews," 6 December 1786. Public Record Office RG 6 670, "London and Middlesex Quarterly Meeting Burials," 22nd day 11 mo 1786.

Chapter 5

Defying James Boswell

After her husband's death, Knowles sought solace in her strong religious faith, but she also explored a new form of supernatural power. While her legal and social status increased as a wealthy widow, she became less visible for a time, leaving few first person accounts. She served as an affectionate parent to her maturing son and continued to practice polite Quakerliness, sending poems, drawings, and advice to young friends. As a widow, Knowles deepened her long relationship with Anna Seward. Despite their many differences, the two women politely discussed religion, politics, fame, and literature. Unlike Seward, however, Knowles actively supported the emerging abolition movement, advocating liberty for African slaves. Knowles reentered the public arena and became embroiled in "Johnso-mania," when Hester Thrale Piozzi insulted her artwork. Moreover, according to Knowles and Seward, Boswell misreported her confrontation with Johnson. Again claiming the right of self-representation, Knowles published her defense of Quakers as Christians. She also restated her arguments that, as a young unmarried woman, Jane Harry was a responsible moral agent, duty bound to choose her religion.

Newly and unexpectedly widowed, Knowles grieved for the loss of her husband but found comfort in exchanging letters with female friends. She fondly recalled Thomas's affection for her and his strong religious convictions. "Many have been the kind letters sent during the time of my deepest distress," she wrote a Quaker friend on Christmas Day, 1786. "My soul at seasons can rejoice in his humble triumph over approaching death," she continued, indicating his certainty of salvation. "Nor did he close without expressing a lively hope," she concluded, "that the time would come when he should receive his Dear wife at that gate, which he said was already open for him!"[1] Her words testify to the mutual love and strong faith undergirding their marriage.

She struggled to achieve the fortitude and resignation to God's will expected of genteel and devout widows.[2] She sought to transcend her grief by writing about her beliefs to two close women friends. To her Quaker friend, she repeated her prayer to God, "Thou *gavest* what Thou has taken away, Blessed be thy adorable name!"[3] Anna Seward told a mutual acquaintance that, "The ever ingenious widow has answered my letter of condolence in an highly religious strain and in that strong, beautiful language, which, on all occasions, flows from her pen."[4]

While Knowles grieved deeply, she gained wealth and legal rights as a widow.[5] As "sole Executrix" of her husband's will, she received significant financial assets in addition to all his "goods, books," and other personal belongings. His legacy included "two shares in the navigation from Leeds to Liverpool" and property in Whitechapel, Edinburgh, and Brighthelmstone.[6]

In the eyes of one of her Anglican acquaintances, Knowles's financial assets as a widow increased her social standing. Mary Cobb lived near Lichfield where she entertained Johnson and assisted Boswell in collecting information for his biography.[7] According to Seward, Cobb, the widow of a prominent banker, pronounced Knowles, "'a bank-bill whom any man would accept on sight.'" Knowles seemed puzzled by the financial simile, but Seward impatiently dismissed her lack of understanding. "Fy!," Seward exclaimed, "In calling Mrs. Knowles a bank bill, is it not saying that everyone is ready to accept her?"[8]

Further proving this point, William Wolseley, a Captain in the Navy and member of the Staffordshire gentry, repeated rumors that Knowles planned to marry a wealthy Anglican. On a visit to Lichfield, Wolseley told Seward, who reported it all to Knowles, that "a man of large fortune" would renounce the Church of England "for the Mary of the Meeting House." According to Seward, Wolseley, with a "meaning smile and nod of confirmation," told "of marriage vestments preparing" and "announced Bath the scene" of the wedding.[9] Despite Wolseley's knowing ways, Knowles did not remarry, just as other widows of her time remarried less frequently than widowers.[10]

This interest in Knowles's future expressed by Cobb, Seward, and Wolseley indicates her integration into the polite provincial society of Staffordshire. There, as in other parts of the country, the social distinctions among Anglicans, Dissenters, the lesser gentry, and the professional classes could sometimes become porous and permeable.[11] Her example shows how economic assets could outweigh religious differences in determining the social status of a widow.

Few first person accounts have been located for the early period of Knowles's widowhood. A later letter from Seward, discussed below, indicates that Knowles left her home in Lombard Street after her husband's death. She may have moved to "Basinghall Street, Number Seven" during this time, since she described living there with her son in an undated letter. She told an unnamed correspondent that, "our staircase and part of the rooms are now painting," suggesting that she was refurbishing a new home for her and George, probably then in his teens.[12]

Boswell's journal provides a brief glimpse of her dispensing religious advice during a visit to Charles Dilly. In October 1787, Boswell noted that he felt "Very ill but obliged to hurry into City," to borrow money from Dilly to repay a pressing debt. Encountering Knowles, Boswell reported that she "told me she knew the cause of my uneasiness, the want of reconciling the soul to God." His entry shows how Knowles again couched her religious advice in nonsectarian terms without specifically referencing her Quaker beliefs. Boswell evidently agreed with her analysis, briefly indicating his concurrence by writing, "I thought so."[13]

Knowles continued to correspond with Seward. Although Seward did not preserve Knowles's letters, she included several of her epistles to Knowles among those she selected for publication after her death. Seward's published letters, admittedly subjective and sometimes misdated and erroneous, still reveal much about her views of Knowles and their political interests and literary tastes.

Based on comments in Seward's letters, Knowles seems to have traveled in the country, sometimes writing vivid and satiric descriptions of the places she visited. In October 1787, Seward thanked Knowles for "Your letter from Buxton, so all yourself in wit and spirit." Provincial spas, like Buxton, became increasingly popular with the polite leisured classes. Women often outnumbered men, and the mixed but genteel company offered acceptable diversions for a widow. Replying to a letter from Knowles, Seward wrote, "Its' pictures of Buxton have science in them to delight a philosophic amateur, and grotesque original humour to divert the merest John Bull, if there should be an atom of risibility in his composition."[14]

By exchanging literary letters, Knowles and Seward participated in the developing social networks linking female writers. Seward gained a national reputation with the publication of *Louisa: A Poetical Novel* and became widely known as "the Swan of Lichfield." Distrustful of the increasingly commercialized world of London publishing, she used her letters to express alternative standards and aesthetic judgments, cultivating her own literary coterie of correspondents.[15]

Knowles served as a link between Seward and a group of well-connected women writers in London. "Thank you for your charming portraits of Mrs. Lort and Mrs. Hunter; one the child of wit; the other of imagination," Seward wrote Knowles.[16] Mrs. Lort must have been Susannah Norfolk Lort, whose husband, Reverend Michael Lort, studied antiquities and knew Johnson, Boswell, and Hester Thrale. Mrs. Hunter was surely Anne Home Hunter, a well-regarded lyrical poet and wife of John Hunter, surgeon to George III and collector of medical curiosities. A contemporary remembered Anne Home Hunter for her brilliant "social, literary parties ... among the most enjoyable of her time, although not always to her husband's taste."[17] Knowles kept Hunter informed about Seward, and Seward later told Knowles, "Mrs. Hunter is very good to inquire after me and my pursuits."[18]

Knowles, Hunter, and Seward exchanged views on fame, with Seward urging Knowles to embrace her public reputation and Hunter to acknowledge her inspiration. "So your fair friend, Mrs. Hunter, disavows poetic inspiration," Seward wrote Knowles, "when you and she would exalt simplicity ... you put me in mind of the children of Israel worshipping the calf in Horeb." Praising "the wit and oratory of Mrs. Knowles, and the poetry of Mrs. Hunter," Seward declared, "O! To be sure it was simplicity solely who set 'Mary Knowles upon one leg in the temple of fame.'" Seward later explained that here she was "Alluding to a humorous description [Knowles had written] of herself in one of her letters."[19] Knowles recognized her fame even though she felt ambivalent about it.

Seward embraced fame and expected Knowles to do the same. Describing her as "the celebrated Quaker Lady," Seward had no patience for what she considered Knowles's too polite dismissals of her fame. Seward rebuffed Knowles's protestations of modesty, using the anti-Catholic language of her time. "What a buzzard does the same mock modesty make of our celebrated M. Knowles,"

Seward wrote her friend, "or rather what a jesuit, winking and catching, with infinite adroitness, at false interpretation."[20]

Seward assessed Knowles's literary and conversational abilities in letters to two friends. "Comic humour and declamatory eloquence are Mrs. Knowles's forte and in them she is unrivalled," she wrote the poet Helen Maria Williams on Christmas Day, 1787. Seward differentiated between male and female writers, adding, "I speak of her own sex, for in wit and classic spirit who may transcend Mr. Hayley?"[21] Although Seward praised Knowles's wit and eloquence, she did not rate her poetry highly. "I love Mrs. K–, [and] think her letters and conversation abound with genius," she commented to another friend. Yet, Seward added, "I cannot admire her verses."[22]

Knowles and Seward enjoyed a multifaceted and complex relationship, based not only on mutual admiration but also on divergent literary opinions and religious views. The two continued to differ markedly concerning the military. As a pacifist, Knowles seems to have questioned the morality of Seward's celebration of a recent military victory. As a proud nationalist, Seward replied, "I have always considered General Elliot's defense of Gibraltar as a truly great, patriotic, and heroic action." She concluded, "It was impossible I could think of the Gibraltar defense in any way inimical to morality."[23]

The women also discussed their religious differences, with Knowles offering a two-layered and gendered metaphor illustrating her view of the Church of England. According to Seward, Knowles referred to the Anglican Church as "the great Diana of Ephesus,"[24] evoking classical female beauty as well as a New Testament warning about material excess in religious worship. Seward credited the metaphor enough to include it in her published letters. Her appreciation of Knowles's allusion suggests how the women's shared knowledge of the classics and Biblical scriptures enabled them politely to discuss their differing religious views.

Despite their differences, Seward commended Knowles's company and conversation to young Thomas Christie of Edinburgh, who later founded *The Analytical Review*. In January 1788, Seward wrote Christie praising "the wit, the information, and the eloquence of Mrs. Knowles!" This combination, Seward continued, "renders her conversation delightful, whether we adopt or combat her opinions. I congratulate you upon the pleasures it will afford you."

Knowles had, however, developed one new interest that Seward could neither understand nor share. As Seward told Christie, "The new, the strange enthusiasm about animal magnetism, has seized her violently. She fervently assures me that it is a great, important discovery in the powers of nature; capable of being highly useful in the cure of diseases." Seward puzzled over Knowles's acceptance of these ideas despite "all the native strength of her understanding." To Seward, Knowles's interest in animal magnetism demonstrated "a portion of metaphysical faith, which carried her a great way up the lunar heights of system."[25]

Knowles's new interest reflected her strong belief in the mysterious operations of divine power, but it also demonstrated her affluence and involvement in popular culture. According to James Jenkins, "Animal Magnetism, or the art of removing maladies by volition, aided with gentle motion of the hands, was now greatly in vogue." As Jenkins explained, "This science (if such a science really existed) was first professed by Messmer at Vienna in 1776." Dr. DeMainauduc, one of Messmer's French students, and his assistant, Ann Prescott, operated an office in Bloomsbury Square where they gave lessons for 200 guineas each.[26]

Jenkins further described a comic conflict between Knowles and James Phillips, the Quaker printer and bookseller, concerning animal magnetism. According to Jenkins, the skeptical Phillips "ridiculed it highly in a poetic Epistle to Mary Knowles." Never one to shrink from conflict, Knowles "smartly replied ... which (I think)," Jenkins later recalled, "produced a rejoinder" from Phillips. While no records of this mock controversy have been found, it ended, according to Jenkins, "without his [Phillips's] conversion, or her professing to have been imposed upon."[27]

Knowles's fascination with the supernatural also caused tensions with another Quaker male, her friend and neighbor, Joseph Woods. In March 1788, Woods confided to a mutual friend that Knowles "hears what is marvellous with such a willingness to believe, that I cannot imbibe all her narrations."[28] The good natured but real disapproval of Phillips and Woods concerning Knowles's exploration of the supernatural indicates how she tested the boundaries between rationalism and mysticism among late eighteenth-century Quakers.

Yet these internal Quaker skirmishes paled, as Knowles became involved in what pundit Peter Pindar dubbed "Johnso-mania," as several writers rushed to publish all kinds of information about the well-known man.[29] In 1787, the recently remarried Hester Thrale Piozzi published 325 letters written by Johnson to her and members of her family. The highly popular two-volume set included Johnson's letter written on 16 May 1776, after his first meeting with Knowles, referring to her "sutile pictures." In the published version, however, either Piozzi or the printer mistook the *s* in the unfamiliar word *sutile*—meaning stitched—for the letter *f*, so the printed letter read "futile pictures."[30]

Although Knowles's friend Joseph Woods questioned her belief in the supernatural, he considered her a genius and resented what he took to be Johnson's slight. Woods wrote a mutual friend in March 1788, asking, "Hast thou seen Mrs. Piozzi's Letters of Dr. Johnson?" He observed ironically, "M. Knowles has the honour of being mentioned by the profound Moralist as 'A Mrs. Knowles the Quaker who works the futile Pictures!'" Reflecting on the insignificance of worldly achievement, Woods appealed to his correspondent, "What, I ask, is Genius when it is so easily depreciated?"[31]

Yet a careful reader soon discovered the mistake, which caused enough of a stir to become the subject of a bet between two literary men. In April 1788, the Reverend Michael Lort, the antiquarian husband of Susannah Norfolk Lort, "desired a sight of the original letter in order to determine a wager." Lort examined the manuscript and wrote Bishop Thomas Percy, the influential literary patron, that, "There it plainly appeared that a dash has been put across the long *s*," changing the letter to *f*. The dash had been added later, said Lort, "perhaps by the printer or the corrector of the press." Lort assured Percy that the word "should be *sutile*." Familiar with Knowles's needle painting, Lort told Percy, *sutile* was "a word, though not to be found in his Dictionary, yet very aptly made to express the mode of painting, viz. in needlework ... made by Mrs. Knowles."[32]

Piozzi, however, steadfastly refused to recognize the error. "It was no mistake," she wrote privately much later in her life. Although admitting that another antiquarian also "said it should be *sutile*," she justified her version by saying, "as Pictures they are futile ... The moth, the sunshine everything may destroy the beautiful work – alas!"[33]

Piozzi disclaimed personal ill will by frostily denying any acquaintance with Knowles. "Against Mrs. Knowles I could have no malice," she wrote years later, "I knew her not."[34] Despite this statement, Piozzi certainly knew of Knowles, whether the two ever met directly or not. Johnson described Knowles, as seen in Chapter Three, in his letter to Piozzi, as Piozzi herself revealed in her published letters. Moreover, Piozzi and Knowles had mutual acquaintances in Boswell and Seward.

Knowles, for her part, seemed determined not to read anything else written by Piozzi. Piozzi later produced a book about her travels in Italy, but, according to Seward, Knowles refused to read it. In a letter to Knowles, Seward expressed surprise to find "it possible you have not read the Piozzan travels."

"You, who profess to interest yourself in the female right to literature and science, ought not to turn such a cold, incurious eye toward anything which advances the progress of that claim," Seward chided Knowles.[35] By using the phrase, "the female right to literature," Seward recalled the title of the poem written nearly 40 years earlier by her father. Yet Seward also included science, an interest shared by the two women. For Seward, their common commitment to female education took precedence over this personal difference.

As Knowles and Seward acquired increasing public recognition, their letters provided opportunities to discuss the challenges and opportunities that accompanied their fame. In a letter written in April 1788, Seward compared Knowles to an unnamed woman writer whose letters had recently been published. "Mrs. – has perhaps as much wit as anybody," Seward wrote Knowles, "but she has not so much efflorescence of fancy, eloquence, clearness and depth in the reasoning powers, as M. Knowles."[36]

In this letter, Seward again scolded Knowles for her professions of modesty. "I entreat you not to expect that mock modesty can ever pass muster with me from your pen," she informed Knowles. "Maria," she wrote, using a Latinized version of her friend's name to evoke the classical spirit, "thou knowest this and hast never, in thy secret heart, felt Mrs. – accomplished as she is, thy superior in the order of ingenious being. Therefore, ... I am ... vexed at the fibs of thy humility."[37]

Yet Knowles measured up to Seward's high standards of independent thinking more often than not. Writing soon after to another correspondent, Seward described Knowles as one "with whom I have maintained the most intimate connection from my earliest youth." She continued, "yet are we each of high and independent spirit, and by no means see every object of genius, literature, and conduct, in the same light." The two women got along so well, according to Seward, because "we hold our minds open to conviction." Moreover, "neither of us fancy that greater and wiser people than ourselves must necessarily have violated that greatness and that wisdom, whenever they acted, or spoke, or wrote contrary to *our* ideas."[38]

While Knowles and Seward remained close friends, they differed significantly over the increasingly important issue of the abolition of the British slave trade. The informal committee that Thomas Knowles helped found had grown into the larger and more religiously diverse London Abolition Committee, which assumed leadership for involving the public in demanding parliamentary action against the slave trade. By 1788, the committee was conducting a nationwide campaign using a variety of tactics to demonstrate the evils of the slave trade to the public and to unpersuaded Members of Parliament.[39]

Josiah Wedgwood, already becoming famous for his distinctive pottery ware, joined the committee and sent abolitionist tracts to Seward, suggesting she write a poem on the subject. Seward informed him that his letter and the tracts convinced her to support abolition, but she declined to write a poem because she feared it might harm her literary reputation. Seward reminded Wedgwood about the abolition verse written by Ann Yearsley, a former milkmaid patronized by Hannah More, the evangelical Bluestocking. Acutely conscious of her place in national literary life, Seward told Wedgwood, "I cannot prevail upon myself to give my scribbling foes new opportunity ... by speaking to the world of the inferiority of my attempt to that of the unlettered milk woman's."[40]

Knowles, perhaps spurred by the memory of Jane Harry Thresher, did not share Seward's compunction concerning writing about abolition. No evidence has been found that members of the London Abolition Committee, several of whom she knew personally, called on her to write an abolitionist poem for publication. Yet an unnamed friend did ask her to compose a poetic inscription for a tobacco box, the kind of request often made to recognized writers.

In June 1788, Knowles produced the following set of couplets:

Tho various tints the human face adorn,
To glorious Liberty Mankind are born;
O, May the hands which rais'd this fav'rite weed
Be loos'd in mercy and the slave be freed![41]

This seemingly simple poem is important in a number of ways. First, it presents a female expression of the radical commitment to "glorious Liberty." Like Richard Price's *Observations on the Nature of Civil Liberty*, described earlier, Knowles viewed liberty as the birthright of all. For her, liberty encompassed politics as well as religion, and her brief verse reminded the owner of the tobacco box about this important political issue. For her, as for other late eighteenth-century radicals, liberty had become a rational, nonsectarian, universal, human right.

Moreover, Knowles specifically supported liberty for all, regardless of skin color, and called for the liberation of slaves. The London Abolition Committee had debated about whether to focus on emancipation of slaves or abolition of the slave trade, but they pragmatically decided to focus first on ending the slave trade only.[42] Unlike the male committee members, Knowles eschewed the more moderate goal of abolition and openly advocated freeing all slaves.

Finally, by making her radical views known in this form, Knowles participated in and furthered the broadening of political participation that accompanied and fueled the popular abolition movement.[43] Her verse, like the tobacco box it adorned, fulfilled a social purpose. Appearing on the tobacco box, the verse would probably be seen not only by the owner but displayed to others. Moreover, Knowles's words were copied and preserved separately, so the verse probably circulated among her friends as a social text, as had her earlier writings.

By transforming a request for a literary inscription into a political statement against slavery, Knowles also demonstrated a keen awareness of the connections between English consumption and colonial slavery. Individual British and American Quakers in the 1760s and 1770s, like John Woolman, had taken the lead in "moralizing consumption" and suggesting abstention from slave products as a way to diminish the profits of slavery. Yet the wide scale abstention movement in Britain did not take hold until the 1790s, and then it focused on sugar, with a strong appeal to women consumers.[44] Knowles wrote her poem three years before this national movement, and she focused on a product more often associated with males. For Knowles, radical rights and responsibilities transcended gender roles.

While Knowles and Seward differed in their degree of support for abolition, they remained united in their common interest in Whig politics. Their correspondence, like the friendships of elite women, provided an important venue to discuss civic events and express their political views.[45] Seward began a letter dated 1 February 1789 by asking, "And what became of my brilliant Mrs. Knowles? I long for her spirited and ever eloquent remarks, upon the sudden, barefaced, disgraceful adoption of Tory principles, by those who so lately affected to triumph in the blessings of the Revolution."[46]

Whigs had recently celebrated the centenary of the Glorious Revolution, but in December, during debates on the Regency Bill, the radical Whig leader Charles James Fox rashly claimed that Parliament had no right to limit the Prince of Wales's jurisdiction as Regent. By doing so, Fox challenged the principle of parliamentary supremacy, a core concept of the revolution and the chief Whig political principle. Seward clearly stated her opinion of this action, and she expected her friend to have an equally strong point of view. Through letters like this, Knowles and Seward, as middling women, participated in political discourse by developing and expressing informed opinions.

While Knowles discussed politics with Seward, she did not neglect the emotional needs and education of her teenage son. In August 1788, she and George spent two weeks in Lichfield, where they visited Seward. Seward shared Knowles's fond affection for "dear George" and urged the two to come again.[47] In February 1789, Seward inquired warmly after "George's learning," indicating that Knowles and her son studied the odes of Horace together.[48] Seward sent mother and son some of the verses she had prepared for publication and expressed pleasure "that my sonnets pleased your Telemachus," referring to the child of Ulysses and Penelope, the faithful wife and talented weaver.[49] Judging by these comments, Knowles, George, and Seward used classical references to establish a common context for their cross-religious friendship.

An undated letter by Knowles to an unnamed friend reveals the warm and loving relationship between her and her son, as George reached maturity. Knowles wrote her friend that George looked forward to visiting "thy two sprightly Boys (so late a Boy himself)." She closed by asking her friend to "accept George's and my love," indicating that both would visit soon.[50]

In June 1789, more than two years after her husband's death, Knowles placed her son in a London counting house and moved to a residence nearby. The opinionated Seward did not approve of her new location or of George's profession. "At length our brilliant Mrs. Knowles takes an house in Lombard Street again," Seward wrote to a mutual friend. Ambivalent about life in London, Seward found it "a strange situation for such a spirit to choose, when city closeness, city noise, and city dirt are no longer necessary to produce pecuniary advantages." The reason for moving to the new residence at No. 53 Lombard Street, as Seward explained but did not approve, was "its vicinity to the counting house in which, with all her ample fortune, she has placed her son," George, just turned 17.[51]

Seward's comments reveal important differences between the two women concerning the acquisition of wealth and ideas about Christian simplicity expressed by both Anglicans and Quakers. Pointing out how "the thirst of riches" could be "fatal to Christian peace and Christian virtue," Seward wondered that such "a pious character" as Knowles "can wish a beloved child to imbibe the desire of increasing an affluent property." While Seward voiced her concerns, Knowles evidently did not consider placing George in business, despite her already considerable wealth, as incompatible with her Quaker beliefs.

Knowles and Seward also differed over her proper economic role as a mother. Indicating that George, like his mother, had "such a love of books and the pencil," Seward pointed out, "His dependence upon you, his attachment to your person, your abilities, your virtues form a bulwark about him against the vices of youth." Seward further argued that, "The fortune which he will inherit from you, as the reward of his good conduct, is more than competent to the elegant comforts of life."[52] Seward believed Knowles had a religious duty to discourage her son from increasing the already ample fortune he would inherit, while Knowles evidently considered it her duty to enable him to take an active role in business.

Despite their serious political, social, and religious differences, the friendship between Knowles and Seward encompassed emotional and personal support. Seward expressed fondness for Knowles in letters to others, describing her to a mutual acquaintance as one of "the oldest friend[s] I have upon earth."[53] In a letter written in February 1790, Seward addressed Knowles as "My beloved" and sought personal advice about health from her.[54]

Like other forward-thinking women of her day, Knowles advised Seward to exercise vigorously. "I remember your injunction in a long past letter," Seward wrote her, "to tear along the gallery, clawing, like a wild cat, at the windows."[55] Knowles's language, as quoted by Seward, is striking in two ways. The first is the advice "to tear along the gallery," evoking vigorous, even fierce, activity. The second is her exhortation to behave like a clawing wild cat, again evoking fierceness, instead of counseling Seward to imitate a gentler animal.

While Knowles may have encouraged unconventional behavior, she also visited the fashionable seaside town of Brighthelmstone. She may have owned property there inherited from her husband. She seemed to be familiar with the town, writing Seward about seeing the Prince of Wales and other notables. "I am charmed with your portraits of our Princes at Brighthelmstone," Seward replied. Knowles observed the prince's mistress, Mrs. Fitzherbert, closely enough to detect a resemblance with Seward. "If I had not so often seen ordinary phizes resemble beautiful ones, I should be flattered that you think me so like the buxom widow who tows our plump heir-apparent about by the heart-strings," said Seward.[56]

As close personal friends, Knowles and Seward seemed undisturbed by their occasional political and religious differences, and took comfort in their mutual support and affection. Seward closed her long and heart-felt letter written in February 1790 by saying, "Neither you nor I, my dear Mrs. Knowles, ought to apologize to each other for our sincerity." It was, as Seward said, the "sincerity of an almost life-long friendship."[57]

While Knowles enjoyed a long friendship with Seward, she also continued to mentor young people through poetry and art, producing a botanical drawing and verses as gifts. Botanical drawing constituted an acceptable art form for some prosperous and well-educated Quakers. Dr. John Fothergill, for example, employed a team of artists, including at least one woman, to make drawings of the more than 3,000 species in his extensive gardens.[58] Yet in her verses and drawing, Knowles did not document botanical species as much as transform them into objects of contemplation and instruction.

In an undated manuscript poem, "Address'd to the amiable M. B., with a set of Paints by M. K.," Knowles hailed "Polly – lovely, Fair, / Gay, witty, young and debonair." Knowles seems to have intended the terms "gay," "witty" and "debonair" to be compliments not indications of defects. While it is not known whether Knowles addressed a Quaker or not, her approving use of these terms suggests that she did not consider them to be incompatible with Quakerliness.

Knowles encouraged Polly to use the paints, "With lightest touches aim to trace, / The Charms of Flora's blooming Race." Describing the drawing of flowers not only as an innocent recreation but as a source of moral inspiration, she noted, "Sages their Pens in Morals guide, / Let them sometimes from pencils slide." Knowles believed that painting flowers could teach universal moral lessons drawn from nature. For her, as for Quakers like Dr. John Fothergill, botanical art could serve higher scientific and moral purposes, further indicating that late eighteenth-century Quaker attitudes toward visual culture encompassed rich complexities.

In Knowles's verse, the flowers became reminders to young women and men of the importance of virtuous behavior. Narcissus recalled the self-obsession of the classical youth and served to "Warn the Beau's before too late / ... less such sad monuments they be / Of self conceit and Vanity!" For Knowles, "the Lilly's snowy pride" became the "Emblem of the unspotted Bride." For her, the red rose represented "the tender blooming Maid!" which she hailed as "thou most perfect work of Nature."[59]

Another short manuscript poem attributed to Knowles is named, "Sent with the drawing of a Moss Rose Bud." It combines floral imagery, reflections on the transience of beauty, and advice to a young man about marriage. She sent a drawing of a "Moss crowned Bud of crimson Hue / The pride of Flora's train" to "Remonstrate to the Swain." The drawing reminded the suitor "That bloom will soon decay / That Female charms than these more Frail / Will quickly fade away."

Perhaps reflecting on her youthful experiences as a recognized beauty, Knowles advised the young man to consider good character and intellectual compatibility as more lasting virtues in a wife than physical appearance. "Say Virtue, sweetness, modest sense / The happiest choice will prove," she wrote. Indicating that intellectual compatibility could grow while external appearances faded, she observed, "When minds congenial mutual glow / then years new charms supply." Perhaps speaking from her own experience of an affectionate marriage, she concluded, "The highest happiness we know / is intellectual joy."[60]

By creating visual and literary art about flowers, Knowles participated in the increasingly fashionable practice of botanical studies among prosperous middling females.[61] By presenting these art forms as promoting a virtuous life and sound morals, she reconciled botanical art and Quaker principles. Through these poems and images, she contributed to the social integration of Quakers into polite life and served as a mentor to young people, regardless of their religious backgrounds.

Settled once again into Lombard Street, Knowles continued to practice Quaker hospitality, opening her home to her cousin who attended the Friends' Yearly Meeting. In May 1790, Morris Birkbeck spent ten or 12 days with his "Cousin Knowles." Birkbeck, a childhood friend from Settle, traveled to North America, and, upon returning to England, established a successful insurance company and became a minister. Interested in history and literature, Birkbeck corresponded with Anna Seward about Litchfield lore while staying at his cousin Mary's house.[62]

According to Knowles, James Boswell also called on her, bringing his description of her confrontation with Johnson concerning the young Jane Harry. Knowles later told G. Sael, a bookseller in the Strand, that Boswell "came to her house in order to read to her his own narrative of the dialogue" with Johnson.[63] When Boswell finished reading, Knowles reacted strongly.

Mincing no words, "She then declared it was not *genuine*," as she later told Sael. Knowles said she pointed out "the fabrications and suppressions" in Boswell's version. She maintained that he then admitted omitting parts of the conversation. She later stated, "the truth of several of which suppressions he had heretofore acknowledged."

After listening to Boswell's account, Knowles "read to him her statement of the conversation." She was adamant in "asserting that the conversation began and ended in theological discussion only," stoutly maintaining "that, whatever might be recollected of the chit-chat which occasionally occurred, it was *after*, not *amidst*, the solemn contest" between her and Johnson. She insisted that Boswell then acceded to her points. "Much of this, though greatly disturbed, the force of truth obliged him, at the interview to acknowledge," she told Sael.

Sael later reported that Boswell "pressed Mrs. K. to dine at his house, when two of his friends ... should hear both narratives." Knowles agreed, and the dinner took place at Boswell's home. Knowles told Sael that, at the dinner, "one gentleman confessed, that there was sufficient internal evidence that Mrs. Knowles's was the genuine statement." He reasoned that, "it was in her own forcible style of language ... and it was on the side of probability, that she, thus attacked, should defend her religious principles." According to the statement Knowles gave Sael, "The other [man] also expressed the same opinion, adding that, with her permission, it should be inserted in the Gentleman's Magazine."

Knowles further told Sael that, although Boswell refused to change his text, he agreed not to contest her version if she published it in the magazine. Boswell "persisted in the determination to print his own representation, though earnestly dissuaded by these two judicious and liberal arbitrators," Sael later reported. Yet, said Sael, Boswell "conceded so far as to assure them, that he would not contradict her account so published."[64]

Two separate incidents support some of what Knowles told Sael. On Saturday, 8 May 1790, Boswell noted in his journal, "Mr. Nichols, Mr. Dilly, Mr. Malone, Molly Knowles."[65] Although Boswell provided no further details, John Nichols, publisher of *Gentleman's Magazine*, and Edmond Malone, Boswell's literary advisor, could have been the two gentleman arbitrators mentioned by Knowles. Charles Dilly, as Boswell's publisher, may not have wanted to serve as an arbitrator, even though he had presumably been present during the conversation. Nichols could have been the man who suggested that Knowles publish her account in *Gentleman's Magazine*, as she told Sael.

One of Boswell's biographers, Adam Sisman, also presented an example of a later literary dispute, which Boswell referred to a similar form of arbitration. When he strongly disagreed with Malone about the wording of an advertisement for a subsequent text, Boswell suggested putting the matter before a third party. The two men did so and were then able to reach a compromise.[66]

On 16 May 1791, Boswell's much anticipated *Life of Samuel Johnson, LL. D.* appeared in two folio volumes of more than 500 pages each.[67] Anna Seward quickly acquired a copy and began reading. Pausing long enough to write Knowles, Seward dryly observed, "Its quantity of writing makes one wonder at his industry, after the world has complained so long of his idleness." Working her way through the first volume, Seward pronounced what she had read so far to be "on the whole, infinitely entertaining."[68]

Boswell introduced Knowles early in the second volume of his *Life*, noting her entry after the dinner where Johnson met Wilkes in 1776. Boswell identified her as "the Quaker lady, well known for her various talents," but he reported no conversation by her.[69] As literary scholar Helen Pennock South observed, given Knowles's reputation as a talker, it is unlikely she remained silent on this occasion.[70] Moreover, Johnson recounted how he conversed with Knowles, as seen in his letter to Hester Thrale described in Chapter Three.

Perhaps Boswell included no conversation by Knowles because he had neglected his journal keeping during this time, as also noted in Chapter Three. At the time this dinner took place, Boswell had been preoccupied with the pleasures of London, as has been seen. As his biographer Adam Sisman observed, "Boswell's only record of the occasion was some brief notes." Although lacking complete notes, and, as Sisman pointed out, writing "more than a dozen years later," Boswell re-created the now famous meeting between Johnson and Wilkes in an account of nearly 4,000 words.[71]

Instead of reporting anything Knowles may have said on this occasion, Boswell publicly presented her in a sexualized way, repeating a joke concerning her and Johnson he said Wilkes later conveyed to him. Boswell wrote that, after Knowles's entry, "Mr. Wilkes held a candle to shew a fine print of a beautiful female figure which hung in the room, and pointed out the elegant contour of the bosom with the finger of an arch connoisseur." Boswell added that Wilkes "afterwards … waggishly insisted that all the time Johnson shewed visible signs of a fervent admiration of the corresponding charms of the fair Quaker."[72]

While Boswell said Wilkes relayed this story to him, Wilkes told his daughter Polly that he believed Boswell revealed too much about Johnson and that his *Life* contained errors as well as brilliance. Writing to Polly on a hot June day, Wilkes hoped for rain "for the earth is as thirsty as Boswell, and as cracked in many places, as he certainly is in one. His book however is that of an entertaining madman." Wilkes expressed sympathy for Johnson, his former foe, saying, "Poor Johnson! Does a friend come and add to the gross character of such a man?" Wilkes promised to share his copy of Boswell's *Life* with Polly. He said he "will point out numberless mistakes; but there are many excellent things in them."[73]

As many modern scholars have argued, Boswell's portrayal of Johnson, especially concerning women, sometimes reflects the views of the biographer rather than his subject.[74] By publishing this sexual joke about Knowles, Boswell underscored his own awareness of how her presence changed the gender dynamics of what had been the all-male gathering. Yet the passage also indicates that Johnson viewed Knowles in a sexualized manner, at least according to Wilkes and Boswell, two notorious womanizers. If accurate, this vignette provides a glimpse of Johnson as a sexual being rather than "A neutral being between the sexes."[75]

Since Boswell included no conversation by Knowles, it is impossible to tell from his account what she said or did while Johnson's reportedly studied her bosom. No sources have been located that indicate that Knowles ever publicly commented on Boswell's presentation of her on this occasion. She did, however, have plenty to say about Boswell's account of her at the dinner in April 1778, especially about his report of her confrontation with Johnson concerning the then unmarried Jane Harry.

Boswell devoted ten folio pages in volume two of his *Life* to the dinner party at Dillys' that included Knowles and Seward. Since Boswell had made extensive notes in his journal on this occasion, comparing his journal entry to his published account can reveal what changes he made, if any, as a result of the information he received from Knowles, Seward, or other sources. It is important to examine this comparison in detail since the conversation that night continued to be a source of heated disagreement between these three principal participants.

In his published introduction of Knowles at this dinner, Boswell added a flattering phrase evidently borrowed from Seward's description of her. He listed Knowles first among the guests that night, identifying her, in the same words used by Seward in her letter to him, as "the ingenious Quaker lady." He also inserted a description of Seward as "the poetess of Lichfield."[76]

Boswell added a footnote to his introduction of Knowles calling attention to the mistake made by his rival, Hester Thrale Piozzi, concerning Knowles's needle paintings. The note pointed out that, "Dr. Johnson, describing her needlework in one of his letters to Mrs. Thrale, Vol. I, p. 326 uses the learned word *sutile* which Mrs. Thrale has mistaken, and made the phrase injurious by writing '*futile* pictures.'"[77] Modern scholarship revealed that Boswell added this note at the last minute. Boswell instructed the typesetters, "'If the note can be printed without deranging the press work, well – If not, leave it out.'"[78] Although Boswell seemed indifferent, the seemingly simple statement showed Piozzi as unlearned, underscored his own credibility, and presented himself as Knowles's defender against this injury.

While seeming to flatter and defend Knowles, Boswell undermined her arguments in favor of women's liberty with the addition of a single word. He prefaced the beginning of his published description of her discussion concerning female liberty by writing, "Mrs. Knowles affected to complain that men had much more liberty than women."[79] Adding the word *affected* cast Knowles's ensuing remarks as a rhetorical strategy rather than a straightforward statement of advocacy on behalf of women's liberty.

Yet, in his published version, Boswell also added a strong statement in support of equal liberty for women he said Knowles made, which is not found in his journal. After protesting that women had less indulgence allowed them than men, Boswell reported Knowles as saying, "'It gives a superiority to men, to which I do not see how they are entitled.'"[80] Whether or not Knowles spoke these exact words, the sentiment is certainly compatible with her commitment to liberty and her previous statements about women's roles.

Perhaps seeking to mollify Knowles, Boswell changed the sequencing of some of the remaining conversation from that noted in his journal. Knowles, as has been seen, insisted that her dialogue with Johnson concerning Harry did not occur amidst other social chitchat. In his published *Life*, Boswell repositioned the sequencing of some topics noted in his journal to place the contested dialogue last. This repositioning, however, created some incongruous transitions.

In his journal, Boswell ended his account of the dinner with the humorous confusion about whether a certain man was a "Prig" or a "Whig." In the revised sequencing, he placed this jocular discussion earlier. In the published version, immediately following this joke, Boswell reported that he said, "I expressed a horrour at the thought of death." Without accounting for this incongruity, he proceeded to describe the discussion concerning that somber subject.[81]

In addition to placing the disputed dialogue between Knowles and Johnson as the concluding conversation of this dinner in his published *Life*, Boswell described Knowles's initiation of the subject of Jane Harry more sympathetically than in his journal. Boswell no longer suggested that Knowles wanted to vindicate herself from the charge of persuading Harry to become a Quaker. Instead, he now wrote that Knowles spoke "in the gentlest and most persuasive manner" and "solicited" Johnson's "kind indulgence" for her friend. Furthermore, he distanced himself from Johnson's harsh reaction by stating his own opinion that Harry's decision "was sincerely a matter of conscience."[82]

Boswell seems to have incorporated a few comments from Seward's letter to him in introducing the conversation that followed. He expanded his description of Harry, although he did not name her. Evidently based on Seward's information, he added that Johnson "had shewn much affection" to Harry, and "she ever had, and still retained, a great respect for him."

He also added a new sentence describing Knowles's overture to Johnson concerning Harry. While Boswell attributed the quote to Knowles, it seems to be paraphrased from Seward's account. He portrayed Knowles telling Johnson that, "'the amiable young creature was sorry at finding that he was offended at her leaving the Church of England, and embracing a simpler faith.'"[83]

In describing the actual exchange between Knowles and Johnson, however, Boswell followed his journal entry closely, incorporating none of the additional information provided by the two women.[84] He added nothing from Seward's account concerning Knowles's repeated solicitations for Johnson's sympathy. He included none of Knowles's arguments concerning her defense of Quaker beliefs or the moral agency of Jane Harry. Nor did he include his own statement, quoted by both women, that Knowles had chafed the mighty literary lion.

In ending his account of the evening, Boswell understandably omitted his journal notes concerning his remarks about holding a rich Quaker in his arms like a lamb, but this omission left another gap to fill. He ended his report of the contested conversation by saying that Johnson "rose again into passion, and attacked the young proselyte in the severest terms of reproach, so that both ladies seemed to be much shocked." This statement accords with the information provided by Knowles and Seward, describing Johnson's angry reaction to Knowles's persistent pleas on behalf of Harry.[85]

Adding this new statement, however, created another difficult transition when Boswell observed, "we were all delighted upon the whole with Johnson." To smooth over Johnson's "occasional explosions of violence," Boswell inserted the extended metaphor comparing Johnson's temperament with "a warm West Indian climate" that he had originally developed in his journal to explain Johnson's angry outburst against Americans. In his published account, he portrayed Johnson's anger at the Americans as comic, although he described it in his journal as harsh and grating. Moving the weather metaphor to the conclusion of his published account, Boswell ended by saying, "the same heat sometimes produces, thunder, lightening, and earthquakes in a terrible degree."[86]

Why did Boswell choose not to include the information provided by Seward and Knowles after specifically discussing each of their accounts with them? Scholars may never know for sure. Yet some indications can be found in Boswell's own words.

In the advertisement to his *Life*, Boswell portrayed Johnson as "a departed Hero," describing his own efforts as his biographer "in the pious office of erecting an honourable monument to his memory."[87] Well aware of Johnson's sometimes problematic social behavior, Boswell acknowledged that he wanted to show that Johnson behaved politely and not as the brutish bore described by some. "How very false is the notion, which has gone round the world," Boswell observed later in his text, "of the rough, and passionate, and harsh manners of this great and good man." While Boswell admitted that Johnson may have been "sometimes too desirous of triumph in colloquial contest," he insisted that, "by much the greatest part of his time he was civil, obliging, nay polite in the true sense of the word."[88]

One of Boswell's first, and least sympathetic, editors, John Wilson Croker detected gaps in the published narrative of Johnson's confrontation with Knowles. Croker noted that Boswell "evidently slurs over the latter part of the conversation." Croker explained these gaps by writing, "It may however be suspected that Boswell was himself a little ashamed of Johnson's violence."[89]

According to Seward, Boswell had previously expressed regret for Johnson's bad behavior in this confrontation, as described in Chapter Four. Boswell further indicated his regret by introducing Knowles more sympathetically and offering his own opinion that Harry changed her religion for conscience-sake. As polite conversation, especially concerning religious differences, became the hallmark of genteel society, Boswell could not include the women's accounts of Johnson's rude and angry behavior, as literary scholar James Woolley wrote, "for the deepest rhetorical reasons."[90]

Moreover, including Seward's descriptions of Johnson's angry remarks about Harry or Knowles's account of Johnson's uninformed view of Quakerism would have revealed Johnson as not only impolite but also bested by a woman in one of the most important literary coteries of the day. The accounts by the two women showed Johnson behaving badly about Harry and arguing badly with Knowles. If, as has been suggested, Boswell sometimes projected his own sexual attitudes toward women onto Johnson, in this case, Boswell might have omitted information to protect Johnson's reputation regarding his treatment of these two women.

Another well-known contemporary female reported that Johnson argued badly and misrepresented his behavior toward her. In her *Letters on Education* published in 1790, Catharine Sawbridge Macaulay Graham insisted that Johnson greatly embellished the now famous anecdote where he supposedly asked her footman to sit down to dinner to refute her arguments about equality. Observing that "Dr. Johnson would argue loosely and inaccurately when he thought he had a feeble antagonist; and ... victory, not truth, was often the thing sought after," Graham insisted that Johnson misrepresented what actually happened.[91]

If Johnson's attitudes and behavior toward women are to be fully understood, then scholars should consider Knowles's and Seward's accounts, as well as that of Graham, precisely because they have not been filtered through Boswell. Publishing his biography one year after Graham's *Letters* appeared, Boswell may not have wanted to repeat another incident where two well-known women portrayed Johnson as not only behaving badly but also arguing badly The accounts of Seward and Knowles should certainly not be ignored simply because Boswell chose not to include them in his *Life*.

When Seward wrote Knowles shortly after the publication of Boswell's *Life*, she had not yet read the second volume, but she had heard that, "it contains the memorable conversation at Dilly's, but without that part of it which I made minutes, and in which you appear to so much advantage over the imperious and gloomy intolerant." Seward believed that, "The omission is surely unjustifiable." She assured Knowles that, "I gave Mr. Boswell my memoir." She insisted that, "though it by no means contained all that was said, it contained nothing but what was said by you and the despot." Finally, she told Knowles, "Mr. B. might have given so much more as you and he could recollect, but he should not have omitted those highly characteristic sentences" she herself had supplied.[92]

Knowles expressed not only disappointment, but also outrage, about Boswell's presentation of her dialogue with Johnson. She wrote to John Nichols, publisher of *Gentleman's Magazine*, that she had been "illiberally used" by Boswell. Referring to herself in the formal third person style, she pointed out that, "many besides Mrs. K. have complained of his fabricated dialogues." Nichols credited her letter enough to include it in his *Illustrations of the Literary History of the Eighteenth Century*.[93]

Although Knowles did not name others who complained, she might have been thinking of her acquaintance, Catharine Sawbridge Macaulay Graham. As noted above, Graham publicly denied the accuracy of the story concerning her footman before Boswell published his *Life*. Despite Graham's protests, Boswell repeated Johnson's version of the anecdote concerning her in his *Life*.[94] Graham died in June 1791, only a few weeks after Boswell's *Life* appeared. She did not publicly contest Boswell's version of this incident, but she could have expressed displeasure to friends and colleagues.

In her letter to Nichols, Knowles indicated that he had invited her to publish her account in *Gentleman's Magazine*. "Mrs. Knowles will ever think herself greatly obliged to Mr. Nichols for his polite attention and kindness to her," she wrote him, adding, "Mr. N. acts with his wonted good nature respecting his magazine. Mrs. K. perhaps may consider what to do in this respect."[95] Although the dating of this letter as published is unclear, the reference supports the idea that Nichols was one of the two gentleman arbitrators who first heard Knowles's version of the dialogue and suggested that she publish it in *Gentleman's Magazine*.

One month after Boswell's *Life* appeared, Knowles publicly defied Boswell by publishing her own account of her dialogue in the June issue of *Gentleman's Magazine*. She presented her decision to publish as an act of defiance in the strong language of a radical resisting intolerance and scorning submission. She wrote a brief prefatory letter, using the pseudonym "A Child of Candour," saying she presented her account as a "Very striking" example of "the mild fortitude of modest Truth ... finely contrasted with the boisterous violence of bigoted sophistry." Such sophistry, she protested, had been too "long accustomed to victory over feigned or slight resistance, and in a certain circle, to timid and implicit submission."[96]

A later source indicated that Knowles "published the dialogue herself, under the signature of *A Child of Candour*."[97] Nichols confirmed her authorship in his *Illustrations of the Literary History of the Eighteenth Century*. "The narrative of Boswell ... not proving satisfactory to Molly Knowles (as she was familiarly styled)," he wrote, "she gave the Dialogue between herself and the sturdy Moralist, in her own manner, under the signature of 'A Child of Candour.'"[98]

While using a pseudonym, she did not conceal that the published dialogue came from her. The opening sentence of her prefatory letter in *Gentleman's Magazine* stated, "I have been favoured, by Mrs. Knowles, with the perusal of the following Dialogue." She closed her letter by saying, "I have obtained permission to publish the Dialogue; and I wish it to appear in your excellent Magazine."[99]

Based on Knowles's strong language in her letter, her use of "child" does not seem to imply a diminutive term but rather additional evidence of the truth of her account. The word *child*, transcending gender and suggesting purity and innocence, seems to have been used by other learned ladies. Seward had earlier described two of Knowles's women friends as one the child of wit and the other of imagination, as has been seen. By pairing "child" and "candour," Knowles may have wanted to underscore the purity of her motives in publishing her version of her dialogue.

"An interesting Dialogue between the late Dr. Samuel Johnson and Mrs. Knowles" followed her brief letter. Printed in full, Knowles's version of the contested conversation occupied nearly three typeset columns, about a page and a half in *Gentleman's Magazine*. In it, Knowles did not fully name her long dead friend, referring to her only as "Jenny H –." She said nothing about the young woman's personal story, perhaps from a sense of delicacy about repeating Johnson's angry words, or perhaps because of her grief over her friend's early death. She focused instead on her own explanation of Quaker theology and on her friend's undoubted duty as a moral agent to choose her religion.

Although the 58-year-old widow had taken a much less public role in the literary life of London since her husband's death, she now stepped into the most public of all literary arenas, the pages of *Gentleman's Magazine*, to defend her friend and her religion, and, once again, to practice self-representation. Like earlier devout women of the seventeenth century, her deep commitment to her religious beliefs made publication a duty, regardless of prevailing views about the propriety of women appearing in the public sphere.[100] Moreover, her published account not only explicated her religious views but also reflected her equally strong commitment to the moral agency of women. By publishing her vindication of the moral right of Jane Harry to determine her own religion, Knowles chose, as she said, resistance over submission to established authority. By publicly demonstrating her continued claim to self-representation as a woman in June 1791, she committed a radical act at a time when the French Revolution presented the most serious challenge yet to English radicals.

Notes

1 Temporary MSS 403 [Braithwaite Papers], Box 7, Packet 15, File 3, Number 38, "[Priscilla Far]mer, [Bingley, B]irmingham, 12th 25 1786."
2 Vickery, *Gentleman's Daughter*, pp. 87–126.
3 Braithwaite Papers, 7, 15, 3, 38, "[Far]mer, 12th 25 1786."
4 *Letters of Anna Seward*, vol. 1, p. 247.
5 Brigid Hill, *Women, Work and Sexual Politics in Eighteenth-Century England* (London, 1994), p. 250.
6 Public Record Office, Prob 11, 1147, quire 573.
7 Sisman, *Boswell's Presumptuous Task*, pp.75, 212–13.
8 *Letters of Anna Seward*, vol. 1, p. 346.
9 Ibid.
10 Hill, *Women, Work and Sexual Politics*, p. 241.
11 Vickery, *Gentleman's Daughter*, pp. 32–7.

12 *Journal of the Friends Historical Society*, 29 (1932): 48.
13 Irma Lustig and Frederick Pottle, eds, *Boswell: The English Experiment, 1785–1789* (New York, 1986), p. 149.
14 *Letters of Anna Seward*, vol. 1, p. 347.
15 Brewer, *Pleasures of the Imagination*, pp. 604–12.
16 *Letters of Anna Seward*, vol. 1, p. 112.
17 *Dictionary of National Biography*, vol. 12, pp. 140–41, "Michael Lort (1725–90)," vol. 10, pp. 284–5, "Anne Hunter (1742–1821)," "John Hunter (1728–93)."
18 *Letters of Anna Seward*, vol. 2, p. 300.
19 Ibid., vol. 1, pp. 46–7.
20 Ibid., vol. 2, p. 106.
21 Ibid., vol. 1, pp. 391–2.
22 Ibid., vol. 1, p. 67.
23 Ibid., vol. 1, p. 348.
24 Ibid., vol. 1, p. 346.
25 Ibid., vol. 2, pp. 6–8.
26 *Records and Recollections of James Jenkins*, pp. 220–21.
27 Ibid.
28 Matthews MSS, Joseph Woods to William Matthews, 27 March 1788.
29 Peter Pindar, Esq. [Dr. John Wolcot], *Bozzy and Piozzi, or the British Biographers: A Town Eclogue* (London, 1786).
30 Hester Lynch [Thrale] Piozzi, *Letters to and from the late Samuel Johnson, LL.D.* (2 vols, London, 1787), vol. 1, p. 326.
31 Matthews MSS, Joseph Woods to William Matthews, 27 March 1788.
32 John Nichols, *Illustrations of the Literary History of the Eighteenth Century* (8 vols, London, 1817), vol. 6, pp. 494–5. Chapman, ed. *Letters of Samuel Johnson*, vol. 2, p. 131.
33 A. Hayward, ed. *Autobiography, Letters and Literary Remains of Mrs. Piozzi* (2 vols, London, 1861), vol. 2, p. 61.
34 Edward Fletcher, *The Life of Samuel Johnson by James Boswell with marginal comments and markings ... by Hester Lynch Thrale Piozzi* (3 vols, London, 1938), vol. 3, p. 1.
35 *Letters of Anna Seward*, vol. 2, pp. 101–7.
36 Ibid.
37 Ibid.
38 Ibid., vol. 2, p. 109.
39 Jennings, *Business*, pp. 22–52.
40 *Letters of Anna Seward*, vol. 3, pp. 28–30.
41 Library of the Religious Society of Friends, MSS Vol. 334 [Gibson MSS, vol. 1], p. 193, "Inscription for a Tobacco Box, 6mo 13 1788."
42 Jennings, *Business*, p. 36.
43 J. R. Oldfield, *Popular Politics and British Anti-Slavery: The Mobilisation of Public Opinion against the Slave Trade, 1787–1807* (London, 1998), pp. 155–84.
44 Claire Midgley, "Slave Sugar Boycotts, Female Activism and the Domestic Base of British Anti-Slavery Culture," *Slavery and Abolition*, 17/3 (1996): 142.
45 Sarah Richardson, "'Well Neighboured Houses:' The Political Network of Elite Women, 1780–1860," in *Women in British Politics, 1760–1860*, pp. 60–65. Elaine

Chalus, "'To Serve My Friends:' Women and Political Patronage in Eighteenth-Century England."
46 *Letters of Anna Seward*, vol. 2, pp. 225–6.
47 Ibid., vol. 2, pp. 151–2.
48 Ibid., vol. 2, pp. 225–6.
49 Ibid., vol. 2, pp. 298–300.
50 *Journal of the Friends Historical Society*, 29 (1932): 48.
51 *Letters of Anna Seward*, vol. 2, p. 284.
52 Ibid., vol. 2, p. 390.
53 Ibid., vol. 2, p. 232.
54 Ibid., vol. 2, pp. 389–92.
55 Ibid.
56 Ibid.
57 Ibid.
58 David Sox, "Sydney Parkinson (1745–1741): Quaker artist with Cook's *Endeavour* voyage," *Journal of the Friends Historical Society*, 59/3 (2002): 231–5. Shteir, *Cultivating Women*, pp. 1–4, 53.
59 Braithwaite Papers, 5, 9, 1, 37, "Address'd to the amiable M. B. / with a set of Paints by M. K."
60 Ibid., No. 36, "Sent with the Drawing of a Moss Rose Bud."
61 Shteir, *Cultivating Women*, pp. 53–107.
62 Library of the Religious Society of Friends, MSS Vol. 150 [Luke Howard MSS], No. 29, "To Anna Seward, Lichfield, 5/15/1790." "Morris Birkbeck (1734–1816)," *Journal of the Friends Historical Society*, 8/1 (1911): 9–15.
63 *Gentleman's Magazine* (Supplement 1796): 1074.
64 Ibid.
65 Marlies Danzinger and Frank Brady, eds, *Boswell: The Great Biographer, 1789–1795* (New York, 1989), p. 48.
66 Sisman, *Boswell's Presumptuous Task*, p. 277.
67 James Boswell, *Life of Samuel Johnson, LL.D.* (2 vols, London, 1791).
68 *Letters of Anna Seward*, vol. 3, pp. 72–9.
69 Boswell, *Life of Johnson*, vol. 2, pp. 83–9.
70 Helen Pennock South, "Dr. Johnson and the Quakers," *Bulletin of the Friends Historical Association*, 44/1 (Spring, 1955): 26.
71 Sisman, *Boswell's Presumptuous Task*, p. 200.
72 Boswell, *Life of Johnson*, vol. 2, p. 89.
73 *Letters from the Year 1774 to the Year 1796 of John Wilkes Esq. Addressed to his Daughter, the late Miss Wilkes* (4 vols, London, 1804), vol. 4, pp. 5–6.
74 Greg Clingman, *James Boswell: The Life of Johnson* (Cambridge, 1992), p. 69. Basker, "Dancing Dogs," Lustig, "The Myth of Johnson's Misogyny."
75 Kemmerer, *"A neutral being between the sexes,"* pp. 23–7.
76 Weis and Pottle, eds, *Boswell in Extremes*, p. 282. Boswell, *Life of Johnson*, vol. 2, p. 223. Portfolio MSS 3, 126, "Notes of a Conversation."
77 Boswell, *Life of Johnson*, vol. 2, p. 223.
78 R. W. Chapman, "Boswell's Revision of the Life of Johnson Reprinted from the London Mercury, 1927," in *Johnson and Boswell Revised by Themselves and Others:*

Three Essays by David Nichol Smith, R. W. Chapman, and L. F. Powell (Oxford, 1929), p. 29.
79 Weis and Pottle, *Boswell in Extremes*, p. 284. Boswell, *Life of Johnson*, vol. 2, p. 225.
80 Weis and Pottle, *Boswell in Extremes*, p. 282–90. Boswell, *Life of Johnson*, vol. 2, p. 225.
81 Weis and Pottle, *Boswell in Extremes*, p. 290. Boswell, *Life of Johnson*, vol. 2, p. 229.
82 Weis and Pottle, *Boswell in Extremes*, p. 288. Boswell, *Life of Johnson*, vol. 2, p. 231.
83 Weis and Pottle, *Boswell in Extremes*, pp. 288–9. Boswell, *Life of Johnson*, vol. 2, p. 231. Portfolio MSS 3, 126, "Notes of a Conversation."
84 Weis and Pottle, *Boswell in Extremes*, pp. 288–9. Boswell, *Life of Johnson*, vol. 2, pp. 231–2.
85 Weis and Pottle, *Boswell in Extremes*, p. 289. Boswell, *Life of Johnson*, vol. 2, p. 231. Portfolio MSS 3, 126, "Notes of a Conversation." [Knowles], *Gentleman's Magazine*, (1791): 502.
86 Boswell, *Life of Johnson*, vol. 2, p. 232.
87 Ibid., vol. 1, p. x.
88 Ibid., vol. 2, pp. 90–91.
89 Croker, *Boswell's Life of Johnson*, vol. 4, p. 157.
90 Woolley, "Johnson as Despot": 145.
91 Catharine Macaulay Graham, *Letters on Education with Observations on Religious and Metaphysical Subjects* (London, 1790), pp. 167–8.
92 *Letters of Anna Seward*, vol. 3, pp. 72–9.
93 Nichols, *Illustrations of the Literary History of the Eighteenth Century*, vol. 4, p. 831.
94 *James Boswell: Life of Johnson*, (New York, 1992), p. 281.
95 Nichols, *Illustrations of the Literary History of the Eighteenth Century*, vol. 4, p. 831.
96 [Knowles], *Gentleman's Magazine* (1791): 500.
97 *The Literary Panorama* (2 vols, London, 1807), vol. 2, p. 1069.
98 Nichols, *Illustrations of the Literary History of the Eighteenth Century*, vol. 4, p. 831.
99 [Knowles], *Gentleman's Magazine* (1791): 500
100 McDowell, *Women of Grub Street*, pp. 17–18.

Chapter 6

The French Revolution and a New Note

As the increasing violence of the French Revolution divided Britons, readers of *Gentleman's Magazine* debated Knowles's presentation of her confrontation with Johnson. Her account also appeared in *Lady's Magazine*, where a reader raised the issue of gender. In this heightened political atmosphere, Knowles, a radical utopian, and Seward, a polite Whig, differed strongly concerning the events in France. Despite her radical opinions, Knowles maintained her connection to King George III and continued to practice polite Quakerliness. She publicly defended Quaker dress and beliefs, wrote a humorous essay describing a coach accident, and entertained a proposal of marriage. Boswell, also affected by revolutionary politics, added a new note to his *Life*, publicly implying that her account of her confrontation with Johnson was not authentic. After Boswell's death, his editor continued this insinuation. Knowles again publicly insisted on the accuracy of her statement, even as serious internal divisions began to threaten Quaker unity.

Knowles publicly defied Boswell in the pages of *Gentleman's Magazine* at a time when escalating violence created international tensions concerning the revolution in France. Many Britons, like Anna Seward, had first hailed the fall of the Bastille as a blow for freedom. In a letter to Knowles dated 25 July 1789, Seward linked French actions to the American Revolution and English liberty. "So France has dipt her lilies in the living streams of American freedom, and bids her sons be slaves no longer," she wrote, "few English hearts, I hope, there are, that do not wish victory."[1] By February 1790, however, Seward had become, in her own words, "a colder sceptic." She told Knowles she believed "France is almost wholly a nation of Deists," based on what she had been told by "numbers" of others "who have had opportunities of seeing and knowing."[2]

In contrast, Knowles maintained, according to Seward, a "benevolent faith, concerning the progressive state of virtue and true piety" in France. Knowles may have been less concerned about the charges of French Deism, having been accused by Johnson of being little better than a Deist herself. Like other radicals, Knowles remained hopeful about the future of the French people as the National Assembly adopted the Declaration of the Rights of Man and Citizen, including liberty, property, security, and resistance to oppression.[3]

Knowles's benevolent faith in progress must have been related to her belief in human perfectibility, just as it was for her contemporary, Mary Wollstonecraft. For Quakers like Knowles, human perfectibility remained rooted in the teachings of George Fox, who wrote, "the law of God, that is perfect, answers the perfect principle of God in everyone."[4] Although not a Quaker, Mary Wollstonecraft also believed in human perfectibility. Feminist scholar Barbara Taylor described Wollstonecraft's religious belief as "that unwavering faith in divine purpose that, suffusing her radicalism, turned anticipation of 'world perfected' into a confident political stance."[5] For both women, religion and radicalism were inseparable.

Seward did not share their radical optimism. In May 1791, she told Knowles she began "to apprehend" the French were "pushing the levelling principles into extremes" with "the confiscation of hereditary estates." Like other Whigs, she read Thomas Paine's *Rights of Man, Part I*. She indicated to Knowles that she agreed with his ideas, but added. "I do not believe those who have obtained power in France will respect its maxims enough to govern themselves by them."[6]

Feelings ran high throughout Britain in the summer of 1791 as members of the Revolution Society planned dinners celebrating the second anniversary of the fall of the Bastille, while Church and King conservatives voiced their opposition. On July 14, 1791, peaceful celebrations took place in many parts of the country. In Birmingham, however, a Church and King mob destroyed the laboratory of Dissenting scientist Joseph Priestley and the homes and businesses of other Nonconformists and radicals.[7]

In this increasingly adversarial political context, public debate about Knowles's published version of her dialogue assumed larger significance. Were Quakers Deists? Or were they, as Knowles insisted to Johnson, genuine Christians, sharing many beliefs—if not practices—with members of the Church of England? Could a Quaker woman have bested Samuel Johnson in a religious debate?

In the months following her publication, readers of *Gentleman's Magazine* debated these issues while voicing different points of view about Knowles, Johnson, and Quakers. The debate began in July 1791, one month after her account appeared, when "W. C." questioned both Johnson's learning and Quakers' Christianity. Writing from Shropshire, "W. C." asserted that, if true, Knowles's version "perfectly convinces me of what for many years I suspected, viz. that Dr. Johnson was but a very superficial Divine." "W. C." added, however, that Quakers were "certainly" Deists.[8] In August, "M. N." disagreed, replying that, "Mrs. Knowles in the Johnsonian dialogue alluded to, fully clears their Society of the Doctor's insinuation of Deism."[9]

Another correspondent, "M. S.," also wrote in August to say that she or he "knew Dr. J., is acquainted with Mrs. Knowles, and loved and respected Jenny H." Based on this knowledge, the writer deemed Knowles's account "a true portrait" of Johnson, who "controverts the opinion of his adversary, not by reason and argument, but by ill-manners and insolence." Citing first-hand experience, the writer added, "I can, at least, aver it corresponds exactly with whatever I have met in his company."[10]

At the same time, the writer stated that Knowles influenced Harry, without naming her, to become a Quaker. "M. S." observed, "That Mrs. K. was the means of converting (I do not say perverting) the mind of J. H. to Quakerism, can hardly be doubted." This was "not much to be wondered at," "M. S." added, given "the abilities of the one, and the easy, good-natured disposition of the other."[11]

In September, "A Constant Reader of the G. M." challenged the Quaker critic and presented new information about the dispute between Knowles and Johnson. In answer to the first correspondent, "W. C.," The "Constant Reader" alluded to the reports by Knowles and Seward that Knowles had chafed Johnson. "From the bigoted malignity of his [W. C.'s] strictures," wrote the "Constant Reader," "I strongly suspect he is as much '*chafed*' with the reading of the dialogue, as the good Doctor himself was in his weak and peevish support of his part of it."[12]

The "Constant Reader" then announced that he or she had "in my possession, a copy of an extract of a letter from a celebrated literary female to the Biographer of Dr. Johnson, containing *her* account of the dispute between the Doctor and M. Knowles." This description matches the manuscript "Notes of a Conversation between Dr. Johnson and Mary Knowles, in a Letter to Boswell," preserved in the Library of the Religious Society of Friends, discussed in Chapter Four. Noting that, "some particulars relative to the principal subject of the dispute are mentioned in the above said letter," the "Constant Reader" presented an "Extract of a Letter from S. to B." This published extract corresponds to the opening paragraphs of the longer manuscript in the Library, suggesting that the manuscript may have been the source used by the "Constant Reader."

In the extract published in *Gentleman's Magazine*, the "Constant Reader" for the first time publicly named "Miss Jenny Harry" as the subject of the dispute. While manuscript copies of Seward's account with its preface concerning Harry had been circulating at least since 1785, neither Boswell nor Knowles had publicly revealed Harry's full name. The "Extract of Letter from S. to B." recounted how Knowles met Harry, including the story that Harry's father forced her to choose between becoming a Quaker or inheriting £100,000.

The published extract ended with Knowles's opening plea on behalf of Harry and did not recount the dialogue that followed. "Here follows the account of the Doctor's surly reply, and of the whole conversation," the "Constant Reader" concluded, "which, I think differs chiefly in manner only from that given in the Magazine" by Knowles.[13] For this correspondent, Jane Harry, rather than Knowles or Johnson, was the primary subject.

Amid these serious religious debates, a pundit issued a poetic challenge to Knowles concerning Quaker dress. "A Poetic Correspondence Between Mrs. Knowles, the Celebrated Quaker, and Captain Morris" appeared in the October 1791 issue of *Gentleman's Magazine*. The brief identification of Knowles as "the Celebrated Quaker" indicates her widespread reputation as an exponent of her faith. The magazine introduced Captain Morris in more detail as "the respectable Author of a Collection of Spirited and Elegant Odes on the Subject of Liberty" and "not the famous Song-writer." This differentiated Thomas Morris from his younger brother, Charles Morris, also a captain, who composed Whig election ballads and socialized with John Wilkes and the Prince of Wales.[14]

In a short prefatory letter addressed to Knowles, Morris facetiously acknowledged that she had bested Johnson. He protested in mock humility, "When I consider that the following lines are addressed to the Lady who subdued that Goliath of Literature, Doctor Samuel Johnson, I think myself scarcely justified in sending them." Morris added somewhat gingerly, "Johnson was a great Bear, I am but a little one."

Morris named his concern as Quaker clothing but referenced gender by saying, "You will please to observe that I meddle only with the men's dress." Morris assured Knowles that he intended "leaving the Ladies to draw what conclusions they may think proper concerning their own." By addressing his verses on men's dress to Knowles, Morris evidently expected her to answer on their behalf, indicating his view of her as a spokesperson for Quaker males as well as females.

Morris signed his letter, "Your *friend*, in the *refined* sense of the word, and a Quaker in *spirit*, Tho, Morris."[15] This letter conveyed affection for Knowles and sympathy for Quaker beliefs, but also ambivalence about Quaker dress. In the fashion-conscious circles frequented by Thomas Morris and his brother Charles, dress became a distinguishing—and questionable—characteristic of Quakers.

Following his letter, Morris presented "A Bone for Friend Mary to Pick," 40 lines of verse written in a light tone and mock heroic mode. In his opening lines, he further indicated that he knew Knowles personally, and the two had previously discussed their religious differences. "When I once disapprov'd of an old-fashioned dress," Morris began, "Friend Mary was pleas'd her dissent to express." His brief reference again demonstrates Knowles's wide-ranging social connections, especially with Whigs and radicals, and her willingness to engage in polite disputation about religion. Continuing in this familiar vein, Morris wrote, "I own my dear Mary, it gives me much pain, / That the Meek should in trifles resemble the Vain."

After this polite opening, Morris turned to his criticisms, comparing Quaker dress to the distinctive clothes worn by some Catholics and Jews. "In these petty fancies [Quakers] take after the Jew," he charged, "And give to appearances more than their due." He also drew a parallel between the clothes worn by Quakers and "the low farce of Saint Benedict's crew."

Morris argued that Quaker dress detracted from their serious religious beliefs. "These old-fashion'd trappings I cannot admire," he declared, "The large hems of garments must laughter inspire." Professing to admire the teachings of George Fox, Morris wrote, "let us covet his grace, not the shape of his hat." Morris further questioned why Quakers would wear distinctive clothing but not practice widely accepted Christian sacraments. "If baptism by water be useless esteem'd, / If e'vn the Lord's Supper superfluous be deem'd," he asked how a broad-brimmed hat or "a lank head of hair" could be seen as indications of "the purest in heart?" Morris ended by expressing both admiration and frustration concerning Quakers, whom he professed to honor. "Such trifling is sport to the wits of the schools," he argued, "And the best of all Christians are laugh'd at as fools."[16]

Morris's challenge may have reflected more widespread opinions, since another contemporary also commented on unfavorable attitudes regarding Quaker dress. Thomas Clarkson, the Anglican abolitionist and Quaker sympathizer, wrote a few years later, "I know of no custom among the Quakers which has more excited the curiosity of the world than this of their dress." Clarkson admired Quakers for withstanding the "powerful attacks of the varying fashions of the world" but commented that the "world had been more than ordinarily severe on the Quakers" in this regard.[17]

Furthermore, comments by two associates of Knowles indicate changing internal and external standards of Quakerliness concerning dress and participation in popular pastimes. Quaker chronicler James Jenkins later observed that Friends' dress in London became more uniform and drab in the last decades of the eighteenth century. He noted that when he returned to London in the 1770s, "The colour of the cloathes of the young men were marone light mixtures, bright snuff, pea-green, and peach bloom." Comparing these colors to those worn later, he observed, "the dark ones so much now in vogue, they deemed only fit for their grandfathers."[18] In a letter to an Anglican friend in 1790, Seward described a Quaker acquaintance by saying, "He retains none of that rigidity which teaches many of his sect to fancy criminality in fashionable apparel, and in partaking the public amusement."[19]

Confronting these changing attitudes directly, Knowles again entered the public arena of *Gentleman's Magazine* to defend Quaker beliefs in a poetic reply to Morris entitled, "The Bone Pick'd." Her longer and more closely argued verses directly followed those from Morris in the October issue of *Gentleman's Magazine*. At 118 lines, her rejoinder was more then three times longer than his challenge. Like him, she, too, wrote in polished couplets, but she adopted a more serious tone and used iambic pentameter.

In "The Bone Pick'd," Knowles eschewed Morris's courtly courtesy and directly challenged his points. After two lines politely praising his poetic fluency, she immediately questioned his reasoning. "Thou begg'st the question quite too much, my friend," she charged, "Nor does thy verse to clear discussion tend."

Knowles, as had Morris, denigrated Catholics and Jews, strongly denying any resemblances to Quaker modes of dress. "Talk not of Friar Benedict, or Jew," she admonished Morris, "They're not in point, thy inf'rence will not do." In her view, "For sordid alms, and love of power, they dress, / The specious Pharisee, and artful Priest!" Quakers, she insisted, "have nobly scorn'd these motives base, / Nor do such schemes their history disgrace." Asserting that Morris reasoned wrongly, she countered, "My friend, indeed, has taken narrow ground, / These people [Quakers] with those wretches [Catholics and Jews] to confound."[20]

By making these unfavorable comparisons with Catholics and Jews, Knowles again displayed the limits of her religious toleration. Like some other radicals, she saw no inconsistency in supporting toleration for Dissenters, while denying the claims of those who were not Protestants. Throughout her life, Knowles sought to win acceptance for Quakers by distancing them from Catholics and Jews. By publishing these views in *Gentleman's Magazine*, she supported greater toleration for Quakers but reinforced limited toleration for those of other religions.

After denying Morris's comparison of Quakers with Catholics and Jews, Knowles set about analyzing and refuting each of his critical points, employing humor as well as reason. "Our list of errors let me now review," she wrote, "That they may have their examination due." She observed, for example, that not all Quakers had "long lank hair" since some "kind Nature *chuse* to curl." She portrayed Quaker dress as preferable to military uniforms, a direct jibe at him as a captain. "Why quarrel with our modest Quaker" shirts, she asked him. Moving from the defensive to the offensive, she followed, "Should they be decked like *military* flirts?"

Resuming her serious tone, Knowles turned to a deeper explanation of Quaker dress. Arguing that Friends followed the teachings of Jesus Christ, not George Fox, in their dress, she asked, "Do not we read, our Great Example wore, / A plainer garb than e'er was known before?" Again, she asked, "Don't his Apostles recommend restraints / Of *dress*, as well as conduct, to the Saints?" Knowles pointed out that the Church of England also warned against excess in dress. "Behold your *own* Priest-made baptismal vow," she countered, "That will not pomp or vanity allow." Quakers constituted true Christians, she argued, because, "We wish to *practice* what ye all *profess*, / Renunciation of a gaudy dress."

As she had done in her published dialogue with Johnson, Knowles equated Quakers with the earliest and purest Christians. George Fox, she maintained, "Referr'd them [his heart-struck converts] to the holy lives of those / First, gen'rous Christians, ere dark Popery rose." Returning to her renunciation of Catholic dress, she added, "Ere the proud Pope (ah, base example!) drest, / With gold and pearls his Antichristian vest."

Knowles also criticized the practice of paying clergy, as she had done in her reply to Clericus nearly 30 years earlier. Referencing an image often used by early Quakers, she lamented the Catholic origins of the paid priesthood by saying, "Oh, shepherds false! betrayers of the fold!" Linking these early priests to contemporary paid clergy, she asked, "Have not the flocks *e'er since* been bought and sold?" She answered her own question, "Down to this very day the practice reigns; / Of hireling pastors this poor world complains!"

Turning Morris's jesting questions to serious purposes, Knowles urged him to "Look in the Scriptures for thyself – research / Read in the earliest pages of the Church." Compare Friends with those who "profess now-a-days," she continued,

"And then let Quaker scruples merit thy praise, / Confess their language and their simple mode, / Are most congenial to the Christian code." Knowles portrayed Quaker faith and simplicity as the best hope in a sinful age. She characterized the current time as a period "Where soul-defiling pleasure – luxury / With all its sinful waves, run mountain high."

Amidst this decadence, she portrayed Quakers, in language reminiscent of the early Friends of the seventeenth century, as "a small city on a hill." She prayed that, "By genuine goodness [they will] be distinguished still." In closing, she appealed to Morris to renounce luxury and adopt Quaker simplicity. "Come, then, my friend, – leave this degenerate age/ ... Relinquish learned honours, wit and fame." Her final line challenged Morris to "Take up thy daily cross – despise the shame / Boldly for *truth* thy testimony bear."[21]

In "The Bone Pick'd," Knowles revisited some of the themes and modes of her earlier published and manuscript writings. She distanced Quakers from Catholics and Jews, and argued against the payment of priests as she had in her *Compendium on Water Baptism*. She identified Quakers with the early Christians, as she did in her published dialogue with Johnson. She interspersed humor with serious reflections as she had in her unpublished verses on fashion and the financial practices of Lord North.

In many ways, she maintained the latitudinarian views she expressed earlier. By publishing her verses in *Gentleman's Magazine*, for example, she focused more on external public opinion than internal Quaker differences. Moreover, while she supported simplicity and "renunciation of a gaudy dress," she did not denounce fine clothes, as such, or prescribe certain types of clothes or behaviors for Quakers.

Yet, perhaps reflecting the increasingly adversarial politics of the time, "The Bone Pick'd" also contains heightened language denouncing Catholics and Jews and defending Quakers as the only true Christians in a degenerate age. In the advice Harry said Knowles gave her and in Seward's version of the dialogue with Johnson, Knowles underscored the goodness of people of all faiths. But as radicals and Dissenters faced Church and King mobs, Knowles portrayed Quakers as alone in withstanding the pernicious luxuries of a consumer age.

Like her *Compendium on Water Baptism* and other earlier writings, "The Bone Pick'd" became an important enough statement of Quaker beliefs for some Friends to copy and preserve in manuscript as a social text. Quakers in London and Nottingham made and preserved at least three manuscript copies.[22] These carefully kept manuscripts indicate that Friends valued and circulated her poetic exchange at a time when Quakers, like other Dissenters, faced increasing suspicions and fears.

Yet if "The Bone Pick'd" proved popular with some Friends, another reader of *Gentleman's Magazine* criticized Quakers and questioned Knowles's theology. In November 1791, "R. B." wrote a long and angry letter, expressing disdain of Quakers as Deists. At the end of the letter, "R. B." added, "And Mrs. Knowles herself, in the curious Dialogue (if genuine) acknowledges their disbelief in the resurrection, the fundamental article of the Christian faith."[23]

On 30 December 1791, "A Female" requested "admission for the following lines" in *Gentleman's Magazine* in reply to the charges made by "R. B." There followed a 34-line poetic "Review of the Observations Respecting the Quakers," signed "Oxonia."[24] This poem has not been definitely attributed to Knowles, but it is characteristic of her subject matter and way of writing. Her authorship seems likely even though she did not sign her name or use her earlier pseudonym. Since "R. B." had not addressed her directly, as had Morris, she, perhaps, saw no need to reveal her identity in addition to acknowledging her gender. Perhaps she chose "Oxonia" as a pseudonym to suggest a strong female connection to learning and wisdom, as opposed to "Lavinia," the name she had used earlier, connoting youthful beauty and rural life.

The brief verse, written in the couplet form often used by Knowles, opened with a sturdy defense of Quaker principles. "While blasphemy, a charge as false as base, / Is thrown on Fox, his memory to debase," she began, continuing, "Then think not thou, whose pen is dipped in gall / That weak attempts like thine can cause their fall." The "Female" enumerated Quaker tenets, pointing out, as Knowles had done in earlier writings, that Quakers shared core Protestant beliefs.

To demonstrate Quaker belief in the trinity, the writer set forth a tripartite set of conditional statements, beginning, "If to believe in Heaven's Eternal Lord, / ... If to believe in the Incarnate Word, / Who on Mount Calvary resign'd his breath/ ... If in the blessed Holy Ghost to trust." Appealing to logic not emotion, she drew the rational conclusion, "If a belief like this with truth agrees, / The Quakers' faith is sound – then call them what you please."

"Oxonia" also specifically answered the charge concerning Quaker views on the resurrection, again pointing out that Friends shared core New Testament beliefs. "The resurrection they do not deny; / On that their best, their brightest hopes rely," she explained. "Their creed is Scripture-built – but, to be brief," she pithily pointed out, "As Paul believ'd it, such is their belief." The "Female" ended her succinct reply by calling on all "ye lib'ral minds, from rancour free / What semblance of the Deists can you see?" She concluded by asking, "Has not R. B. a fund of ignorance shown, / Or which is worse a heart to malice prone?"[25]

By appealing mainly to logic rather than emotion and calling for understanding and enlightened good will, "Oxonia" not only effectively defended Quakers but also supported polite discussion of religious differences. The brief verses evince the rational appeal of much of Knowles's earlier writing. Whether written by her or by another woman, Knowles's poetic reply to Morris engendered further public discussion of religion by a female.

While readers of *Gentleman's Magazine* debated Knowles's defense of her Quaker beliefs, *The Lady's Magazine* published "An Interesting Dialogue between the late Dr. Johnson, and Mrs. Knowles, the Quaker," in September 1791, three months after it first appeared in print. One of a number of publications aimed specifically at female readers, *The Lady's Magazine*, in the words of its title, served as an *Entertaining Companion for the Fair Sex, appropriated solely for their Use and Amusement.*[26] Publication of Knowles's dialogue in this female-oriented magazine must have highlighted the gender aspects of her controversy with Johnson.

Mary Wollstonecraft's *Vindication of the Rights of Woman*, appearing in early 1792, certainly highlighted gender issues; and, in March of that year, a "Lover of Truth" wrote to *The Lady's Magazine*, focusing on the gender dynamics in Knowles's confrontation with Johnson. Perhaps playing devil's advocate, a "Lover of Truth" asked, "Is it not a matter of astonishment that the ingenious author of the Rambler, should be defeated in argument by a woman?" The "Lover of Truth" reported that, although Johnson's defeat had at first seemed improbable, as she or he continued to reread Knowles account, "the more do I admire the ingenuity, as well as justness of her replies." The "Lover of Truth" hastened to "declare myself an entire stranger to the name of Mrs. Knowles, that I am not a member of the Society of Quakers, and I am a passionate admirer of the superior talents of the late Dr. Johnson." The "Lover of Truth" ended by pointing out that Johnson had judged Quakers without having read Barclay's *Apology* and suggesting that interested persons should read it and come to their own conclusions.[27]

While the "Lover of Truth" admired Knowles's religious arguments, as political opinions became more sharply divided in the spring and summer of 1792, her longtime friend Anna Seward criticized her continued support of the French Revolution. Seward, like other moderates, vehemently opposed the ideas widely distributed in Thomas Paine's *Rights of Man, Part II*. Writing to a genteel female friend in the country, Seward criticized "Paine's pernicious and impossible system of equal rights." She characterized his writings as "calculated to captivate and dazzle the vulgar, to make them spurn the restraints of legislation, and to spread anarchy, murder, and ruin over the earth."[28]

Sharp tensions emerged when Knowles visited Seward in Lichfield in August 1792. "Mrs. Knowles, the witty and the eloquent, was amongst us, on a week's visit," Seward wrote in her usual favorable terms in the same letter to her genteel friend. Yet her tone suddenly changed, "She made flaming eulogisms upon French anarchy, which she calls freedom," Seward said, "and uttered no less vehement philippics against everything which pertains to monarchy."[29]

Women's studies scholar Harriet Guest distinguished between what she called "the polite and provincial liberal whiggery" of Anna Seward and "the radical utopianism of city whigs," like the recently deceased Catharine Sawbridge Macaulay Graham. Knowles shared Graham's radical commitment to liberty and the right to resist tyranny, as has been seen. Knowles's belief in the possibility of human perfectibility made her, like Graham and Wollstonecraft, a radical utopian. By asserting republican principles, she created tensions with Seward, but she also provides an example of the continuation of female expression of radical ideas after Graham's death.[30] More research is needed on the transmission of radical ideology in the late eighteenth century by middling women like Knowles to assess more fully their philosophical links with younger female radicals, like Wollstonecraft.

Knowles also continued to associate with Quaker male radicals, including a mysterious French nobleman turned revolutionary. James Phillips, the Quaker bookseller with whom she disputed about animal magnetism, became an active abolitionist and close associate of Thomas Clarkson. Clarkson visited France and openly supported the revolution, and Phillips seems to have shared his views.[31] Phillips corresponded with persons in France, including Jean de Marsillac, a Quaker convert from a landed Calvinist family in the Languedoc. Marsillac visited London, and, in 1792, he sent copies of his French translation of the life of William Penn to a number of London Friends, including Knowles.[32] So while Seward began to fear and distrust the French, Knowles and other Quakers maintained at least one connection there.

Despite the deepening political and religious divisions spreading across the nation, Knowles demonstrated her personal independence and close family ties by traveling alone in a public coach from Birmingham to London. After a visit to the Lloyds, Knowles set out for home on Christmas Day, 1792, in a coach she described as "overweighted with Birmingham wares." Knowles later recounted how, "5 miles beyond Stratford, the axletree suddenly broke while going too fast on the rough road." Then, "Our coach tumbled over!"

Knowles transformed the accident into a humorous dialogue, indicating her style of travel, self-possession, and comic sensibility. An experienced traveler carrying what she considered her necessities, Knowles showed a great deal of command over both herself and the coachman. While one coachman returned to Stratford for help, the other tried to conduct the passengers to a nearby alehouse. Sorely tossed and tumbled but not seriously injured, Knowles refused to budge without her pattens, or overshoes, and "*Sac de nuit*," presumably containing her nightclothes and other personal items.

In a good-natured portrayal of herself and the befuddled coachman, she recounted their conversation in dialogue form: "Coachy – 'Why you cannot be more bespatter'd than you are;' Madam –'I know that, but I won't every moment put my feet into *fresh* cold spatter, so give me my pattens.'" Evidently, the "Coachy" complied, and the group proceeded to the alehouse where they found a warm fire and reviving spirits.

Knowles's report of this accident includes a glimpse of her loving relationship with her son George. She continued her saga by saying that another coach eventually appeared and delivered the passengers to London. "We arrived safe in the port of the Bull and Mouth [Inn] between 11 and 12 at night," wrote Knowles, "where my dear Boy had been anxiously waiting from 3 in the afternoon."[33]

Upon returning to London, Knowles wrote her cousin, Sampson Lloyd III, about the climate of political repression in the capital. The king had called up the militia and warned against sedition in response to continued riots and unrest. Addressing her cousin as "my hearty brother in political philosophy," Knowles told Lloyd that, "the force of the centre of power, has so effectually silenc'd discussion here, that I am given to understand no subject is so cautiously enter'd upon as the doctrines of government." Referring to the leader of the radical Whigs, she added, "no, not even Charly Fox keeps up his subsequent speeches the independence he at *first* exhibited."[34]

Anna Seward reacted very differently to the changing political climate. In January 1793, she wrote a friend that, "It is not to the credit of Mr. Fox that he stands almost alone" in supporting the French.[35] The execution of King Louis XVI further polarized British opinion and propelled Seward and many others into horrified revulsion of the French leaders.[36] On 1 February 1793, when France declared war on Britain, opposition to the revolution became, for Seward and many others, a national duty.

The deepening political divisions within Britain finally shattered the often strained but never before broken friendship between Knowles and Seward. In June 1793, Seward visited Buxton, and there she met "a group of Quakers, from Dublin." As she reported to a friend, "They introduced themselves to me, as connected with Mrs. Knowles by the bands of distant consanguinity, and near friendship." Despite her earlier remarks about Knowles and her support of the revolution, Seward seemed well disposed to these Irish Quakers, saying, "They are all social, friendly, and well-informed, two of them having shining talents."[37]

Yet after this letter of June 1793, no further references to Knowles appear in Seward's published correspondence, covering three more volumes and 16 additional years before her death in 1809. Perhaps Seward's correspondence to and about Knowles continued, but Seward did not deem the letters of sufficient general interest to be included among those she copied out for publication. Yet the complete lack of references to Knowles suggests that their friendship had ended. A comment by a contemporary memoirist that Knowles "for many years was the confidential friend of Miss Seward" further indicates that their friendship had a limited time span.[38]

Boswell, too, had been affected by the changing political climate. In 1791, he wrote an anonymous poem protesting what he saw as the pernicious impact of female abolitionists. In "No Abolition of Slavery, or, The Universal Empire of Love," Boswell equated slavery with sexual desire and described the Parliamentary leaders who supported abolition as unmanly and unduly influenced by intellectual women. Belittling many of the abolitionists in the House of Commons by name, he wondered how one of them, "a Roman free and rough," could "Descend to weak blue stocking stuff, And ... feelings soft and kind, Till you emasculate your mind."[39] Boswell clearly intended for his poem to be comic, but the verses reveal serious connections in his thinking about women, Africans, and subordination.

As the French Revolution became more threatening to many Britons, Boswell saw Johnson as an ever more important symbol of British moral superiority. According to biographer Adam Sisman, in November 1792 when Boswell celebrated the profits from the sale of the first edition of his *Life*, he toasted "the pious memory of Dr. Johnson," followed hard by "the favorite Tory toast, 'Church and King.'"[40] In December 1792, Boswell signed a Declaration of Loyalty and joined the fiercely conservative Association for Preserving Liberty and Property Against Republicans and Levellers.[41]

Boswell was now compiling corrections and additions to the first edition of his *Life*, which he also planned to incorporate into a revised second edition. By July 1793, he regarded Johnson as Britain's chief defense against French radical ideas. In the advertisement to his expanded but less expensive second edition, he wrote of his hopes that Johnson's "strong, clear, and animated enforcement of religion, morality, loyalty, and subordination ... will ... prove an effectual antidote to that detestable sophistry which has lately been imported from France, under the false name of philosophy." For Boswell, Johnson became the bulwark against the political uncertainty threatening to engulf Britain. "I have Johnsonified the land," he declared in the advertisement to the second edition. It now became imperative that Britons, threatened by foreign ideas "will not only *talk* but *think* Johnson."[42]

In this heightened political context, Boswell completed what Adam Sisman termed many "lengthy" and "not always impressive" footnotes.[43] *The Principal Corrections and Additions to the First Edition of Mr. Boswell's Life of Dr. Johnson* sold separately for six pence, as well as being included in the second edition. In one of his newly added notes, Boswell questioned Knowles's credibility and denied the authenticity of her version of her dialogue.

He began the new note by asserting that, "Mrs. Knowles [was] not satisfied with the fame of her needlework, the '*sutile pictures*' mentioned by Johnson, in which she had indeed displayed much dexterity." He directly raised the issue of her gender. "Nay," he continued, Knowles was not content "with the fame of reasoning better than women generally do, as I have fairly shewn her to have done."[44]

By again referring to the "sutile pictures," already explained in a footnote in the first edition and retained in the second, Boswell acknowledged Knowles's artistic accomplishment while again reminding readers of Piozzi's mistake. Yet, at the same time, he suggested that Knowles was ungrateful and rapacious for fame, two characteristics considered especially unsuitable for women. By portraying her ability to reason as unusual among women, he complimented her while denigrating the abilities of women in general. Again presenting himself as generous and fair, he repeated his assertion that she sought fame.

Having cast Knowles in this unfavorable light, Boswell continued, she "communicated to me a dialogue of considerable length, which after many years had elapsed, she wrote down as having passed between Dr. Johnson and herself at this interview." He declared that, "I had not the least recollection" of the dialogue supplied by Knowles and "did not find the smallest trace of it in my 'record' taken at the time." Suggesting that her account was fabricated, he wrote, "I could not, in consistency with my firm regard to authenticity, insert it in my work."[45]

Although intending to discredit her account, Boswell acknowledged that she gave him her version prior to the publication of his first edition. This supports what Knowles told Sael, the bookseller, as described in Chapter Five. Moreover, although Boswell denied having any record of the dialogue he did, as has been seen, make notes in his journal concerning Knowles's defense of Harry. Finally, since he later discussed the conversation with both Seward and Knowles, he had some recollection of it at that time.

Referring to Knowles's published account in *Gentleman's Magazine* Boswell said, "It relates chiefly to the principles of the sect called Quakers." He recognized that in her version "no doubt the Lady appears to have greatly the advantage of Dr. Johnson in argument, as well as expression." He ended by observing, "From what I have now stated, and from the internal evidence of the paper itself, any one who may have the curiosity to peruse it, will judge whether it was wrong in me to reject it, however willing to gratify Mrs. Knowles."[46] With this final show of double-edged politeness, Boswell again presented himself as a gallant gentleman trying to please a lady, while portraying Knowles as an ambitious female willing to sacrifice authenticity for fame.

If, as Knowles maintained, Boswell promised, "that he would not contradict her account so published,"[47] why did he now change his mind and add this damning footnote? The answers to this question can best be found in Boswell's own words in the newly added footnote and in his advertisement to the second edition. Moreover, Boswell may have felt that the danger from France required this action.

Boswell plainly named his first concern in the opening sentences of his footnote, the increasing fame of Knowles. Her literary fame had certainly grown since the publication of her account in *Gentleman's Magazine*, as evidenced by the responses from readers and her poetic exchange with Captain Morris. Moreover, most of the published responses supported her presentation of Johnson, even though some questioned Quaker beliefs. Sael, the bookseller, later suggested that the positive reception given Knowles's account may have prompted Boswell's footnote. "How far her Magazine-statement circulated or suppressed his own was perhaps best known to himself," Sael observed, "when he thought it proper to place the severe *note*, which appeared in his second edition."[48]

Boswell also named another reason for refuting Knowles's account in the advertisement to his second edition, the need to preserve the principle of "subordination" in the face of the French-inspired threat of equality. Boswell's earlier poem upholding slavery specifically linked subordination of women with the subordination of Africans. Since he now believed subordination to be essential to preserving the British way of life, he may have felt that he must disprove Knowles's demonstration that she, a radical woman intellectual and abolitionist, in his own words had bested "Dr. Johnson in argument, as well as expression."

In his *Principal Corrections* and the additions to his second edition, Boswell also included several footnotes questioning the information provided by Seward and accusing her of attacking the memory of Johnson.[49] Seward disputed his charges in a letter printed on the front page of *Gentleman's Magazine* in October 1793. Boswell responded in November, and the two traded increasingly heightened charges of inaccuracy and bad behavior in December 1793 and January 1794. Finally, in January, Boswell announced that, "I committed to the flames those sheets of '*Johnsonian Narratives*,' with which I was favoured by her."[50] Among those sheets, Boswell evidently burned Seward's letter containing her account of the disputed dialogue between Knowles and Johnson.

While Seward publicly and repeatedly confronted Boswell, Knowles took no part in their debates conducted in the popular magazine. According to Sael, the bookseller, Knowles remained silent because she did not think Boswell would change his mind or his account. As Sael later explained, Knowles, "despairing of successful admonition" to Boswell, "deferred speaking to him."[51]

In January 1795, Boswell began work on a third edition of his *Life of Johnson*, but, according to Adam Sisman, he drank heavily and had difficultly concentrating. In April, he became gravely ill at a meeting of the Literary Club. "Nineteen episodes of gonorrhea had taken their toll," as Sisman pointed out. On 19 May 1795, Boswell died at his home in London at age 54.[52]

Although Knowles had not publicly disputed Boswell's footnote concerning her, one unnamed book owner bound a manuscript copy of her version of the dialogue into the corresponding volume of Boswell's published *Life*. In November 1796, a letter appeared in *Gentleman's Magazine* calling attention to a listing "In Mr. Sael the bookseller's catalogue, lately published." The writer "met with the following article" in the catalogue: "'Life of Dr. Johnson by Boswell – In these volumes are inserted, neatly written in MS. containing twelve pages, the spirited conversation between *Dr. Johnson and Mrs. Knowles, omitted by Boswell from certain motives*, in which Mrs. K. had evidently the superiority in argument over the great Lexicographer, in the vindication of her amiable friend.'"

The correspondent to *Gentleman's Magazine* observed, "It is here obviously meant to convey an insinuation, that Mr. Boswell was led to this omission by sinister motives; and that he was willing to defend Johnson's character, at the expense of truth." The letter writer echoed Boswell's argument that "he could not have inserted it with that strict fidelity, which was his first object, as an 'honest chronicler,' to deserve." The writer concluded that, "Mr. Sael has given us no reason to disbelieve" Boswell's account.[53]

The writer of this letter identified him or herself only by the initials "J. B." Although lacking evidence for a more complete identification, it seems worth noting that Boswell's youngest son, also named James Boswell, was then a studious young man of 18. James Boswell, the younger, cared for his father in his dying days and became closely associated with his father's collaborator and literary executive, Edmond Malone.[54] Since the younger Boswell later became a literary scholar careful of his father's reputation, he could have written this letter.

In a reply dated "Strand, Dec 16," published in *Gentleman's Magazine*, G. Sael, the bookseller, answered "J. B." "Since I first published a Catalogue of Books," Sael explained, "it has been my practice to annex, by way of *note*, whatever might appertain to their rarity and estimation." Sael further explained that he obtained such information, "either from what I might have gathered from my own reading, or collected from incidental circumstances."[55]

A published catalogue supports this part of Sael's letter. The catalogue described Sael as a "Bookseller, No. 20, Newcastle Street, Strand, London," who specialized in an "Extensive collection of Curious Books, with ancient MSS, Missals and Authors of Uncommon Rarity, collected with much labour from various Parts of the Kingdom, and some Elegant Libraries lately offered for Sale." In 1794, his collection numbered more than 4,900 items, "now selling, for ready Money only."[56]

In his letter to *Gentleman's Magazine*, Sael explained that, "The life of Dr. Johnson by Mr. Boswell falling into my hands, in a library I lately purchased, I found affixed to it, in MS, a very interesting and spirited conversation, said to have passed between Dr. Johnson and Mrs. Knowles." After reading the letter from "J. B.," Sael said he "endeavoured to possess myself of the truth of the fact, and have lately obtained an opportunity of consulting *that lady*, respecting the authenticity of Mr. Boswell's statement, as also of the MSS. bound up in the book now in my possession."

Sael visited Knowles, reporting that, "She politely attributed candour to my disposition, and was obligingly communicative on the subject." He recounted how she told him that Boswell came to her house to read his draft of the dialogue, she denied the truth of it, and the two submitted their accounts to gentleman arbiters, as described in Chapter Five. Sael ended by saying, "notwithstanding what Mr. B. has thought proper to say, she continues to assert the *truth* of her own publication as it appeared in the *Gentleman's Magazine* ... to which I refer your correspondent [J. B.], or to my MS. which differs but little from my recital." Despite the assertions of "J. B.," Sael, a man well-acquainted with books, found no reason to doubt the truth of Knowles's version of her dialogue.[57]

Knowles did not publicly comment on this letter from Sael, perhaps because she was preoccupied with internal differences among Quakers. When Britain went to war with France, Quakers again came under attack for their pacifism. In August 1793, for example, rioters smashed the windows of 150 Quakers in Birmingham who refused to display lighted candles in celebration of a military victory.[58] Some Friends responded by limiting contacts with non-Quakers and restricting their social and cultural activities.

In an undated poem written sometime after 1794, Knowles challenged what she portrayed as unfavorable views expressed by some Quakers concerning botanical art. She addressed her poem to "Friend Pope," who, given Knowles's medical connections, might have been Margaret Pope, wife of a prominent Quaker physician, Robert Pope.[59] Knowles entreated Pope to send her "a milk-white Foxglove," which she proposed to draw and return as a picture.

Remarking on the attitudes of some Quakers, Knowles observed that, "Strict Friends on this subject sometimes make a racket." She found it amusing that some of these same Friends devoted much time to tending the plants in their gardens, adding, "I smile in observing their own blooming bracket." Pointing to what she saw as an inconsistency, she asked, "And when zealously pleading, against waste of time, / Should they still in festoons teach their woodbines to climb?"

While Knowles previously sent drawings and verses about botanical subjects as gifts, she indicated that some Quakers now viewed her botanic art unfavorably. With arguments more comic than combative, she appealed for reconciliation. "Then hear loving Friends! Let your candour appear, / Nor on poor imitation be very severe." she humorously begged. "No rich gardens have I – Epicurean treat! / I paint flow'rs of no fragrance." she protested, "my Fruit I can't eat."[60]

In a marginal note to this poem, Knowles quoted a reference from Thomas Paine, whose father was a Friend. Knowles noted, tongue in cheek, that, "Paine, in one of his books, pleasantly says, 'Had Quaker taste presided at the Creation, what a drab-coloured world we should have had!'" Although Knowles did not identify the source of the quotation, it came from Paine's *Age of Reason* first published in Paris in 1794 and issued in London one year later.[61]

Since well-read women and men often copied out and circulated memorable quotations as part of their varied modes of intellectual exchange, Knowles may have read or heard only this one satiric comment from Paine's book. Yet given her record of ecumenical reading, she might well have analyzed his entire text. Paine described his book as an "investigation of true and fabulous theology." In it, he embraced Deism, denied the divinity of the Scriptures, and proclaimed that, "It is only by the exercise of reason that man can discover God."[62] Knowles wrote in her marginal note, "How mistaken is the satire of profligate Paine!"[63] Yet, she seems to have based her judgment on his presentation of Quaker beliefs rather than his doctrines of political equality that horrified Seward.

Concerning Quakers and the creation, Paine further added, "Not a flower would have blossomed its gaieties, not a bird been permitted to sing." In her poem, Knowles countered his claim, while underscoring her own point concerning the inconsistency of appreciating nature but not nature paintings. "Dame Nature, they have no desire should dress plain," she wrote, refuting Paine, "Mere drab coloured plants, wou'd not so much engage 'em, / To strip birds of fine plumage, me thinks wou'd enrage 'em."[64] While Knowles refuted Paine's claim, she also seemed to join in his satire against strict Quakers.

Although Knowles commented on what she saw as the inconsistencies of some Friends, she continued to be a sought-after visitor among wealthy and ecumenical Quakers, such as Samuel Hoare, who frequently socialized with those of other faiths. A successful banker and founding member of the London Abolition Committee, Hoare owned a home in Hampstead and a country estate in Norfolk, where he often entertained Evangelical Anglicans of the Clapham Sect, such as William Wilberforce, as well as fellow Quakers.[65] Sarah Hoare, Samuel's daughter, later recalled favorite visitors remembering that, "Mrs. Knowles, who was also a very amusing companion, came to stay with us" around 1796.[66]

By 1798, at age 65, Knowles left her home in the busy commercial district of Lombard Street and moved to Number 17, Ely Place, a quiet enclave between

Holborn and Smithfield. She now lived within the compass of Peel Monthly Meeting, located at the sign of a baker's peel, not far from St. John's Gate. Perhaps because of its location, this meeting, numbering 270 members in 1786, included more servants and apprentices than the more affluent one in Gracechurch Street.[67] On 21 February 1798, the Peel Women's Meeting reported, "A minute of Grace Church Street Monthly Meeting recommending Mary Knowles" had been brought in and read. On 21 March, the women assigned reported favorably on their visit to Knowles, and she duly became a member of the Peel Meeting.[68]

By then, radical voices had been effectively silenced in Britain, and, despite her earlier support of French republicanism, Knowles renewed her acquaintance with King George III. Although Knowles criticized monarchy as a form of government in France, she, like many British radicals, remained loyal to the person of the king. As historian John Dinwiddy wrote, although "the great majority of the English middle-class reformers ... rejoiced at the downfall of Popery and Bourbon despotism, [they] were by no means democrats or revolutionaries themselves." Like them, Knowles had emphasized, not the overthrow of the British monarchy, "but constitutional balance, elimination of corruption and independence."[69]

The king, although troubled by debilitating vicissitudes of health, continued to be well-disposed towards Quakers. When he heard about the speaking talents and ecumenical views of a visiting Quaker minister from Philadelphia, he invited him to Buckingham House. William Savery, the visiting minister, was, according to Knowles's old friend Dr. John Coakley Lettsom, a man of great "chearfulness, with animated conversation" and a "lenient disposition." As a minister, according to Lettsom, "he endeavoured to promote religion by exhibiting the true enjoyments annexed to virtue rather than by enforcing the throes consequent on vice." Speaking throughout Britain, Savery attracted large crowds of all faiths.[70]

According to Savery's journal, published later, on 2 March 1798, he "dined at Benjamin West's in co. with George Dillwyn," an American Quaker whose brother, William, helped found the London Abolition Committee. After dinner, Savery "went with West, Dillwyn, and Mary Knowles in a carriage to Buckingham House."[71] While Savery's manuscript account of this meeting has been lost, Lettsom later reported that the king asked Savery about the Americans "for whom he expressed a continuance of parental regard." Savery assured the king, said Lettsom, that Americans, and especially American Quakers, continued to hold him in high esteem.[72]

Like the presentation of her son at court more than 20 years before, Knowles and her Quaker friends used a private social visit to underscore their status as faithful subjects. This meeting also definitely links Knowles to the American-born court painter, Benjamin West, who continued to have close ties with both the king and queen. Even more importantly, the visit demonstrates her long-lasting relationship with the royal family.

Knowles also continued to participate in popular culture. In 1799, her name appeared among the subscribers to the second edition of *The Balnea: Or, an*

Impartial Description of All the Popular Watering Places in England written by George Saville Carey.[73] The author, the son of Henry Carey who claimed to have composed "God Save the King," arranged public entertainments in London, Bath, Buxton, and other popular spas. Since Knowles had participated in the fashionable amusements at Buxton, Brighthelmstone, and Batheaston, she had personal experience with some of the places described in Carey's book.

Perhaps more importantly, Carey dedicated his book to Mary Linwood, who, like Knowles, excelled in the art of needle painting. According to a nineteenth-century Quaker, "It was Mary Knowles who taught her art to Miss Linwood."[74] Since Linwood spent her youth in Birmingham, where Knowles once lived and frequently visited, the two could have met there.

Carey's dedication to Linwood evoked the current contests concerning the status of embroidery as art. In her *Letters on Education*, written in 1790, the late Catharine Sawbridge Macaulay Graham regretted that, "The art of needle-work ... has been too much depreciated in modern days," adding, "I would rather see it resume all its former importance."[75] Carey, too, regretted the declining status of embroidery. In his dedication to Linwood, he wrote, "Had you lived in the mythological days of old, the transcendent labours of your ingenious hands would have raised your name to a state of immortality."[76]

Although the Royal Academy of Art excluded needlework from their shows, the enterprising Linwood first exhibited her needle paintings in Leicester Square and later opened a gallery in Hanover Square.[77] According to art expert Marcia Pointon, "The main challenge to the Royal Academy by the 1790s was probably Miss Linwood's exhibition of needlework."[78] Knowles had once proudly proclaimed her employment in the art of the needle and may have known Linwood. Her subscription to *The Balnea* could have indicated her support for Linwood, even though, Knowles, as a Quaker, did not publicly display her own artwork.

At age 66, Knowles had not lost her sense of humor or, evidently, her attraction to men. In 1799, she received a proposal of marriage from a much younger man which she answered in a poetic "Reply to a Love Letter Addressed to Her, when Old, by a Young Man." She began in a mock serious tone, "This love letter of dearest Frank's / I with the earliest, warmest thanks ... read your ardent lines, professing, / How sweet such delicate caressing." Tongue in cheek, she continued, "How sweet th' intelligence must be/ That you are *fallen in love with me*."

Shifting to an openly comic mode, she made pointed remarks about their different ages and appearances. "Such instances are very rare," she wrote, "And may well make old maidens' stare." She professed to be flattered to receive the attentions of "you so lively and so pleasant, / with brow so fair and eyes so bright, / With chin so round and teeth so white." Yet she compared their match to "Dryden's young May tied to December, or January so the rhyme is," observing dryly, "A case in point – in point of *time* is, / This case 'tween you and I may be."

In her mature years, as in her youthful memoirs, Knowles mocked the idea of women waiting passively for proposals. She comically portrayed herself as "I too long of hope forlorn, / like a poor nightingale on a thorn." She continued facetiously, "When faithless lovers fly away," what could she do but "set warbling forth 'ah well a day.'"[79]

Knowles satirically subverted gender expectations by proposing a double wedding between her and Frank and a contemporary couple comprising an older man and a much younger bride. Knowles would have been well aware of the withering public criticism heaped on her acquaintance Catharine Macaulay two decades earlier when she married the much younger William Graham. By proposing a double marriage between herself and Frank along with an elderly groom and younger bride, Knowles equalized the gender differences in the two cases and upheld the liberty of women to chose partners of any age.[80]

Although Knowles's friendship with Seward seems to have ended, Seward's version of Knowles's dispute with Johnson appeared in a short-lived provincial publication in 1798. J. Mitchell of Carlyle printed *The Satellite or Repository of Literature, composed of Miscellaneous Essays (Chiefly original) intended for the diffusion of Useful and Polite Knowledge.* The first issue featured a "Conversation Between Mrs. Knowles and Dr. Johnson, sent to Mr. Boswell for Publication."

The editors explained that, "This paper was sent to Mr. Boswell by Miss Seward for the purpose of being inserted in the Life of Dr. Johnson; but we believe was never published." In the opinion of the editors, Seward's account "bears such strong marks of authenticity that we admit it into this Miscellany without hesitation." They added that it provides "another instance of the intolerant disposition of that great man," Dr. Johnson.[81] This printed version, cited by literary scholar James Woolley, is substantially the same as the manuscript copy of Seward's letter to Boswell in the London Library of the Religious Society of Friends, described in detail in Chapter Four.[82]

Since both she and Seward had publicly disputed Boswell's account, Knowles must have been dismayed to find his damning footnote questioning her authenticity continued in the third edition of the *Life of Johnson*. Boswell had not completed the revisions for this edition before his death. Edmond Malone, as his literary executor, made the final changes with additional notes and supplementary materials. In 1799, Charles Dilly published this third, "revised and augmented" edition in four volumes, which has come to be considered the definitive or standard text.[83] Knowles may have expected better from Malone. As has been seen, he might have been one of the arbitrators whom she said listened to her account before publication of the first edition of Boswell's *Life*.

As soon as the third edition appeared, Knowles immediately and publicly challenged the presentation of her confrontation with Johnson, just as she challenged Boswell's original publication eight years before. In 1799, John and Arthur Arch of London issued an eight-page *Dialogue Between Dr. Johnson and Mrs. Knowles*, selling for six pence. The booklet included her version of the confrontation as originally printed in *Gentleman's Magazine* and a brief introductory preface, presumably written by her. This preface no longer contained the radical language of defiance used in 1791 but instead explained the sequence of events leading up to and following Boswell's publications, closely following what Knowles told Sael.

Written in the third person, the preface opened by stating that, "Mr. Boswell, for reasons best known to himself (but which are guessed at by others), refused to admit into his book, Mrs. Knowles's account of her Theological Dialogue with Dr. Johnson." The writer pointed out that Boswell had "previously applied to her" for her account and "had frankly acknowledged the truth of the particulars therein, which he afterwards thought proper to suppress." Not only had he suppressed her account, but "Mr. Boswell, then in his second edition, by a marginal note, and surely by means in a liberal style, disavows any recollection of matter different from his own statement."

Since "In the third edition, his note is continued," the writer hoped the recent republication "will be deemed a sufficient inducement and apology for offering now to the public, the above-mentioned Dialogue, as a supplement to the new edition of Mr. Boswell's book." The preface ended by observing that rival biographers, like Hester Thrale Piozzi and Sir John Hawkins, "may perhaps be sometimes charged with inaccuracy," but "there are several persons who figure in Mr. Boswell's book, who are much dissatisfied with his representations and colloquial arrangements."[84] Although this preface did not reference the radical right to resistance, as had the letter from the "Child of Candour," Knowles again insisted that Boswell's version was incomplete and steadfastly persisted in publishing her defense of Quaker beliefs and arguments in favor of Harry's moral agency to choose her religion.

The eight-page publication, encompassing the three-page preface and five-page dialogue, circulated both in bound form and as tracts. The London Library of the Religious Society of Friends contains two copies of the unbound dialogue in tract format.[85] The British Library contains another copy, handsomely bound in brown leather with the title stamped in gold leaf on the cover.[86] These varied formats demonstrate that Knowles's dialogue reached a range of readers as an inexpensive tract but was also valued enough to be bound and preserved.

During this period of war abroad and repression at home, it may have seemed even more important for Knowles publicly to defend Quakers from Johnson's charges of Deism. As the century came to an end and Knowles rounded 66, her Quaker faith continued to form the bedrock of her thoughts and actions. Yet as the new century began, the increasing tensions caused by the prolonged war and internal political turmoil threatened even that Quaker bedrock.

Notes

1 *Letters of Anna Seward*, vol. 2, p. 289.
2 Ibid., vol. 2, p. 387.

3   Ibid.
4   *George Fox: The Journal*, p. 17.
5   Taylor, *Wollstonecraft*, p. 4.
6   *Letters of Anna Seward*, vol. 3, pp. 76–7.
7   Edward Royle and James Walvin, *English Radicals and Reformers* (Lexington, 1982), pp. 44–7. Mrs. Catherine Hutton Beale, ed. *Reminiscences of a Gentlewoman of the Last Century: Letters of Catherine Hutton* (Birmingham, 1891), pp. 71–93.
8   *Gentleman's Magazine* (July–December 1791): 631–2.
9   Ibid., 693.
10 Ibid.: 700.
11 Ibid.: 700–1.
12 Ibid.: 798.
13 Ibid.: 798–9.
14 Ibid.: 948. *Dictionary of National Biography*, vol. 13, "Thomas Morris," pp. 978–88.
15 *Gentleman's Magazine* (July–December 1791): 948.
16 Ibid.
17 Thomas Clarkson, *A Portraiture of Quakerism*, vol. 1, pp. 258–76.
18 *Records and Recollections of James Jenkins*, p. 15.
19 *Letters of Anna Seward*. Vol. 2, pp. 359–60.
20 *Gentleman's Magazine* (July–December 1791): 948–9.
21 Ibid.
22 Library of the Religious Society of Friends, John Thompson MSS and Temporary MSS 28. Dictionary of Quaker Biography, "George Bott (1748?–1820)." Durham, North Carolina, Duke University, Perkins Rare Book and Manuscript Library, "Papers of Hanna Bott."
23 *Gentleman's Magazine* (July–December 1791): 1,019.
24 Ibid., (Supplement, 1791): 1,223.
25 Ibid.
26 *The Lady's Magazine* (Sept. 1791): 489–91.
27 Ibid., (March 1792): 142.
28 *Letters of Anna Seward*, vol. 3, pp. 159–60, to "Lady Gresley."
29 Ibid.
30 Harriet Guest, *Small Change: Women, Learning, Patriotism, 1750-1800* (Chicago, 2000), p. 265. Kathryn Gleadle, "British Women and Radical Politics in the late Nonconformist Enlightenment c. 1780–1830, " in *Women, Privilege and Power*, pp. 137–8.
31 Jennings, *Business*, p. 69.
32 Norman Penney, "Life and Letters of Jean de Marsillac," *Journal of the Friends Historical Society*, 15/2 (1918): 49–56; 16/1 (1919): 18–22; 16/3 (1919): 81–90.
33 E. F. Howard, "Mary Knowles and the Lloyds of Birmingham," *Friends Quarterly Examiner*, (1934): 90–96.
34 Ibid.
35 *Letters of Anna Seward*, vol. 3, p. 201.
36 Ibid., vol. 3, p. 203.
37 Ibid., vol. 3, p. 266.
38 Ashmun, *Singing Swan*, p. 107.

39 [James Boswell], *No Abolition of Slavery: Or the Universal Empire of Love* (London, 1791). James G. Basker, *Amazing Grace: An Anthology of Poems About Slavery, 1680–1810* (New Haven, 2002).
40 Sisman, *Boswell's Presumptuous Task*, pp. 274–5.
41 Kevin Gilmartin, "In the Theatre of Counterrevolution: Loyalist Associations and Conservative Opinion in the 1790s," *Journal of British Studies*, 41/3 (July 2002): 292–328.
42 James Boswell, *The Life of Samuel Johnson, LL.D.* (2nd edn, 3 vols, London, 1793), p. xv–xvii.
43 Sisman, *Boswell's Presumptuous Task*, p. 276.
44 James Boswell, *The Principal Corrections and Additions to the First Edition of Mr. Boswell's Life of Dr. Johnson* (London, 1793), p. 23. Boswell, *Life of Johnson* (2nd edn), vol. 3, p. 84–5.
45 Ibid.
46 Ibid.
47 *Gentleman's Magazine* (July–December 1796): 1,074.
48 Ibid.
49 Boswell, *Principal Corrections and Additions*. Boswell, *Life of Johnson* (2nd edn).
50 *Gentleman's Magazine* (July–December 1793): 875, 1,099–1,101; (January–June 1794); 32–5.
51 Ibid., (July–December, 1796): 1,074.
52 Sisman, *Boswell's Presumptuous Task*, pp. 282–6.
53 *Gentleman's Magazine* (July–December 1796): 924.
54 Sisman, *Boswell's Presumptuous Task*, p. 288.
55 *Gentleman's Magazine* (July–December 1796): 1,074.
56 G. Sael, *Extensive Collection of Curious Books ... Offered for Sale* (London, 1794).
57 *Gentleman's Magazine* (July–December 1796): 1,074.
58 W. B. Stephen, ed., *Victoria County History of Warwickshire*, vol. 3, *The City of Birmingham* (London, 1964), pp. 279–80.
59 Library of the Religious Society of Friends, Temporary MSS 403 [Braithwaite Papers], Box 7, Packet 15, File 3, Number 43, "M. Knowles to Friend Pope." Dictionary of Quaker Biography, "Dr. Robert Pope, (1748–1827)."
60 Braithwaite Papers, 7, 15, 3, 43, "M. Knowles to Friend Pope."
61 Thomas Paine, *The Age of Reason: Being an Investigation of True and Fabulous Theology* (London, 1795), p. 45.
62 Ibid., pp. 1–4.
63 Braithwaite Papers, 7, 15, 3, 43, "M. Knowles to Friend Pope."
64 Paine, *The Age of Reason*, p. 45. Braithwaite Papers, 7, 15, 3, 43, "M. Knowles to Friend Pope."
65 Jennings, *Business*, p. 94.
66 Sarah and Hannah Hoare, *Memoirs of Samuel Hoare*, edited by F. R. Pryor (London, 1911), p. 24.
67 Beck and Ball, *London Friends Meetings*, p. 201.
68 Library of the Religious Society of Friends, "Registers of the Members of the Peel Monthly Meeting, 1798–1805," "Peel Monthly Meeting, Women's Minutes, 1795–1805."

The French Revolution 143

69 J. R. Dinwiddy, *Radicalism and Reform in Britain, 1780–1850* (London, 1992), pp. 174–5.
70 "William Savery: A Sketch by Dr. Lettsom," in Job Sibley, *Discourses Delivered by William Savery of North America at Several Meetings of the People called Quakers and Others* (London, 1806), p. iv.
71 Jonathan Evans, *A Journal of the Life, Travels, and Religious Labours of William Savery* (London, 1844), pp. 581–2.
72 "William Savery: A Sketch by Dr. Lettsom."
73 George Saville Carey, *The Balnea: Or, an Impartial Description of All the Popular Watering Places in England* (2nd edn, London, 1799), pp. iii–iv.
74 Theodore Compton, *Recollections of Tottenham Friends*, pp. 33–4.
75 Catharine Macaulay Graham, *Letters on Education*, pp. 64–5.
76 Carey, *Balnea*, p. x.
77 Swain, *Embroidered Georgian Pictures*, p. 20.
78 Marcia Pointon, *Hanging the Head: Portraiture and Social Formation in Eighteenth-Century England* (New Haven, 1993), pp. 2–3.
79 Library of the Religious Society of Friends, Portfolio MSS 3, Folio 124, "Reply to a Love Letter Addressed to Her, when Old, by a Young Man."
80 Ibid. Hill, *Republican Virago*.
81 *The Satellite or Repository of Literature, composed of Miscellaneous Essays (Chiefly original) intended for the diffusion of Useful and Polite Knowledge*, 1 (1798): 8.
82 Woolley, "Johnson as Despot." Portfolio MSS 3, 126, "Notes of a Conversation."
83 James Boswell, *Life of Samuel Johnson, LL.D.* (3rd edn, 4 vols, London, 1799).
84 [Mary Morris Knowles], *Dialogue Between Dr. Johnson and Mrs. Knowles* (London, 1799).
85 Tracts Vol. 534, No. 1; Box 44.
86 [Knowles], *Dialogue Between Dr. Johnson and Mrs. Knowles*.

Chapter 7

"Help Me To Pray"

During the long period of warfare abroad and repression at home, internal tensions concerning theology, radicalism, and gender seriously divided Quakers. These tensions boiled over in the protracted controversies surrounding Hannah Barnard, a visiting minister from New York. Despite these tensions, Knowles maintained her radical views and close Quaker connections, and she also remained an important public figure. Publications in England and America featured stories about her, and engravings of her circulated on both sides of the Atlantic. When the fourth edition of Boswell's *Life of Johnson* repeated his footnote questioning her authenticity, her version of the confrontation with Johnson again appeared in print. This time her name appeared first in the title. Yet as she faced death and changing standards of Quakerliness, Knowles experienced deep anxieties. The woman who had so often before practiced radical self-representation struggled with severe self-doubt.

Under the duress of the long war with France, Friends, even within the same family, disagreed about how to put their pacifist principles into action. In Birmingham, for example, Samuel Galton and his son, closely related to the Lloyds, reacted very differently to the concerns expressed by some Friends about the gun factory they owned and operated. In the 1790s, local Quaker leaders asked the Galtons to stop manufacturing guns being used by the military. The father agreed and gave up his part of the business. Samuel Galton, Jr., however, refused, saying, "men are not responsible for the abuse of what they manufacture."[1]

Tensions over the French Revolution also contributed to what James Jenkins described as a "revolt" by young Friends in Ireland, who called themselves "New Lights." As Jenkins explained, they took that name because they claimed to have received "New Light upon sundry important points of discipline, and by which, they professed to discern much wrong in the practical exercise thereof." Jenkins suggested that many of these New Lights held "democratic" political principles. He told how one young dissonant behaved rudely to a visiting Quaker disciplinarian, calling the visitor an "aristocrat."[2]

According to Jenkins, the New Lights also questioned "the truth of many historical passages of the Old Testament."[3] Knowles's cousin, Morris Birkbeck, may have agreed with them, at least in theory. In 1798, he published *Some Animadversions on the Supposition of the Scriptures Being the Only Principal and Perfect Rule to Salvation*, the tract written more than 50 years earlier by Richard Morris, his and Knowles's grandfather. In a brief introduction, Birkbeck explained that he chose to publish the tract at this time because "it seems to me to point out, not only what the scriptures are, but, with much force and perspicuity, to prove what they are not."[4]

In London, a comment made by a country Quaker seems to indicate changing standards of Quakerliness in female apparel. In 1799, Elihu Robinson attended the London Yearly Meeting, noting in his diary that, "there was a very large gathering," including "many not of ye Society." He noted he had difficulty distinguishing female Friends from the visitors "as many young Women who profess with us appear very Gay!"[5] His use of the word "gay" seems to indicate disapproval of Quaker women who wore bright colors or fashionable dress.

At the turn of the century, the tensions among Quakers concerning theology, radicalism, and gender began to coalesce around Hannah Barnard, a ministering Friend from Hudson, New York, whom Knowles knew personally. The controversies surrounding Barnard and her visits to England and Ireland, as described in detail by James Jenkins, threatened the organizational unity of British Quakers. Knowles commented on these controversies, which had a major impact on her cousin, Morris Birkbeck.

Barnard arrived in London in 1799 and immediately entered into a dispute concerning relationships between Quakers and members of other faiths. Reflecting a significant power differential, the Women's Yearly Meeting in Britain, established in 1784, could not consider issues concerning discipline, the sole purview of men. Barnard, along with other female Friends, thus went before the men's meeting, to ask them to reopen a decision prohibiting other religious groups from using Quaker meetinghouses. When the men declined, Barnard insisted so persistently that one male Friend described her behavior as "the greatest obstinacy he had ever witnessed." Finally, the men requested Barnard and her allies to withdraw from the meeting. Not long after, she left London for Ireland.[6]

The next year, 1800, Knowles wrote a humorous poem, advising a young female acquaintance about proper Quaker behavior and poking fun at those who criticized gay Friends and wanted to limit interactions with members of other faiths. She addressed her 34-line verse to "Ann Blakes junior," probably the daughter of one of Morris Birkbeck's business partners.[7] In it, Knowles, now rounding 67, portrayed herself as an ancient tabby, giving advice to a youth.

"Tis order'd, that we ancient Tabbies, / By all the monthly meeting Rabbis," she wrote, "That we should keep our gay young people, / From every house that has a steeple, / Or building popish or socinian. / Or any not of our opinion." By identifying strict Quaker leaders with rabbis, whom she portrayed as rigid rule keepers, she continued to reflect and further the prevailing anti-Semitism. At the same time, by jesting about "gay young people," she diffused the seriousness of that term as a criticism.

Keenly aware of gender dynamics, Knowles mentored her young friend through gentle satire. "So am not I in duty bound," Knowles playfully asked the young woman, "to warn thee of this dang'rous ground … Have not I sufficient said?" Perhaps recalling her own exchange with Clericus four decades earlier, she asked, "Can we of beauty be too careful, / While dashing Fellows are so snareful?" Never one to enforce strict rules, the ancient tabby soon relented and became the young girl's accomplice instead. She concluded her poetic advice by saying, "If thou *wilt* go to that place, / Put *my* slouch bonnet o'er thy face."[8]

Hannah Barnard, meanwhile, traveling in Ireland, associated with New Lights and supporters of the French Revolution. "The writings of the French republicans had filled her head with their political nonsense about Liberty and Equality," Jenkins said. Barnard manifested her political views in her ministry, according to Jenkins, and offended some Friends by insisting that masters and mistresses sit with their servants during religious meetings. In Ireland, "she frequently disturbed the arrangements made by friends of the place," Jenkins reported, "by ... mingling up, rich, and poor, clean, and dirty promiscuously together."[9]

Returning to London in 1800, Barnard requested a certificate from the men's Yearly Meeting to travel as a ministering Friend to Europe. The men denied her request after an Irish Friend argued that she "had proven herself 'not to be one with Friends, in some important points of doctrine.'" The Morning Meeting of Ministers and Elders asked her to desist from traveling as a minister and return to New York.

Barnard not only refused to follow this directive, but she persistently proceeded to challenge the authority of a succession of meetings. The Morning Meeting referred her case to the Devonshire House Monthly Meeting in London within whose compass she then lived. After deliberating many weeks, the monthly meeting agreed that she should return home. Undeterred, Bernard appealed to the London and Middlesex Quarterly Meeting, but that meeting upheld the judgment of the monthly meeting. Undaunted, Barnard announced that she would appeal to the men's Yearly Meeting of 1801.

Gender constituted one factor in this controversy. A female Friend in England appealed to Barnard's husband, perhaps hoping he would restrain her. James Jenkins reported that the Friend "sent an account to America which made her [Barnard's] husband extremely uneasy. Jenkins said the female Friend complained to the husband about Barnard's "Blasphemy, Lies and Impertinence."

Jenkins linked Bernard's impertinence to being an American. "With respect to impertinence that probably referred to the firmness with which she [Bernard] defended every thing which she undertook to defend," Jenkins later mused, trying to present the complaints against her fairly. "In this, she was truly American," he continued, noting that Americans "have always appeared to me, to be of all men, the most tenacious."[10]

As the men's Yearly Meeting considered Barnard's appeal, Knowles commented on the controversy and indicated her personal acquaintance with her. On 1 June 1801, Knowles wrote her longtime friend Mary Farmer Lloyd that, "We are unhappily engaged this annual meeting in a sort of metaphysical disquisition that puzzles many uncultivated minds, and grieves many more."[11] In making this observation, Knowles implicitly distinguished between well-educated Quakers, like herself and Lloyd, and those less educated, indicating internal tensions between these two groups. Jenkins later explained the "metaphysical disquisition" by saying that some Quakers believed that Barnard held socinian, or unitarian, views, stressing the unity of the Divine and questioning the divinity of Christ.[12]

"I do not agree with Hannah Barnard and have told her so," Knowles wrote Lloyd, indicating she knew Barnard personally. Although she did not support Barnard's views, Knowles told Lloyd, "I sincerely wish the controversy may be conducted with that charity, that we, as a people profess." Knowles added that she considered Barnard "a very clever and agreeable woman."[13]

Although Knowles considered Barnard agreeable, the men's Yearly Meeting most likely did not. The Yearly Meeting referred her case to a committee, and on 1 June 1801, the same day Knowles wrote Lloyd, the committee rejected Barnard's appeal and again asked her to return home. With persistence remarkable even for an American, Barnard appealed this decision to the meeting as a whole. The Yearly Meeting appointed a nine-member Committee of Appeals made up of men Friends from all parts of the country. After several lengthy and emotionally charged discussions, the appeals committee upheld the original decision. Barnard now had no choice but to return to New York where she was later disowned.[14]

This highly charged dispute strained the unity of British Friends and divided the family of Morris Birkbeck. According to Quaker accounts, Morris Birkbeck, Jr., left the Friends "about the time of the Barnard controversy" and emigrated to the American frontier of Illinois. A later descendant intimated that Birkbeck, Jr., left England because of his radical views. Before leaving, he had been active in the efforts to abolish the British slave trade. After settling in Illinois, he became interested in Robert Owen's ideas and helped establish the utopian community at New Harmony, Indiana.[15] Like Knowles, the younger Birkbeck combined radical political views with a utopian faith in human perfectibility.

Like her young cousin, Knowles may have been sympathetic to Barnard's radical political ideas, although she did not agree with her religious views. In her letter to Mary Farmer Lloyd, Knowles did not denigrate Barnard's radical political principles the way Jenkins did in his memoirs. Jenkins wrote that Barnard had "imbibed from the Revolutionists of France, (who were then republicans,) the utter dislike of kings, and priests, wishing the downfall of hierarchical power."[16] Knowles, herself, had expressed similar views only a few years before, according to Anna Seward. Since Knowles was not a minister, she, unlike Barnard, may have enjoyed somewhat more freedom to express her radical political views, especially to non-Friends like Seward.

Jenkins linked Knowles to another contemporary radical, the political writer Gilbert Wakefield, who died in 1801. Jenkins described Wakefield as "celebrated," and "a writer in divinity and politicks of considerable eminence."[17] Another contemporary described Wakefield, an Anglican who became a unitarian, as "a political fanatic," who vehemently opposed England's war with France and strongly supported liberty.[18] According to Jenkins, Knowles knew Wakefield personally. "Mary Knowles used to say of him," Jenkins recalled, "'in conversation, he is the mild and agreeable companion, but, when he sits down to write, he generally dips his pen in the gall of bitterness.'"[19]

Despite the tensions within the British Quaker organization stemming from theological and political differences, Knowles remained dedicated to her faith and to her Quaker friends. As shown in her letter of June 1801, Knowles still valued the friendship of her former bridesmaid, Mary Farmer Lloyd. "The pleasure that arises from the unexpected salutation of a distant, long absent, *dear* friend, is an animated sensation that I think the pathetic pen of poetry can alone describe," she wrote Lloyd with feeling. "Suffice it to say, that to the sweet sounds of thy amity, I am a delighted Respondent."

Mary Lloyd now had 15 children. One of her daughters, perhaps Anna Lloyd, had recently visited Knowles. Anna later married Isaac Braithwaite and became a well-known Quaker minister. "I was as much pleased with thy dear Daughter's company, as she cou'd be with mine," Knowles told Mary Lloyd. She assured the doting mother that her daughter's visit "confirms me in my early, shall I say *our* early opinion of her natural temperament."

This letter also indicates that Knowles remained on close and loving terms with Rachel and Sampson Lloyd III and their large family at Farm. Knowles shared the family's grief at the premature death of Sampson Lloyd IV. "Please to remember me most kindly to the Family at Farm," she wrote Mary Lloyd, adding, "my sympathy has been tenderly engag'd – as was my regard for him whom they also deplore." At age 68, Knowles seemed reconciled to her own death. "I trust they are supported," she concluded, still referring to the Lloyd family, "by the consciousness, that they themselves and all of us, are swiftly advancing to the end of all things *here*!"[20]

While Knowles cherished her Quaker connections, she also remained an important public figure, appearing twice in a newly established magazine for women. *The Lady's Monthly Museum or Polite Repository of Amusement and Instruction* was, in the words of its title, "*an Assemblage of whatever can tend to please the Fancy, interest the Mind or exalt the Character of the British Fair.*" The magazine further proclaimed its founding in 1798, "*by A Society of Ladies.*" The title and ownership presents females as producers as well as consumers of commercial printing. In the first number, "The Proprietors" explained that while the "writers are anonymous," the "Chief Contributors are Ladies of established reputation in literary circles."[21]

Each month the magazine profiled a notable female, indicating changing attitudes toward women in the public gaze. A profile in 1800, focusing on the needle painter Mary Linwood, acknowledged the earlier work of Knowles. "Among the cultivators of this new method of painting, the names of Lady Yates, of Mrs. Wright and of Mrs. Knowles deserve to be respectfully noticed," the profile pointed out.[22] This reference demonstrates that some contemporaries viewed Knowles as a talented visual artist independently of her religious and literary achievements.

In November 1803, *The Lady's Monthly Museum* featured a profile of Knowles, including a brief biography stressing her artistic and religious accomplishments. Noting that a traditional education "alone could not satisfy her active mind," the article described how she turned to the "polite arts" of poetry, painting, and "more especially the imitation of nature in needlework." The story described her needle painting of the king as "her grand undertaking," recounting how she became friends with the royal family. The unnamed writer also mentioned Knowles's travels on the continent, including her presentation to royalty there.

Stressing Knowles's strong religious beliefs, the writer quoted her as saying, "'Even arts and sciences are but evanescent and splendid vanities, if unaccompanied by the Christian virtues!'" In this way, Knowles again presented her beliefs as Christian rather than uniquely Quaker. The profile included a full reprint of her version of her confrontation with Johnson. Without questioning its authenticity, the writer observed that the dialogue demonstrated "that she is no contemptible advocate for the principle of the respectable society of Friends."

Although the profile made no mention of Boswell or his derogatory footnote, the writer stressed Knowles's modesty, perhaps in reaction to his insinuation that she desired fame. "She has written on various subjects, philosophical, theological, and poetical, some of which have been published with her name, but more anonymous," the profile noted. "We are informed her modesty retains in manuscript far more than has appeared to the public," the writer noted.[23]

Despite this mention of her modesty, the article also included an engraving of her. Each issue of *The Lady's Monthly Museum* included an image of the featured female, so the proprietors may have commissioned this one by an artist identified as Mackenzie. The engraving shows the head and shoulders of Knowles facing left in profile. The image shows she has aged since creating her self-portrait in midlife, but she is dressed the same and is portrayed with a slight smile on her pleasant-looking face. A small lace cap sits atop her otherwise unadorned hair. She wears a dark dress with a fichu, or scarf, tied over her bosom and a simple black ribbon around her neck. As an added touch indicating her intellectual achievements, rows of books appear in the background among the conventional drapery.[24]

By permitting this engraving, Knowles once again tested the boundaries of acceptable Quaker attitudes toward visual art, especially for women. As art historian Marcia Pointon observed, engravings could be seen as a form of visual information rather than as decorative art.[25] Yet few other early nineteenth-century engravings of Quaker English women have surfaced, dating from before those of the well-known female reformers of the Victorian age.[26]

As part of the fast-growing print trade, a lively market had developed for the production and consumption of engravings of notable politicians, heroes, beauties, and other celebrities.[27] The engraving of Knowles, as a celebrated public figure, seems to have circulated independently of the magazine. Two copies of the engraving, individually printed on heavy paper, are preserved in the Library of the Religious Society of Friends. These engravings indicate that reproductions of her image were sold or otherwise distributed, and these two copies more than likely once belonged to Quakers.[28]

The original engraving and an adaptation also made their way to America. Two different images of her are preserved in the Quaker Collection at Haverford College Library in Haverford, Pennsylvania. A copy of the original engraving from *The Lady's Monthly Museum* shows Knowles facing left with the rows of books behind her, as described above. The words "Published by Vernor and Hood," who also published *The Lady's Monthly Museum*, appear at the bottom of the reproduction (Illustration Four).

The Haverford College Quaker Collection also includes an adaptation of the original engraving. The profile is somewhat larger with a plain background. In it, Knowles faces right, but the image seems to be drawn from the one in *The Lady's Monthly Museum* (Illustration Five). Since engravings of well-known Britons were frequently traded and pirated by Americans, it is possible that the adaptation was made to be circulated and sold in the United States. Quakers in Philadelphia had long commissioned and collected portraits, as discussed in Chapter Two, so there might have been a larger market for her engraving there.

Knowles's public reputation definitely extended across the Atlantic by 1804. That year, Daniel Lawrence, an American printer with Quaker connections, mentioned her, although not by her full name, in a preface to his publication of *A Brief Account of the Vision and Death of the Late Lord Lyttleton*.[29] Thomas, the son of Baron George Lyttleton, had been, unlike his well-respected father, notoriously "vain, impudent, and unfaithful." The son died suddenly in 1779, at age 35, after telling friends of a vision of a mysterious lady in white who foretold his death.[30] For months afterwards, according to a notation made at the time by Hester Thrale, "Lord Lyttleton's Death and Dream fill[ed] everybody's mouths."[31]

In 1803, articles appeared in the Charleston, South Carolina, *Courier* and the *New York Daily Advertiser*, alluding to new information recently brought to light about the untimely death of the young lord more than 20 years earlier.[32] The next year, Lawrence produced his *Brief Account*, explaining that he "sought for and attained the original writing" on which the newspaper stories had been based. "The original (at present in our possession)," he announced," is in the handwriting of Mrs. M – K –." He further identified Knowles as "a lady distinguished in the literary world, for her piety and learning, and for her dispute with the celebrated Dr. Johnson, on the right of private judgment in matters of religion."[33]

Like the writer of her profile in *The Lady's Monthly Museum*, Lawrence did not question the authenticity of Knowles's account. Lawrence may have been unaware of the controversy between her and Boswell concerning the text of her dialogue with Johnson. Yet, in any case, as he indicated, he admired her learning and piety and considered her a reliable source of information.

Lawrence further explained in his preface how the new information recorded by Knowles reached him. The American publisher named as his source William

Illustration 4 [first name unknown] Mackenzie, *Mrs. Knowles*, 6.8 in x 3.7 in, engraving, 1803, Haverford College Library.

"Help Me To Pray"

Illustration 5 [artist unknown], *Mrs. Knowles*, 5.1 in x 3.2 in, engraving, date unknown, Haverford College Library.

Wolseley, now an admiral in the British navy. Wolseley was the career naval officer with family connections in Staffordshire who years earlier had told Seward that Knowles planned to remarry, as described in Chapter Five. According to Lawrence, Wolseley "verbally narrated" the details of his account to Knowles. After listening to Wolseley's words, Knowles "wrote them down, in his presence for Mr. W – S – of the City of Philadelphia, who was in England in the year 1798." W. S. most probably was William Savery, the Philadelphia Friend with whom Knowles visited the royal family that year.

According to the account as written by Knowles, Wolseley revealed that he had been with Lyttleton "when these extraordinary events occurred." Wolseley said he had been a guest at the home of the young lord and tried to comfort the dying man. At the exact moment of Lyttleton's death, according to Wolseley, another friend, who lived 30 miles away, insisted that the dying man visited him and bid him farewell.[34]

Knowles's interest in the Lyttleton story could have been related to a similar long-held story in her own family, interpreted as a spiritual manifestation of supernatural power. The Lyttleton legend, as elaborated by Wolseley, bears a strong resemblance to a ghostly story concerning the death of Knowles's aunt, Sarah Morris Birkbeck, more than six decades earlier. Birkbeck, a Quaker minister, became deathly ill while on a religious visitation in a far away county. Her young children, including Mary's cousin Morris Birkbeck, ever afterwards insisted that their mother visited them in their nursery at the moment of her death.[35] The story of her aunt's death and the Lyttleton legend reflect Knowles's lifelong interest in the mysterious operation of the divine spirit.

The Lyttleton story and Knowles's connection to it also had enduring interest for others in Britain and America. When Lyttleton's letters appeared in England and America, the American edition, printed in 1807, repeated the story of his vision and death, mentioning Knowles, albeit erroneously and not by her full name. The American edition referred to the publication of an earlier story, supposedly in *Gentleman's Magazine*, but not located there, describing "a talk to be given by Mrs. K –" at the Gracechurch Street Meeting concerning the meaning of Lyttleton's vision.[36] Whether or not Knowles actually gave the talk, she did evince an ongoing interest in this supernatural story.

Knowles also continued to be recognized as an influential female in Britain, respected for her religious writings. Mary Pilkington awarded Knowles special distinction among the many famous women featured in her *Memoirs of Celebrated Female Characters Who Have Distinguished Themselves By Their Talents and Virtues in Every Age and Nation* published in 1804. A professional writer by necessity, Pilkington supported herself by her pen while her husband served in the navy. She displayed the changing attitudes toward women in the public gaze by claiming that her *Memoirs* contained "the most extensive Collections of Illustrious Examples of Feminine Excellence ever Published in which the virtuous and the vicious are painted in their true colours." Arranged alphabetically, the 346-page volume featured brief biographies of scores of women, but included engravings of only 12. Knowles, along with needlework artist Mary Linwood and Anna Seward, appeared among those 12.

Pilkington, who seemed to be acquainted personally with Knowles, described her as "no less distinguished for the possession of superior talent, than for a blameless purity of life." Recognizing "her religious tenets" as "those of Quakerism," Pilkington added that, "the utmost liberality of sentiment is displayed in her mind." She reprinted an excerpt from Knowles's account of her dialogue with Johnson, introducing it by saying, "The powers of her mind and the truly Christian principles of her persuasion, may be gathered from a conversation that took place between her and Doctor Johnson," Pilkington concluded that, "Superior as Dr. Johnson generally proved himself in argument, it evidently appears that, in this instance, he must have been foiled, and all prejudices with regard to our religious persuasions, is a convincing mark of a contracted mind."[37]

Yet while Knowles's version of her dialogue continued to be credited and reprinted in the early 1800s, so did Boswell's, along with his damning footnote. When Charles Dilly retired suddenly after a long and influential career, Boswell's children sold the copyright for their father's book to Thomas Cadell and William Davies. In 1804, Cadell and Davies published a fourth edition of Boswell's *Life*, edited by Edmond Malone. The young James Boswell, now graduated from Oxford and living in London, assisted Malone. This edition repeated the note Boswell added to the second edition questioning the authenticity of Knowles's account.[38]

The next year, the complete text of Knowles's version again appeared as a tract, this time with her name listed first in the title. The eight-page *Dialogue between Mrs. Knowles and Dr. Johnson*, printed by C. Stower, Charles Street, Hatton Garden, closely corresponds with the earlier edition published by John and Arthur Arch. The tract contained the same prefatory explanation of Boswell's refusal to include her version and her account of her conversation with Johnson.[39]

No evidence has been found indicating whether Knowles, at age 72, directly instigated this publication. Yet since 1791, she had consistently demonstrated that she would not passively accept the republication of what she termed Boswell's incomplete account of her dialogue. The location of the publisher in Hatton Garden, very near her home in Ely Place, suggests she could have supervised the printing. Moreover, either she or the publisher placed her name first in the title indicating her importance as a person of interest to the reading public.

An undated broadside version of *A Dialogue between Mrs. Knowles and Dr. Johnson* also appeared, printed in two colors with the text arranged in columns on a single sheet of large paper. The printer, Thomas Smart, Bookseller, in Huddersfield, must have produced it after 1803 because he included a brief biographical sketch based on the one in *The Lady's Monthly Museum*. Like Stower, Smart reprinted the dialogue as it had originally appeared in *Gentleman's Magazine* and in the earlier tract published by John and Arthur Arch. This broadside version made her account more widely available to a range of readers.[40]

In 1805, C. Stower, the Hatton Street publisher, also reissued Knowles's *Compendium of a Controversy on Water Baptism*, written more than 40 years before. Stower printed the poetic challenge from "Clericus" and "Lavinia's answer," but without giving Knowles's real name. The *Compendium* appeared in a tract format similar to Stower's edition of the *Dialogue between Mrs. Knowles and Dr. Johnson*, published that same year. Four copies of the *Compendium* in two slightly different tract formats are preserved in the London Library of the Religious Society of Friends. One copy of the tract includes the publisher's name and date.[41] Three additional copies appear in a similar format with the initials "M. K." printed at the end, without the publisher and date.[42] The presence of multiple copies of the tract suggests that it circulated widely. The publications bearing Knowles's initials at the end suggest that she financed, or at least cooperated, in the production of it and, perhaps, distributed copies to her friends.

One reader of Stower's edition of the *Compendium* had the tract expensively bound and added some important information to the opening pages. This copy, preserved in the British Library, is beautifully bound in red leather and gold trim with the title printed in gold leaf. On the inside cover, the owner pasted the oval engraving by Mackenzie, originally published in *The Lady's Monthly Museum*, as a memento of the author. The owner must have known Knowles or at least known about her because she or he wrote on the title page, "by Mary Knowles (born Morris) wife of Dr. Knowles of London." On the second page, the owner added the information, discussed in Chapter One, identifying "Clericus" as a clergyman from Coventry named Rand.[43]

The owner also pasted onto one of the front pages a printed copy of "Verses by Mary Knowles." The short poem written by Knowles, as "M. K.," to a female friend, addressed as "Delia," appears in two colors on a single page but does not include a date or publisher. Another copy of the printed "Verses" is also preserved in the British Library in a "Poetical Scrap Book" of writings by women, perhaps assembled by a nineteenth-century collector.[44] The presence of these two copies indicates that the "Verses" circulated, at least to a limited degree, in print.

The brief 12-line "Verses" address some of the same gender-related themes discussed by Knowles in her earlier manuscript poems, but these words also include serious warnings relating to wealth, beauty, and public fame, not found in her earlier works examined here. These "Verses" are also written in an uncharacteristically didactic tone. This new tone and content suggest that her standards concerning polite Quakerliness may have changed.

"An humble outside oft is scorn'd," wrote Knowles, "But see! tis fraught with gold!" While Knowles earlier directed gentle satire at Birmingham Quakers for their concern with fashion, she had not then defended a "humble" appearance. She now warned that, "Pride courts the public eye – It is the body, not the mind / That's deck'd too anxiously." The reference to anxiety is a concern not found in her earlier writings.

"Ah! let this note instruction bring," she urged, "Ye! Who true wealth would win." In her previous poems, Knowles had taught through humor, classical references, and botanical metaphors rather than this kind of direct "instruction." She had also always appeared comfortable with her financial wealth as evidenced in her practice of polite Quakerliness and encouragement of her son to enter business, despite Seward's criticisms. Here, however, Knowles eschewed financial wealth in favor of spiritual blessings. She ended by urging females to transcend outward appearances, public approbation, and economic wealth, writing, "Daughters of the celestial King / All glorious are within!"[45]

Female friendships continued to remain important to Knowles. She treasured her relationship of more than 40 years with Mary Farmer Lloyd, even when one of Lloyd's daughters was disowned as a Quaker. When Priscilla Lloyd married Christopher Wordsworth, brother of the poet, Quaker rules against marrying non-Friends meant that she would be disowned as a Friend. Despite this, Knowles wrote Mary Farmer Lloyd in June 1805 with warm wishes for the young couple and their new son. "It gives me pleasure to hear thy dear daughter is in so hopeful a way, and that her sufferings have been rewarded by a lovely Boy," Knowles wrote Lloyd, with no recriminations. "May he and a grateful Husband," Knowles added, "increase all her comforts."

In this same letter, Knowles told Lloyd that she suffered from "an inflammation of the lungs, which makes country air thought just now quite expedient." Knowles regretted not being able to see Lloyd, then visiting her daughter in London. She hoped Lloyd would be able to visit her later, warmly assuring her that, "a day spent with me at Ely Place wou'd be highly pleasant to thy ever affectionate Friend."[46]

Knowles also renewed her close friendship with Jasper Capper and his family. She had advised Capper, more than 30 years before, about the true qualities of a minister and attended his wedding to Anne Fry, the daughter of her close friends, as seen in Chapter Three. Since then, Jasper Capper, assisted by his wife, established a modest business as a linen-draper in Whitechapel. In 1801, Anne Fry Capper became a recognized Quaker minister.[47]

In late December 1806 or early January 1807, Jasper Capper paid Knowles a visit "which," he wrote his sister Mary Capper, "seemed to revive all that tender affection that we felt for each other in years past." Yet by then Knowles was very ill. On 22 January 1807, Jasper Capper wrote his sister that his wife, Anne, had visited Knowles's sickbed the day before.

Anne Capper reported that Knowles "is sensible of there being but a step between her and death." While recognizing that "The prospect is awful," Anne Capper said that Knowles "appears tender and resigned." Anne Capper further reported that Knowles "has been greatly comforted by a visit from John Eliot and Robert Howard,"[48] two Friends from the Peel monthly meeting.

John Eliot, like Mary Knowles, had struggled with issues relating to wealth and fashion. As a young man, Eliot wore a fashionable hat atop a flowing white wig, sported expensive shoe buckles, and carried a gold-headed cane. Like Thomas

Knowles, he kept a coach and horses. Yet Eliot gave up these fashions and became "a plain Friend" and a minister, known for his generous hospitality to visiting Quakers.[49] A contemporary described Robert Howard, father of Luke Howard the meteorologist, as "a man of singularly strong and sterling character."[50]

Mary Knowles also received comforting visits from her son and other Friends. In his letter to his sister, Jasper Capper noted that another of their sisters, who lived near Knowles, "had been at hand and ready to afford her personal aid, as well as her valuable company." He also noted that George remained an affectionate and dutiful son during his mother's illness. George, who had not married, seemed devoted to his mother. Capper told his sister that, "The attention of Mary Knowles's son has been very commendable."[51]

Although Anne Capper described Knowles as "tender and resigned," two other close friends said she experienced severe self-doubts in the final weeks of her life. James Jenkins, her longtime admirer, indicated that she expressed much anxiety during her last days. Jenkins did not know the exact source of these anxieties, but he wrote, "We may conjecture that her uneasiness arose from a consciousness that her talents had not been sufficiently employed in religious service in the society of which she has always been a member."[52]

Joseph Woods, another longtime friend, also indicated that Knowles experienced doubts and anxieties. Woods attributed her misgivings to her supernatural explorations. He later wrote a mutual friend that, "she expressed some regret for the too great earnestness with which she pursued her investigations into Animal Magnetism."[53]

Woods and Jenkins both commented that Knowles worried excessively about money and did not practice charity appropriate to her wealth. Woods told a mutual friend that, "the Habit of saving money for her son became a sort of ruling passion and stuck with her to the last."[54] Jenkins expressed similar views, saying Knowles may have "deeply regretted that notwithstanding her ample means she had afforded but little relief to 'the widows, and the fatherless in their afflictions.'"[55]

Although Jenkins believed Knowles regretted her lack of charity, Woods described how she took advantage of a legal technicality to ensure that her son received as much of her wealth as possible. Woods later reported that, "M. Knowles is said to have accumulated 50 or 60 thousand pounds, and to have died with only 2000." He explained that, "By a Deed of Gift made on her Death Bed, when she had no expectation of recovery, I am told she made over her property to her son." Woods surmised, "By this means [she was] perhaps evading the probate duty and saving about 500 pounds to her son."[56] Knowles's will dated 10 January 1807 affirms his story. In it, she assigned her entire estate to George.[57]

On 2 February 1807, Anne Fry Capper again attended the sickbed of Mary Knowles. Capper found her remorseful about her past and concerned for her future state. "She was closely tried until near her end," she reported to her sister-in-law, "by not being able to feel the presence of Him, whom she sought ability to pray to and to worship; and upon whom she very frequently called for forgiveness."[58]

While Knowles wrestled with self-doubts, her anxieties can be seen as the final stage in the spiritual development of a sincerely devout woman. In *Daughters of Light*, Rebecca Larson found similar spiritual insecurities expressed by Quaker women ministers in the face of death. "Concern about what happened after death, particularly the fear of future punishment and the consequent desire to guarantee salvation, fueled the ... religious quests" of many female ministers, she found. Larson further observed how near death experiences often provoked a "spiritual crisis," prompting women to question past practices and seek signs of salvation.[59]

Esther Storrs Morris, Mary Knowles's paternal grandmother, had also experienced these kinds of doubts and anxieties on her deathbed. All through her life, according to her husband, Esther had been "Conscientiously concerned for the Promotion of the Honour of Truth in its ancient purity and lustre." Yet, as she lay dying, "she went thro' a great deal of Exercise both outward and inward." Richard Morris found her "often reflecting on her own Unworthiness," saying she feared she was "not deserving the least of the Lord's Mercies to her."[60]

Knowles seemed to experience similar doubts and anxieties, but Anne Capper also noted that Knowles specifically questioned the value of her achievements. "O! How lightly she esteemed all her accomplishments!" Capper wrote, "'What,' as she said, 'the world calls accomplishments!'" All through her life, Knowles interacted with a wide variety of people and expressed ecumenical views, but she now identified her accomplishments as part of the non-Quaker "world."[61]

Knowles's dying doubts reflect the social transformation of Quakers during her lifetime. All her life, she had practiced forms of polite Quakerliness that facilitated the integration of Friends into middle-class society. Yet in facilitating social integration, Knowles had spent a great deal of time with people and philosophies outside Quaker circles. James Jenkins remarked how, "she had mixed much with literary characters, and of different religious sentiments – with the Atheist, the Deist, and the Unitarian, etc." Yet, he concluded, "it did not appear that the religion of her education had been ever abandoned."[62] While her Quaker beliefs were beyond question, the social integration to which she had contributed prompted new definitions of acceptable Quaker behavior, and now she, herself, seemed to question her previous practice of Quakerliness.

Seeking salvation, Knowles echoed the words of Job. "She said to my sister and me," Anne Capper reported after her visit on 2 February, "'I repent in dust and ashes!'" Capper told her sister-in-law, "she appeared very desirous to feel an assurance of acceptance." Capper vividly described how, "Turning toward me, and taking my hand, she said, 'I commend you all to God. Possess Him. Possess Him, if you can, whatever becomes of me!'" Although wracked by self-doubt, Knowles expressed hope for salvation. "'I hope I shall not be cast away forever! I believe I shall not,'" Capper reported her saying, adding "She was quiet when I left her."[63]

Nearly 40 years earlier, when Knowles almost died in childbirth, she had written her then unmarried friend, Mary Farmer, that she "thought I was spared to become more pure, to head the heavenly courts with my redeemer."[64] Now as

Knowles faced death again, her confidence in her salvation seems to have eroded. When Knowles wrote Farmer four decades before, she had not yet achieved fame, wealth, and social status. Those achievements appear to have become burdens to her as she lay dying. While she tested the boundaries of Quakerliness with impunity throughout her life, she developed severe self-doubts in the face of death.

"Early in the morning," Anne Capper continued in her letter to her sister-in-law, describing her visit to Knowles on 2 February 1807, "the nurse heard her say, 'Lord help me to pray; I cannot of myself.'"[65] Knowles's plea for divine assistance in prayer once again paralleled the deathbed experience of her grandmother, Esther Storrs Morris, more than 100 years before. Richard Morris had recorded how, just before her death, his wife had "cried out, 'I cannot pray loud enough and praise the Lord enough.'"[66]

These pleas reflect a core Quaker belief, expressed by Robert Barclay. "Prayer cannot be offered without the aid of the Spirit," Barclay explained. He further noted that, "We are to wait for the holding out of his scepter, as permission to draw near to him and experience the greater freedom that comes with the enlargement of the Spirit upon us as we turn our hearts to him."[67]

Whether Mary Knowles received the spiritual scepter for which she waited is not known. As Anne Capper explained in her letter, "'Lord help me to pray'" were "her last words." On the morning of 3 February 1807, Mary Morris Knowles died at her home in Ely Place at age 73.

"I trust she found forgiveness and everlasting mercy, for Jesus' sake," Anne Capper concluded.[68] Capper's words are generous and loving. Yet her words also reflect the idea, expressed so poignantly by Knowles herself, that her worldly accomplishments required divine forgiveness.

Far from being ashamed of her dying doubts, Knowles wanted others to learn from them. According to Jenkins, "Agreeably to her desire, her remains were taken ... into the week day meeting of the Peel, where the circumstances of the compunction of her dying hours were adverted to." On 11 February, both Jenkins and Woods attended her burial at Bunhill Fields, where her husband had been interred more that 20 years before. At the graveside, Jenkins said, "a witness of her mental distress, likewise mentioned that the deceased had expressed to her much regret that she had not been a better steward of her time and talents."[69] By admitting her fears and doubts, Knowles became an example to others in death as she had been to many in life.

An unknown reader honored her memory with a carefully bound copy of her brief biography in *The Lady's Monthly Museum*, containing her version of her dialogue with Johnson. A handsome green leather volume preserved in the British Library contains the pages from the magazine along with the "elegant portrait" of her. At the back of the little book, the unnamed owner added an engraving of a weeping woman, the classical symbol of grief.[70]

In a letter written to William Matthews not long after her death, Joseph Woods carefully considered the character of their longtime friend. She "was a woman of extraordinary endowments," he wrote Matthews, who had once exchanged poetry with her in Bath. Because of her accomplishments, and perhaps because of her debates with Boswell and Johnson, Woods believed "her name will be accompanied with some celebrity in the annals of literary ladies."[71]

Despite her dying doubts, these comments by Woods implied pride and approval of Knowles's literary accomplishments. He seemed to regard her fame as a natural result of her outstanding abilities. He appeared to consider her memory as a literary lady to be a fitting tribute to her accomplishments, even for a Quaker.

Woods added two other telling phrases about her, describing her as "a patriot, too, and politician."[72] By calling her a patriot, Woods indicated that she maintained her radical commitment to liberty throughout the complicated political changes of the long eighteenth century. As he surely knew, her radicalism lay solidly rooted in her devotion to religious liberty, which she defended so strongly to Johnson. This commitment to religious liberty in turn formed the basis for her beliefs in liberty for women, Americans, African slaves, and the revolutionaries in France.

In describing Knowles as a politician, Woods indicated that he did not consider politics to be the exclusive purview of males. Throughout her life, Knowles commented on political events and persons in letters, poems, and discussions with her friends. She followed the actions of political leaders and observed candidates' debates during at least one election. She called on King George III to protect Quakers as loyal pacifist citizens. By referring to her as a politician, Woods showed that he took her political views seriously and indicated that others did, too.

Mary Morris Knowles was not unflawed as she herself recognized. Convinced that women deserved liberty, she actively participated in religion, politics, and art. By so doing, she gained fame as a public figure but provoked criticisms and ultimately her own self-doubts. Perhaps it should not be surprising that Knowles, with her independent mindedness and self-managed wealth, would leave a mixed legacy and doubt herself in her dying days. While her longtime friends Joseph Woods and James Jenkins acknowledged her shortcomings, they honored her memory as a devoted Quaker, literary lady, patriot, and politician, too. Her life and death demonstrate the complex connections interlacing religion, gender, and radicalism in the long eighteenth century.

Notes

1 Library of the Religious Society of Friends, Dictionary of Quaker Biography, "Samuel Galton [Junior], 1753–1832."
2 *Records and Recollections of James Jenkins*, pp. 303–5.
3 Ibid.
4 Richard Morris, *Some Animadversions on the Supposition of the Scriptures Being the Only Principal and Perfect Rule to Salvation*, (London, 1798), p. v.

5 Library of the Religious Society of Friends, "MSS Diaries and Memoranda of Elihu Robinson," 9 vols, vol. 5, 22 May 1799.
6 *Records and Recollections of James Jenkins*, pp. 310–12.
7 "Our bibliographers: Morris Birkbeck," *Journal of the Friends Historical Society*, 8/1 (March 1911): 11.
8 Library of the Religious Society of Friends, Howarth MSS, Box 7, Folder 12, Number, 23, "34 lines addressed to Ann Blakes jr. 1800."
9 *Records and Recollections of James Jenkins*, p. 340.
10 Ibid., 342–57.
11 Temporary MSS 403 [Braithwaite Papers], Box 7, Packet 15, File 3, Number 41, "Charles Lloyd, Birmingham for Mary Lloyd / M. Knowles, 6th month 1st 1801."
12 *Records and Recollections of James Jenkins*, pp. 358–62.
13 Braithwaite Papers, 7, 15, 3, 41, "Charles Lloyd, Birmingham for Mary Lloyd."
14 *Records and Recollections of James Jenkins*, pp. 358–62.
15 Dictionary of Quaker Biography, "Morris Birkbeck [Junior], (1764–1825)." Robert Birkbeck, *The Birkbecks of Westmorland*, p. 101. Jennings, *Business*, p. 42.
16 *Records and Recollections of James Jenkins*, p. 341.
17 Ibid., p. 384.
18 *Dictionary of National Biography*, "Gilbert Wakefield (1756-1801)."
19 Ibid. *Records and Recollections of James Jenkins*, pp. 384–5.
20 Braithwaite Papers, 7, 15, 3, 41, "Charles Lloyd, Birmingham for Mary Lloyd."
21 *The Lady's Monthly Museum or Polite Repository of Amusement and Instruction, Being an Assemblage of whatever can tend to please the Fancy, interest the Mind or exalt the Character of the British Fair by A Society of Ladies*. 1 (July–December 1798): i–ii.
22 Ibid., 4 (July–December, 1800): 3–4.
23 Ibid., 11(July–December, 1803): 289–94.
24 Ibid.
25 Pointon, "Quakerism and Visual Culture."
26 Ibid.
27 Brewer, *Pleasures of the Imagination*, p. 456.
28 Library of the Religious Society of Friends, Picture Box K, 1 and 17.
29 *A Brief Account of the Vision and Death of the late Lord Lyttleton* (Stanford, New York, 1804).
30 *Letters of the Late Lord Lyttleton, only son of the Venerable George, Lord Lyttleton* (1st American edition, Troy, New York, 1807), pp. vi, 290–92.
31 Katharine Balderston, ed., *Thraliana: The Diary of Hester Lynch Thrale (later Mrs. Piozzi), 1776–1809* (2 vols, Oxford, 1942), vol. 1, p. 413.
32 Charleston Library Society, *Courier*, 23 July 1803. New-York Historical Society, *New York Daily Advertiser*, 24 August 1803.
33 *A Brief Account of the Vision and Death of the late Lord Lyttleton*, p. 3.
34 Ibid.
35 John H. Ingram, *The Haunted Homes and Family Traditions of Great Britain* (London, 1884), pp. 228–30.
36 *Letters of the Late Lord Lyttleton*, (1st American edn), pp. vi, 290–92.
37 Pilkington, *Memoirs of Celebrated Female Characters*, pp. 218–9.
38 Edmond Malone, ed., *The Life of Samuel Johnson, LL.D. ... by James Boswell, Esq.* (4th edn, 4 vols, London, 1804), vol. 3, p. 323.

39 [Mary Morris Knowles], *Dialogue Between Mrs. Knowles and Dr. Johnson* (London, 1805).
40 Library of the Religious Society of Friends, "Tracts," Vol. O, p. 295, [Mary Morris Knowles], *Dialogue Between Mrs. Knowles and Dr. Johnson* (Huddersfield, no date).
41 "Tracts," Vol. 192, Number 15. [Mary Morris Knowles], *Compendium on Water Baptism* (London, 1805).
42 "Tracts," Vol. 237, Number 13, [Mary Morris Knowles], *Compendium on Water Baptism*; Box 44, 2 copies;.
43 MSS notes in British Library copy of [Mary Morris Knowles], *Compendium on Water Baptism* (London, 1805).
44 British Library, "Poetical Scrap Book."
45 *Compendium* and "Poetical Scrap Book."
46 Braithwaite Papers, 7, 15, 3, 42, "Mr. Wordsworth, M. Knowles, E. Place, 6th 14 1805."
47 Dictionary of Quaker Biography, "Anne Fry Capper, (1756–1821)."
48 "Memoirs of Mary Capper," p. 48.
49 Dictionary of Quaker Biography, "John Eliot, (1734/5–1813)."
50 Dictionary of Quaker Biography, "Robert Howard, (1738–1812)."
51 "A Memoir of Mary Capper," p. 48.
52 *Records and Recollections of James Jenkins*, p. 454.
53 Matthews MSS, Joseph Woods to William Matthews, 18 April 1807.
54 Ibid.
55 *Records and Recollections of James Jenkins*, p. 454.
56 Matthews MSS, Woods to Matthews, 18 April 1807.
57 Public Record Office, Prob 11/1464, quire 592.
58 "A Memoir of Mary Capper," p. 48.
59 Larson, *Daughters of Light*, pp. 71–3.
60 Braithwaite Papers, 7, 15, 4, 1, "A Short Account of the Life and Departure of my lately Deceased Dear Wife Esther Morris."
61 "A Memoir of Mary Capper," p. 48.
62 *Records and Recollections of James Jenkins*, p. 454.
63 "A Memoir of Mary Capper," pp. 48–9.
64 Braithwaite Papers, 7, 15, 3, 37, "Mildenhall 8mo 23d 68."
65 "A Memoir of Mary Capper," pp. 48–9.
66 Braithwaite Papers, 7, 15, 4, 1, "A Short Account of the Life and Departure of my lately Deceased Dear Wife Esther Morris."
67 *Barclay's Apology*, pp. 288–90.
68 "A Memoir of Mary Capper," pp. 48–9.
69 *Records and Recollections of James Jenkins*, p. 454. Matthews MSS, Woods to Matthews, 18 April 1807.
70 *Life of Mrs. Knowles*.
71 Matthews MSS, Woods to Matthews, 18 April 1807.
72 Ibid.

Conclusion

Disconnections and Reconnections

In the years following her death, facts and fictions about Mary Morris Knowles combined and intermingled, presented in popular publications, manuscripts, privately printed memoirs, private and published letters, anecdotes, and scholarly research. Like contemporary views, memories, Quaker histories, and scholarship concerning her became mixed and contested. Changing concepts of gender and standards of Quakerliness influenced how successive generations of Friends viewed her; while, over the decades, her radical political ideas and activities were almost forgotten altogether. After her death, successive editions of Boswell's *Life of Johnson* with its damaging footnote about her went unchallenged. As Boswell's text became canonical, her account became entangled in the politics of scholarship and disconnected from her life story. The persistence of her story demonstrates the need for future research reconnecting the links joining religion, gender, and radicalism in the long eighteenth century.

Just as Knowles questioned herself in her dying days, her contemporaries remembered both her accomplishments and shortcomings. In March 1807, *The Monthly Repository of Theology and General Literature*, designed to promote "the cause of free inquiry and rational religion," carried her obituary, indicating her status as a public figure. The unnamed writer recalled her achievements with both brush and needle. "This lady possessed a variety of talents," the brief notice pointed out, "She was not only known as a painter, but also for her portraits in needlework." The writer also recalled "Her talents for conversation ... recorded by Mr. Boswell ... where she appears to great advantage."

The obituary concluded on a vaguely negative note, however, referring to Knowles's wealth. "Mrs. K. is said to have died very rich," the writer noted, "During the latter years of her life," the writer added, "[she seemed] to have felt rather too much of that propensity which riches so frequently encourage."[1]

At the same time, others honored her publicly and privately. *The Literary Panorama* for 1807 included her among the "Biographical Memoirs" of persons of public interest who died that year. This obituary, drawn largely from the profile in *The Lady's Monthly Museum*, remembered her as both talented and modest. Referring to her disputed dialogue with Johnson, the unnamed writer recounted how Knowles published her own account under the name of the "Child of Candour."[2] Another contemporary, perhaps the meteorologist Luke Howard, whose father Robert Howard had visited Knowles on her deathbed, copied her obituary and preserved it at the London Library of the Religious Society of Friends.[3]

As the long war with France finally ended, many Friends in England increasingly turned inward. Some remembered Knowles's religious words, disconnected from her practice of polite Quakerliness. In 1815, *The Annual Monitor and Memorandum Book* included four lines from her *Compendium on Water Baptism*: "Tis grace alone, we by experience find / Imparts instruction to the attentive mind; / Convicts of error and restrains from sin / For what these are is manifest within."[4] The brief entry, signed simply "Knowles," indicates that readers still knew her name and appreciated her stress on the inner spirit, but there is no trace here of her artistic accomplishments or radical political views.

Her son George died a wealthy bachelor in 1820, while still in his 40s, ending her direct line of descendants. A note in a record book indicates he may no longer have been a Quaker at the time of his death. Still, he was buried with his mother and father in the Quaker cemetery at Bunhill Fields.[5] His will divided his considerable fortune among his cousins on his mother's side, including the son of his aunt Esther Morris Lythall and the children of his uncle Joseph Morris.[6] If he ever wrote any observations about his famous mother, they remain undiscovered.

After her death, Boswell's presentation of her went unchallenged. The same year she died, Cadell and Davies published a fifth edition of his *Life of Johnson*, again edited by Malone with assistance from the young Boswell. The edition continued Boswell's version of Knowles's dialogue with Johnson and the footnote, added to the second edition, questioning her authenticity.[7] For the first time in the 16 years since the publication of the first edition of Boswell's *Life*, Knowles's account did not appear as an alternative text.

Among the three witnesses who wrote their versions of the disputed dialogue, Anna Seward gained the last word by outliving the other two. Before she died in 1809, Seward edited her correspondence for posthumous publication, including her letter to Mompessan containing her version of Knowles's confrontation with Johnson. In preparing this letter for publication, Seward added a note, charging that, "Mr. Boswell has strangely mutilated, abridged, and changed the minutes sent him of this conversation."[8]

Despite Seward's protest, within the next seven years, Boswell's account, along with his harsh footnote concerning Knowles, appeared in three successive editions of his increasingly popular biography. In 1811, Cadell and Davies published the sixth edition of *The Life of Samuel Johnson LL.D.* in four large volumes edited by Malone. The publishers produced a seventh edition that same year bound in five smaller volumes. Malone died in 1812, but in 1816 Cadell and Davies published an eighth edition, which he had edited, continuing Boswell's offending footnote.[9]

The first scholarly treatment of Boswell's text, including a consideration of the disputed dialogue between Knowles and Johnson, appeared in 1831 by the notorious literary critic and Tory politician, John Wilson Croker. By then, Croker was already known as both a painstaking scholar and "a much hated man" because of his sharply expressed political and literary opinions.[10] Determined to identify references to people and events he considered in danger of fading from the historical record, Croker scoured contemporary sources and incorporated new information directly into Boswell's text. He also announced that he added "gleanings" of his own "to clear up obscurities."[11]

The resulting five-volume compilation incorporated Boswell's *Journal of a Tour to the Hebrides* into *The Life of Johnson* and included nearly 2,500 notes added by Croker.[12] Two of those notes are examined here because of their lasting impact on Knowles and her account of her dialogue with Johnson. In addition, the notes added by Croker evince changing attitudes toward race and gender in the nineteenth century.

In presenting the long contested conversation that took place on 15 April 1778, Croker added a footnote concerning Jane Harry and her racial heritage. He stated that, "She was the illegitimate daughter, by a mulatto woman," of an English planter. In this statement, Croker reflected new language concerning legitimacy and racial categorization not found in eighteenth-century descriptions of Harry. Croker also challenged Seward's story of Harry's choice to become a Quaker or receive a large inheritance, saying Seward "made a romantic history" of Harry.[13]

Croker added a lengthy note concerning Knowles in which he attempted to discredit her. "Mrs. Knowles, to her own account of this conversation was desirous of adding Miss Seward's testimony," he claimed, intimating that Seward wrote her version at Knowles's behest. Yet, he went on to observe, somewhat contradictorily, that Seward's version "did not satisfy the fair disputant," Knowles.

Croker asserted, but did not prove, that the accounts of both women lacked credibility. "It is amusing to observe," he commented, that, "there is little accordance between them." He considered the women's accounts spurious because, "They affect to give the precise dialogue in the *very words* of the speakers, and yet do not agree in almost any one expression or sentiment," and "neither preserve a word of what Mr. Boswell reports." He argued that both women "(but particularly Mrs. Knowles) attribute to Johnson the poorest and feeblest trash." Based on these opinions, he concluded that, "we may be forgiven for rejecting both as fabulous."[14]

While Croker acknowledged that, "Boswell was himself a little ashamed of Johnson's violence" that night, he sought to justify Johnson's bad behavior by blaming Knowles. Johnson "was forced into the discussion by the very person by whose unauthorized and underhanded interference so much mischief (as he considered it) had been done," Croker claimed. He provided no proof, however, that Knowles acted in an unauthorized or underhanded way concerning Harry.

"Long as this note is," Croker concluded by citing a letter from Seward saying, "Mrs. Knowles did not hesitate to designate ... [a mutual Quaker friend] as an APOSTATE, although she had not quitted her sect, but only married one who did not belong to it."[15] Croker evidently included this to imply that Knowles did not practice religious toleration. If so, he must have been unaware that the eighteenth-century Quaker organization designated marrying outside their religion as a disownable offense.

Croker's numerous comments and emendations to Boswell's text created quite an outcry among scholars and critics.[16] Yet no one seemed to notice that he had disconnected both Knowles and Seward from their accounts by subsuming their versions to Boswell's text and by judging them in terms of his opinions about Johnson. By attempting to discredit Knowles personally, Croker shifted attention away from her defense of Quakers as Christians and her arguments about Harry's moral agency to choose her religion. Moreover, by erroneously linking Knowles's account to that of Seward, he questioned the accuracy of both women.

By the mid-nineteenth century, changing views about gender and Quakerliness influenced some Quaker memories of Knowles, although many continued to honor her accomplishments. A description of Knowles in an American Quaker publication indicated the persistence of her fame but also the confusion between her and Seward's accounts. *The Friend*, a weekly *Religious and Literary Journal* published in Philadelphia, reprinted Seward's version of the disputed dialogue with Johnson, evidently unaware that it differed from that given by Knowles.

Reflecting changing views relating to gender, the editor of *The Friend* described Knowles as "distinguished her day, in and about London for much singularity and eccentricity of character." The editor further stated that Knowles had "a masculine understanding, considerable literary acquirements, and superior conversational powers, which later recommendations gained for her a ready access to the higher circles and literati."[17] No record has been found of Knowles having been described as having a masculine understanding during her lifetime.

While her *Compendium on Water Baptism* was reprinted in Ireland,[18] references to her in an American Quaker publication indicated differing standards of Quakerliness among nineteenth-century Friends. In 1847, Katharine Capper Backhouse, the daughter of Jasper and Anne Fry Capper who tended Knowles on her deathbed, wrote "A Memoir of Mary Capper," her father's sister. Backhouse recalled Knowles's positive influence on her aunt, and she remembered Knowles's talents with the needle and the brush. Backhouse praised Knowles as "eminent for her great intellectual powers, and for her taste and skill in painting and in needlework; in which arts she excelled in the imitation of nature."

Yet Backhouse believed that Knowles spent too much time with those of other faiths and wasted her talents on useless diversions. "Her conversational powers were so great," wrote Backhouse, "that her company was much sought, and she was thereby induced to mix unprofitably, with many worldly-minded persons, to her great loss." Believing that this kind of socializing was wrong, Backhouse characterized the illness suffered by Knowles before her death as a "mercy" which "permitted" her "to feel the burden of sin."[19]

Although Backhouse questioned her Quakerliness, Knowles served as a source of inspiration to other mid-nineteenth-century Friends. An unnamed correspondent sent a copy of her poetic exchange with Captain Morris to *The British Friend*, suggesting that the poems be published. The verses had been "long in my possession," said the correspondent, "and rarely perused without the point and truthfulness of the 'picked bone' affording me gratification."[20]

In 1851, Wilson Armistead included several pieces by or about Knowles in his six-volume *Select Miscellanies, Chiefly Illustrative of the History, Christian Principles and Sufferings of the Society of Friends*. He reprinted Knowles's *Compendium on Water Baptism* and the "Poetical Correspondence Between Captain Morris and Mary Knowles." In addition, he reprinted an excerpt of the entry on her from Pilkington's *Memoirs*.

Armistead texts also demonstrated fluidity and confusion in sources relating to her. In reprinting an "Interesting Dialogue Between Dr. Johnson and Mary Knowles," he based his text on Seward's account rather than Knowles's version, which included her defense of Quaker beliefs. At the same time, he reported, for the first time in print, the story of Knowles's presentation of her young son to King George III. These reports indicate how personal memories and published sources relating to her were created and contested long after her death.[21]

Despite the earlier characterization of Knowles as having a masculine understanding, a late nineteenth-century female remembered her as an advocate for women. Rachel Lowe, a descendant of the Lloyds, examined Knowles's manuscripts while writing her privately printed recollections of *Farm and Its Inhabitants*. Appreciative of Knowles's high estimation of women's capacities, Lowe commented that, "she argues for the cultivation of women's intellects, describing the happy consequences of a mistress understanding the reason of a pudding-bag bursting."[22]

Quaker historians continued to recall Knowles's accomplishments and her account, although Croker's real and imagined criticisms influenced some of them. In 1888, three historically-minded Quaker men compiled a generally well documented *Biographical Catalogue: Being an Account of the Lives of Friends and others whose Portraits are in the London Friends Institute*. The title of this enterprise indicates that portraiture had become more acceptable and widespread among British Friends since Knowles's lifetime. Knowles merited an eight-page entry, along with a small reproduction of the engraving and excerpts from the biographical profile published in *The Lady's Monthly Museum*.

"By referring to Croker's edition of Boswell's Johnson, it will be seen that Boswell would not admit the accuracy of M. K.'s narrative nor of one given by Anna Seward," the authors observed. Adding that, in relation to Knowles, "there seems an adverse animus in his [Croker's] various allusions made to her," they published all three accounts. They invited readers to examine each "and make choice as to which seems more likely to be correct." Knowles's version thus reappeared in print for the first time since 1805.

Yet, the same authors also added to Knowles's association with masculinity. They quoted Croker as saying "in a note to his edition of Boswell" that, "M. K. was described by her contemporaries as having had a sharp masculine countenance with somewhat of a Puritan expression, and by no means attractive."[23] This comment does not appear in Croker's lengthy footnote, nor has it been located in other writings by Croker. The inaccurate observation thus seems to reflect the authors' views, rather than Croker's writings, concerning her.

The *Biographical Catalogue* included a four-page entry on Jane Harry. This description of Harry indicates hardening nineteenth-century views on race as well as gender. Evidently based on Croker's description of her mother as a "Mulatto," the authors referred to Harry as "a Quadroon," again making a racial distinction not found in her lifetime. The *Catalogue* reprinted Seward's description of Harry, despite Croker's dismissal of it, explaining Harry's decision to become a Quaker. At the same time, the entry also repeated Croker's undocumented assertion that Knowles "exercised somewhat of an underhand influence" concerning the young woman's conversion.[24]

Despite these conflicting views about Knowles, an entry in the *Dictionary of National Biography*, published in 1892, reconnected her with many of her achievements, although not her painting or radical politics. "Miss Fell Smith" wrote the first scholarly study of her life, applying high standards in compiling her brief entry. Charlotte Fell Smith, a Quaker biographer and editor,[25] reminded readers that Knowles, as well as Seward, sent Boswell a report of the disputed dialogue before the publication of his *Life*. Unlike Croker, Fell Smith believed that Seward's version substantiated Knowles's account. "Its authenticity," she wrote, referring to Knowles's account, "was corroborated by Miss Seward, who was present for the interview." Unlike Boswell, Malone, and Croker, Fell Smith argued that the firsthand accounts provided by the women deserved serious consideration.

Fell Smith focused on Knowles's cultural accomplishments but not her radical political activities. Reviewing a range of information about her in addition to the accounts of her disputes with Johnson and Boswell, Fell Smith highlighted her achievements in needlework and religious writing. Perhaps she did not include Knowles's political statements and expertise in painting because she lacked access to the manuscript materials where much of this information is found.[26]

While Fell Smith argued for a serious consideration of the accounts by Knowles and Seward, by the late nineteenth century, the disputed dialogue became further entangled in the politics of literary scholarship concerning Johnson and Boswell. Denouncing the "monstrous medley" that John Wilson Croker made of Boswell's text, Dr. George Birkbeck Hill devoted his life to producing a new edition of Boswell's *Life of Johnson*.[27] His "monumental"[28] six-volume edition first appeared in 1887.

Although Hill replaced many of the notes and additions made by Croker, as literary scholar Kevin Hart argued, Hill added many notes of his own, some of which reflected a "deep continuity" with Croker.[29] Despite his own assiduous scholarship, Hill accepted Croker's dismissal of Seward's account concerning Harry and Knowles. In a footnote referring to Seward's letter describing Harry's decision to become a Quaker, Hill asserted, but did not elaborate, that, "Mr. Croker shows [it] to be inaccurate." As for Seward's account of the contested conversation, Hill also dismissed it by saying, "There is too [in Seward's letter] a long and lifeless report of the talk at this dinner."[30]

Hill examined at least one source relating to Knowles[31] and took the trouble to read her version of the dialogue as published in *Gentleman's Magazine*. He removed Croker's lengthy note disparaging her and added information from Johnson's letter to Thrale describing her. Like Malone, Hill made no comment on the note Boswell added to his second edition questioning her authenticity.[32] Without including the information that many contemporaries accepted Knowles's account as credible, her version remained discredited in Boswell's footnote, and the long contested conversation began to become static and rigid.

In 1895, W. H. Craig declared that the arrival of a new age of female equality had inspired him to write *Dr. Johnson and the Fair Sex: A Study of Contrasts*. Although garbling facts and conflating sources, Craig declared that Knowles "stands out prominently among Johnson's friends, for the reason that, whenever they met, she gave him battle and rarely sustained defeat." Craig referred to Knowles's debate with Johnson concerning women's liberty, but "To pursue this subject," he believed, "might lead to painful mis-conceptions of the Dr.'s well-merited character for devotion to the sex." He concluded by asking that, "at all events, Ladies should give him [Johnson] the benefit of the doubt."[33]

While historians and literary writers focused on Johnson and Boswell, family memories of Knowles remained strong into the twentieth century. Generations of nieces, probably descended from her brother's daughter, Esther Morris Reynolds,[34] remembered her artistic and literary achievements. In 1901, Miss Margarette Reynolds donated the family copy of the needle painting of King George III to the Victoria & Albert Museum, where it remains today.[35] Richenda Elizabeth Reynolds, another relative in the extended family, still "had several things belonging to old Aunt Knowles" in her possession in the early 1900s.[36]

A new generation of Lloyds also fondly recalled Knowles and rejected Croker's negative comments about her. In *The Lloyds of Birmingham with some Account of the Founding of Lloyd's Bank* published in 1908, Samuel Lloyd included a chapter on "Dr. Johnson and Mary Knowles" and a reproduction of her engraving. Lloyd reprinted her account of her dialogue as well as Seward's version. While noting that, "Croker ... tells a different tale," Lloyd did not reprint his comments.[37]

Another Quaker historian, Joseph Joshua Green, provided new information about Jane Harry Thresher, his relative by marriage. Green transcribed family letters relating to her in the *Friends Quarterly Examiner*. He publicly named Thomas Hibbert as her father for the first time, and he uncovered the 28-page letter she wrote, beseeching Hibbert's guidance when she decided to become a Quaker.[38]

Green also seems to have prompted the surprising appearance of an article about Knowles and her dispute with Johnson in the pages of the November 1912 edition of *The Nation*. In "News for Bibliophiles," William E. A. Axon described

Boswell's footnote concerning Knowles as "not altogether candid." Furthermore, in Axon's judgment, "Croker has added a not too candid note" to Boswell's. Axon urged "Johnsonians to obtain, if they can," a copy of Knowles's version, assuring them that, "The Dialogue is lively reading."[39]

Knowles's reputation as a needlework artist proved as persistent in the twentieth century as she had been in the eighteenth. In 1948, Queen Mary acquired the needlework self-portrait created by Knowles at a time when it constituted a radical act of self-representation.[40] The next year, the queen displayed the self-portrait, along with Knowles's needle painting of George III, already in the Royal Collection. Bernard and Therle Hughes described the importance of these two works of art, indicating a renewed appreciation of Knowles's accomplishments. They also reproduced her self-portrait in an article in *Country Life*.[41]

Despite the persistent families memories, Quaker historical accounts, and public recognition of Knowles and her artistic achievements, by the late twentieth century, Boswell's view of her became enshrined in the literary canon. In 1971, L. F. Powell pronounced Boswell's text "sacred" and the "authority" of George Birkbeck Hill's edition "undisputed."[42] As Kevin Hart argued, this "process of sacralisation" of Boswell's text meant that his *Life* became a "tomb for Johnson." Hart argued that instead of an extraordinarily interesting, gifted, and, like all mortals, sometimes flawed human being, Johnson, frozen in Boswell's text, became a historical monument and a piece of "cultural property."[43]

The status of Boswell's text as canonical, to be revered and never challenged or changed in any way, survived postmodernism and extended into the twenty-first century. In his 2001 revision of *The Correspondence and other Papers of James Boswell relating to the making of the Life of Johnson*, Marshall Waingrow described Knowles's account only briefly as "totally discrepant from his [Boswell's] own record."[44] While it is undoubtedly important to preserve Boswell's text as he wrote it, its canonical status should not limit historical debate or remove the possibility of considering Knowles's alternative account simply because it does not agree with what Boswell wrote.

Disconnecting Boswell's text from Knowles's account has meant that some current scholarship relating to *The Life of Johnson* presents conflicting and unsubstantiated views about her. For example, although some contemporaries described Knowles as a wit, as has been seen, a 1999 edition of *The Life* stated that, "She was not a wit."[45] In *Boswell's Presumptuous Task*, however, published in 2000, Adam Sisman described Knowles as "witty."[46] Furthermore, the 1999 edition of *The Life* points to her dialogue with Johnson as proof of the "spontaneous and even festive tolerance" of "Johnson's milieu." Knowles's published account does not support that statement.[47]

Despite these disconnections, recent scholars have rediscovered some of Knowles's important social, religious, and artistic connections. Citing her debate with Johnson about women's liberty, literary scholar Katharine Rogers named Knowles as a feminist forerunner.[48] Historian John Brewer noted her friendship with Anna Seward, one of the influential figures he profiled in his study of eighteenth-century culture.[49] Rebecca Larson saw her as a key example of the changing image of Quakers in the eighteenth century, noting her close relationship with Jane Harry.[50] Margaret Swain documented her achievements in needlework.[51]

This study has closely examined Knowles's life story to explore her connections to three important themes in the long eighteenth century. To recap these themes briefly, Knowles contributed to religious toleration for English Quakers by explaining her beliefs to non-Quakers in print and polite conversations. She facilitated greater understanding of such basic Quaker beliefs as the spiritual nature of Christ and the rejection of water baptism, formal liturgy, and a paid priesthood. She effectively compared Quaker theology to more widely accepted Protestant beliefs and practices. She consistently upheld liberty of choice in religion and promoted toleration for a wide variety of faiths. Yet, she advanced toleration for Quakers by limiting it for Jews and Catholics.

By developing new forms of polite Quakerliness, Knowles helped to develop conventions of Quaker sociability, which facilitated the integration of prosperous Quakers into polite society. She balanced motherhood and family duties with participation in the expanding social and cultural opportunities increasingly available to middling women throughout the Georgian Age. She contributed to enlarging concepts of sociability, including women and men of various faiths and ethnic origins. Her experiences indicate the range of gender roles available to both women and men during the Georgian Age and demonstrate the complexity and inclusivity of concepts of female sociability.

Knowles challenged gender relations within her family and in social and public contexts in a variety of ways. She insisted on choosing her marriage partner and resisted conventional domesticity, developing her own household standards. She had a happy marriage, a loving son, and fond relationships with her extended family, especially the Lloyds. She consistently defended women's liberty, and she attracted fame and public recognition as an artist and religious writer.

Knowles furthered women's participation in politics by expressing strong opinions in letters, poems, and conversations with males and females. She used her relationships with the royal family to support Quaker pacifism and request a political favor. Always a champion of liberty, she advocated for the abolition of slavery. Knowles voiced strong support for the French Revolution, indicating how women participated in the transmission and transformation of radical ideology in the eighteenth century.

Examining these connections points to new areas of research on gender, Quakerism, and radicalism. Knowles's experience suggests the need for further considerations of how Quakers balanced changing aesthetic considerations, social customs, and religious restraints. Future studies could probe the religious tensions between radical beliefs, ethical consumerism, and attitudes toward fashion practiced by prosperous male and female Friends like her. As her life story demonstrates, her Quaker beliefs both fostered radical self-representation and engendered self-doubt. It would be worthwhile to discover whether that same dynamic affected other Quaker women and men.

Future researchers could investigate to what extent other middling women developed socially significant cross-gender friendships and exercised political influence. Additional studies identifying how women like Knowles actively resisted confinement to the domestic sphere and participated in the creation of visual arts are needed to inform modern constructions of femininity. More research is needed on the connections between notions of women's liberty and radical political thinking pre-dating Mary Wollstonecraft's *Vindication*. As yet unstudied women like Mary Wilkes Hayley, for example, only briefly glimpsed here, may have contributed to the transmission of radical political ideology.

Knowles and her connections also demonstrate the need to preserve, catalog, and publish primary source materials relating to women, especially to understudied middling women, and the even less studied Caribbean-born women living in England, like Jane Harry Thresher. Some of the letters, poems, and drawings by Knowles cited in this study remain in private hands, as do all of the sources cited here relating to Thresher. To understand and preserve the rich history of women and men's lives in the eighteenth century, more primary source materials must be collected and made available to researchers interested in the full range of historical records, including popular publications, written memories, and material artifacts.

Finally, this study seeks to encourage future scholars to focus on individual lives and the larger stories they have to tell as a way of informing new theories and understandings of the long eighteenth century. The story of Mary Morris Knowles is a powerful lens through which to view change and continuity not only in her lifetime but also in subsequent memories and scholarship about her. Popular and scholarly interest in her endures because her life explores questions of continuing importance: How does one honor religious ideals of simplicity in an increasingly acquisitive and consumer oriented age? What is the role of gender in shaping the lives of women and men? What does it mean to be radical? By looking forward to future scholarship, the story of Mary Morris Knowles and her connections strengthens the case for new research into the untold stories and activities of diverse women and men from a wide range of religious and social backgrounds.

Notes

1 *The Monthly Repository of Theology and General Literature* 2 (March 1807): 160.
2 *The Literary Panorama*, 2 (1807): 1068–9.
3 Library of the Religious Society of Friends, MSS Volume 150 [Luke Howard MSS], Number 39.
4 *The Annual Monitor and Memorandum Book, arranged upon an Improved Plan for the Year 1815* (York, 1815), p. 13.

5 Public Record Office, RG 6, 416, "Grace Church Street Monthly Meetings Burials, 1795–1837."
6 Public Record Office, Prob. 11/1631, quire 362, "Will of George Knowles, Esq."
7 Edmond Malone, ed. *The Life of Samuel Johnson, LL.D ... By James Boswell, Esq.* (5th edn, 4 vols London, 1807)
8 *Letters of Anna Seward*, vol. 1, p. 97.
9 Edmond Malone, ed. *The Life of Samuel Johnson, LL.D ... By James Boswell, Esq.* (6th edn, 4 vols, London, 1811); (7th edn, 5 vols, London, 1811); (8th edn, 4 vols, 1816).
10 Margaret Drabble, ed. *Oxford Companion to English Literature* (revised edn, Oxford, 1995), p. 244.
11 Croker, *Life of Samuel Johnson*, vol. 1, p. vii.
12 Sisman, *Boswell's Presumptuous Task*, p. 292.
13 Croker, *Life of Samuel Johnson*, vol. 4, pp. 155–6.
14 Ibid., vol. 4, p. 157.
15 Ibid., vol. 4, pp. 157–8.
16 Sisman, *Boswell's Presumptuous Task*, pp. 292–3.
17 Robert Smith, ed. *The Friend: A Religious and Literary Journal* (2nd edn) 1 (1829): 163.
18 *The Irish Friend* 2/9 (9th mo, 2nd 1839): 71.
19 Backhouse, "Memoir of Mary Capper."
20 *The British Friend* 6 (1848): 110–11.
21 Armistead, *Select Miscellanies*, vol. 1, 60–64; vol. 2, pp. 90–104; vol. 3, pp. 93–7; vol. 4, p. 168.
22 Lowe, *Farm and Its Inhabitants*, pp. 45–6.
23 W. Beck, W. F. Wells, H. G. Chakley, compilers, *Biographical Catalogue: Being an Account of the Lives of Friends and others whose Portraits are in the London Friends Institute* (London, 1888), pp. 405–13.
24 Ibid., pp. 333–7.
25 W. Raymond Powell, "Charlotte Fell Smith, Friend, Biographer and Editor," *The Journal of the Friends Historical Society*, 60/2 (2004); 113–42.
26 Charlotte Fell Smith, "Mrs. Mary Knowles (1733–1807)," in Sidney Lee, ed. *Dictionary of National Biography* (London, 1892), vol. 21, p. 302.
27 G. B. Hill, *Life of Johnson* (New York, 1921), p. xxiv.
28 John Wain, *Samuel Johnson: A Biography* (New York, 1974), "Note on Sources."
29 Kevin Hart, *Samuel Johnson and the Culture of Property* (Cambridge, 1999), p. 82.
30 George Birkbeck Hill, ed. *Boswell's Life of Johnson* (6 vols, New York, 1891), vol. 3, p. 340.
31 Library of the Religious Society of Friends, Temporary MSS 28, File 7, two letters from Hill concerning Knowles.
32 Hill, *Boswell's Life of Johnson*, vol. 3, p. 340.
33 W. H. Craig, *Dr. Johnson and the Fair Sex: A Study of Contrasts* (London, 1895), pp. vii, 27, 131–2, 201–2.
34 Dictionary of Quaker Biography, Esther Morris Reynolds (1773–1851) married William Foster Reynolds and had 10 children.
35 Library of the Religious Society of Friends, Picture Box K, Catalogue.
36 Library of the Religious Society of Friends, Portfolio MSS B.

37 Lloyd, *The Lloyds of Birmingham*, p. 34, 110–34, 238. A contemporary of Lloyd, Sir Alfred E. Pease in *The Diaries of Edward Pease, The Father of the English Railways* (London, 1907) reprinted a copy of Seward's account, but this version, based on a later copy, contains many corruptions.
38 J. J. Green, *Friends Quarterly Examiner*, 1913 and 1914.
39 William E. A. Axon, "News for Bibliophiles," *The Nation* (Nov. 12, 1912): 429.
40 Library of the Religious Society of Friends, Picture Box K, 15/4.
41 Bernard and Therle Hughes, *Country Life*.
42 *Boswell's Life of Johnson*, edited by George Birkbeck Hill, Revised and enlarged by L. F. Powell, (6 vols, Oxford, 1971), vol. 3, pp. 284–300.
43 Hart, *Samuel Johnson and the Culture of Property*, p. 182.
44 Waingrow, *The Correspondence and other Papers of James Boswell*, p. 48.
45 Angus Calder, ed. *Boswell: The Life of Samuel Johnson, LL.D.* (Ware, Herts, 1999), p. xviii.
46 Sisman, *Boswell's Presumptuous Task*, p. 88.
47 Calder, *Boswell*, p. xviii.
48 Katharine M. Rogers, *Feminism in Eighteenth-Century England* (Urbana, Il., 1982), p. 31.
49 Brewer, *Pleasures of the Imagination*, pp. 192, 587, 588.
50 Larson, *Daughters of Light*, p. 373.
51 Swain, *Embroidered Georgian Pictures*, pp. 18–20.

Bibliography

Manuscript Sources

Charleston Library Society, South Carolina
Newspaper Collection

Duke University, Perkins Rare Book and Manuscripts Library, North Carolina
Papers of Hannah Bott

Haverford College Library, Pennsylvania
Quaker Collection

Library of Religious Society of Friends, London
Diaries and Memoranda of Elihu Robinson
Dictionary of Quaker Biography
Digest Registers of Births, Deaths and Burials
Howarth MSS
John Thompson MSS
Matthews MSS
Monthly Meeting Records
MSS Vols 150, 334, 347
Portfolio MSS 3, 6, 11
Temporary MSS 1, 5, 28, 403
Thompson-Clarkson MSS

New-York Historical Society, New York
Newspaper Collection

Public Record Office, London
RG 6, Quaker Records
Prob 11

Printed Primary Sources

The Annual Monitor and Memorandum Book, arranged upon an Improved Plan for the Year 1815 (York: W. Alexander, 1815).

Armistead, Wilson, *Select Miscellanies* (6 vols, London: Charles Gilpin, 1851).

Backhouse, Katharine (ed.), "A Memoir of Mary Capper," in William and Thomas Evans, (eds), *The Friends Library* (14 vols, Philadelphia: Joseph Rakestraw, 1848), vol. 12.

Balderston, Katharine (ed.), *Thraliana: The Diary of Hester Lynch Thrale (later Mrs. Piozzi), 1776–1809* (2 vols, Oxford: Clarendon Press, 1942).

Barclay's Apology in Modern English, ed. Dean Freiday (Newberg: Barclay Press, 1991).

Beale, Mrs. Catherine Hutton (ed.), *Reminiscences of a Gentlewoman of the Last Century: Letters of Catherine Hutton* (Birmingham: Cornish Brothers, 1891).

Beloe, Rev. William, *The Sexagenarian: Or the Recollections of a Literary Life* (2 vols, London: F. C. and J. Rivington, 1817).

Binns, George Jonathan. "A Short Account of the Life of Jonathan Binns, M. D." (Liverpool City Library, typescript, 1930).

The Birmingham Directory (Birmingham: Pearson and Rollason, 1777).

Bond, Donald F. (ed.), *The Tatler* (Oxford: Clarendon Press, 1987).

Boswell, James, *Life of Samuel Johnson, LL.D.* (2 vols, London: Charles Dilly 1791).

———, *Life of Samuel Johnson, LL.D.* (2nd edn, 3 vols, London: Charles Dilly, 1793).

———, *Life of Samuel Johnson, LL.D.* (3rd edn, 4 vols, London: Charles Dilly, 1799).

———, *The Principal Corrections and Additions to the First Edition of Mr. Boswell's Life of Dr. Johnson* (London: Charles Dilly, 1793).

[Boswell, James], *No Abolition of Slavery: Or the Universal Empire of Love* (London: R. Faulder, 1791).

The British Friend, 6 (1848): 110–11.

Butterfield, Lyman, "The American Interests in the Firm of E. and C. Dilly, with their letters to Benjamin Rush, 1770–1795," *The Papers of the Bibliographical Society of America* vol. 45 (1951).

Carey, George Saville, *The Balnea: Or, an Impartial Description of All the Popular Watering Places in England* (2nd edn, London, J. W. Myers, 1799).

Chapman, R. W. (ed.), *The Letters of Samuel Johnson with Mrs. Thrale's Genuine Letters to Him* (3 vols, Oxford: Clarendon Press, 1952).

Clarkson, Thomas, *A Portraiture of Quakerism as Taken from a View of the Moral, Education, Discipline, Peculiar Customs, Religious Principles, Political and Civil Oeconomy and Character of the Society of Friends* (3 vols, London: Longman, Hurst, Rees, and Orme, 1806).

"Conversation Between Mrs. Knowles and Dr. Johnson, sent to Mr. Boswell for Publication," *The Satellite or Repository of Literature, composed of Miscellaneous Essays (Chiefly original) intended for the diffusion of Useful and Polite Knowledge*, 1 (1798): 8.

Crosfield, John Fothergill, *The Crosfield Family* (privately printed, 1980).

Danzinger, Marlies and Brady, Frank (eds), *Boswell: The Great Biographer, 1789–1795* (New York: McGraw Hill, 1989).

Deverell, Mary, *Sermons on Various Subjects* (2nd edn, London: William Strahan, 1776).

Evans, Jonathan, *A Journal of the Life, Travels, and Religious Labours of William Savery* (London: Charles Gilbin, 1844).

Fletcher, Edward, *The Life of Samuel Johnson by James Boswell with marginal comments and markings ... by Hester Lynch Thrale Piozzi* (3 vols, London: Curwen Press, 1938).

Gentleman's Magazine.

George Fox: The Journal, ed. Nigel Smith (London: Penguin, 1998).

Graham, Catharine Macaulay, *Letters on Education with Observations on Religious and Metaphysical Subjects* (London: Charles Dilly 1790).

Hayward, A. (ed.), *Autobiography, Letters and Literary Remains of Mrs. Piozzi* (2 vols, London: Longman, Green, Longman and Roberts, 1861).

Hoare, Sarah and Hannah, *Memoirs of Samuel Hoare*, ed. F. R. Pryor (London: Headley Brothers, 1911).

Howard, E. F., "Mary Knowles and the Lloyds of Birmingham," *Friends Quarterly Examiner*, (1934): 91–2.

Hutton, W., *An History of Birmingham to the End of the Year 1780* (Birmingham: Pearson and Rollason, 1781).

[Jenyns, Soame], *A View of the Internal Evidence of the Christian Religion* (London: J. Dodsely, 1776).

Johnson, John, *Memoirs of the Life and Writings of William Hayley, Esq,* (2 vols, London: Henry Colburn, 1831).

Kent's Directory for the Year 1783 (51st edn, London: Richard and Henry Causton, 1783).

Kerby-Miller, Charles (ed.), *Memoirs of the Extraordinary Life, Works, and Discoveries of Martinus Scriblerus* (New York: Russell and Russell, 1966).

[Knowles, Mary Morris], *Compendium of a Controversy on Water Baptism*, (London: C. Hatton, 1805).

[Knowles, Mary Morris], "Lord North and the Quaker," *Journal of the Friends Historical Society*, 17/3 (1920): 77–9.

[Knowles, Mary Morris], *Dialogue Between Dr. Johnson and Mrs. Knowles* (London: J. and Arthur Arch, 1799).

[Knowles, Mary Morris], *Dialogue Between Mrs. Knowles and Dr. Johnson* (London: C. Hatton, 1805).

[Knowles, Mary Morris], *Dialogue Between Mrs. Knowles and Dr. Johnson* (Huddersfield, no date).

The Lady's Monthly Museum.

The Leadbeater Papers: A Selection from the Manuscripts and Correspondence of Mary [Shackleton] Leadbeater (2nd edn, 2 vols, London: Bell and Daldy, 1862).

Letters from the Year 1774 to the Year 1796 of John Wilkes Esq. Addressed to his Daughter, the late Miss Wilkes (4 vols, London: Longmans, 1804).

Letters of Anna Seward, written between the years 1784 and 1807 (6 vols, Edinburgh: Archibald Constable and Co., 1811).

Letters of the Late Lord Lyttleton, only son of the Venerable George, Lord Lyttleton (1st American edition, Troy, New York: Wright, Goodenow and Stockwell, 1807).

The Literary Panorama (London: C. Taylor, Hatton Gardens, 1807).

Lustig, Irma S. and Pottle, Frederick A. (eds), *Boswell: The Applause of the Jury, 1782–1785* (New York: McGraw Hill, 1981).

——— (eds), *Boswell: The English Experiment, 1785–1789*, (New York: McGraw Hill, 1986).

Macaulay, Catharine, *Observations on a Pamphlet Entitled Thoughts on the Cause of the Present Discontents* (London: Edward and Charles Dilly, 1770).

Malone, Edmond (ed.), *The Life of Samuel Johnson, LL.D. ... by James Boswell, Esq.* (4th edn. 4 vols, London: Cadell and Davies, 1804).

——— (ed.), *The Life of Samuel Johnson, LL.D ... By James Boswell, Esq.* (6th edn, 4 vols, London, 1811); (7th edn, 5 vols, London, 1811); (8th edn, 4 vols, 1816).

Memoirs of the Life and Writings of the late John Coakley Lettsom, ed. Thomas Joseph Pettigrew (3 vols, London: Longman, Hurst, Rees, Orme and Brown, 1817).

[Miller, Anna Riggs], *Letters from Italy* (3 vols, London: Edward and Charles Dilly, 1776).

[Miller, Lady Anna], *Poetical Amusements at a Villa near Bath* (2nd edn, London: Edward and Charles Dilly, 1776).

The Monthly Repository of Theology and General Literature, 2 (March 1807): 160.

Morris, Richard, *Some Animadversions on the Supposition of the Scriptures Being the Only Principal and Perfect Rule to Salvation* (London: James Phillips and son, 1798).

The New Complete Guide to All Persons Who Have Any Trade or Concern with the City of London and Parts Adjacent (14th edn, 1775).

Nichols, John, *Illustrations of the Literary History of Eighteenth-Century London* (8 vols, London: John Nichols and son, 1822).

"Notes and Queries [by C. D. Sturge, Birmingham, 1741]," *Journal of the Friends Historical Society*, 4/3 (1907).

Paine, Thomas, *The Age of Reason: Being an Investigation of True and Fabulous Theology* (London: Daniel Isaac Eaton, 1795).

Pilkington, Mrs. [Mary], *Memoirs of Celebrated Female Characters Who Have Distinguished Themselves By Their Talents and Virtues in Every Age and Nation* (London: Albion Press, 1804).

Pindar, Peter, [Dr. John Wolcot], *Bozzy and Piozzi, or the British Biographers: A Town Eclogue* (London: G. Kearsley and W. Foster, 1786).

Piozzi, Hester Lynch [Thrale], *Letters to and from the late Samuel Johnson, LL.D.* (2 vols, London: A. Strahan and T. Cadell, 1787).

[Rack, Edmund, ed.], *Caspipina's Letters ... To which is Added The Life and Character of William Penn, Esq.* (2 vols, Dublin: I. Jones, 1792).

Records and Recollections of James Jenkins, ed. J. William Frost (New York: Edwin Mellin Press, 1984).

Reed, Joseph and Pottle, Frederick (eds), *Boswell: Laird of Auchinleck, 1778–1782* (New York: McGraw Hill 1977).

Ryskamp, Charles and Frederick Pottle (eds), *Boswell: The Ominous Years, 1774–1776* (New York: McGraw-Hill Book Co., Inc., 1963).

Sael, G., *Extensive Collection of Curious Books ... Offered for Sale* (1794).

Tracts, Vol. C. Library of the Religious Society of Friends.

Swedenborg, Emmanuel, *A Treatise Concerning Heaven and Hell, Containing a Relation of many Wonderful Things therein, as heard and seen by the Author* (London: James Phillips, 1778).

Voltaire: Candide and Philosophical Letters (New York: The Modern Library, 1992).

Waingrow, Marshall (ed.), *The Correspondence and other Papers of James Boswell relating to the making of the Life of Johnson* (New York: McGraw-Hill Book Co., 1966).

———, (ed.), *The Correspondence and Other Papers of James Boswell Relating to the Making of the Life of Johnson* (2nd. edn, Edinburgh: Edinburgh University Press, New Haven and London: Yale University Press, 2001).

"William Savery: A Sketch by Dr. Lettsom," in Job Sibley, *Discourses Delivered by William Savery of North America at Several Meetings of the People called Quakers and Others* (London: Darton and Harvey, 1806).

The Works of Alexander Pope, Esquire, vol. 4, *Containing His Miscellaneous Pieces in Verse and Prose* (London: A. Millar and others, 1764).

Wickham, Rev. Hill (ed.), *Journals and Correspondence of Thomas Sedgewick Whalley* (2 vols, London: Richard Bentley, 1863).

Wimsatt, William Jr. and Pottle, Frederick A. (eds), *Boswell for the Defense, 1769–1774* (New York: McGraw Hill, 1959).

Secondary Sources

Abraham, James Johnston, *Lettsom: His Life, Times, Friends and Descendants* (London: William Heinemann, 1933).
Anderson, John Eustace, *A History of the Parish of Barnes in the County of Surrey* (Richmond: privately printed, 1900).
Ashmun, Margaret, *The Singing Swan: An Account of Anna Seward and Her Acquaintance with Dr. Johnson, Boswell, and Others of Their Time* (New Haven: Yale University Press, 1931).
Axon, William E. A., "News for Bibliophiles," *The Nation*, (Nov. 12, 1912): 429.
Barrow, Christine, *Family in the Caribbean: Themes and Perspective* (Princeton: Marcus Wiener Publications, 1998).
Basker, James G., *Amazing Grace: An Anthology of Poems About Slavery, 1680–1810* (New Haven: Yale University Press, 2002).
———, "Dancing Dogs, Women Preachers and the Myth of Johnson's Misogyny," *The Age of Johnson*, 3 (1990): 63–90.
Beck, William and Ball, T. Frederick, *The London Friends' Meetings* (London: F. B. Kitto, 1869).
Beck, W., Wells, W. F., and Chakley, H. G., compilers, *Biographical Catalogue: Being an Account of the Lives of Friends and others whose Portraits are in the London Friends Institute* (London: Friends Institute, 1888).
Bleackley, Horace, *Life of John Wilkes* (London: John Lane, 1917),
Booth, Christopher C., "The Correspondence of Dr. John Fothergill with Sir Joseph Banks," *The Journal of the Friends Historical Society*, 59, 3 (2004).
Brewer, John, *The Pleasures of the Imagination: English Culture in the Eighteenth Century* (New York: Farrar Straus Giroux, 1997).
Brooke, John and Namier, Sir Lewis, *The History of Parliament: The House of Commons, 1754–1790* (London: Her Majesty's Stationery Office, 1964).
Calder, Angus (ed.), *Boswell: The Life of Johnson* (Ware, Hertforshire: Wordsworth Edition Limited, 1999).
Carretta, Vincent (ed.), *Unchained Voices: An Anthology of Black Authors in the English-Speaking World of the Eighteenth-Century* (Lexington: University Press of Kentucky, 1996).
Carroll, Kenneth L., "The Mary and Charlotte Fiasco: A Look at 1778 British Quaker Relief for Philadelphia," *Pennsylvania Magazine of History and Biography*, 52/2 (1978): 212–23.
Clark, Sir George, *A History of the Royal College of Physicians of London* (3 vols, Oxford: Clarendon Press, 1966).
Clarke, Norma, *Dr. Johnson's Women* (London: Hambledon, 2000).
Clifford, James L., "The Authenticity of Anna Seward's Published Correspondence," *Modern Philology*, 34/2 (1941): 113–22.

Colley, Linda, "Radical Patriotism in Eighteenth-Century England," in Raphael Samuel (ed.), *Patriotism: The Making and Unmaking of British National Identity*, vol. 1 *History and Politics* (London: Routledge, 1989).

Compton, Theodore. *Recollections of Tottenham Friends and the Forster Family* (London: Edward Hicks, 1893).

Craig, W. H., *Dr. Johnson and the Fair Sex: A Study of Contrasts* (London: Sampson, Low, Marston and Co., 1895).

Croker, John Wilson (ed.), *The Life of Samuel Johnson LL.D., including a Journal of a Tour to the Hebrides by James Boswell* (5 vols, London: John Murray, 1831).

Cross, David A., *"A Striking Likeness:" The Life of George Romney* (Brookefield: Ashgate, 2000).

Cunningham, Andrew and French, Roger (eds), *The Medical Enlightenment of the Eighteenth Century* (Cambridge: Cambridge University Press, 1990),

Davidoff, Lenore and Hall, Catherine, *Family Fortunes: Men and Women of the English Middle Class, 1780–1850* (Chicago: University of Chicago Press, 1987).

Davies, Adrian, *The Quakers in English Society, 1655–1725* (Oxford: Oxford University Press, 2000).

DeMaria, Robert, Jr., *The Life of Samuel Johnson* (Oxford: Blackwell, 1993).

——, *Samuel Johnson and the Life of Reading* (Baltimore: Johns Hopkins Press, 1997).

Dinwiddy, J. R., *Radicalism and Reform in Britain, 1780–1850* (London: Hambledon Press, 1992).

Donaldson, Barbara, "The Registration of Dissenting Chapels and Meeting Houses in Staffordshire, 1689-1852," in Staffordshire Record Society (eds.), *Collections for a History of Staffordshire*, 4th series, vol. 3 (Kendal, 1960), pp. xxii-iv.

Dresser, Margaret, *Slavery Obscured: The Social History of the Slave Trade in an English Provincial Port* (London: Continuum, 2001).

Ezell, Margaret J. M., *Social Authorship and the Advent of Print* (Baltimore: Johns Hopkins Press, 1999).

Fell Smith, Charlotte, "Mrs. Mary Knowles (1733–1807)," in Sidney Lee, ed. *Dictionary of National Biography* (London: Smith, Elder and Co., 1892).

Fox, R. Hingston, *Dr. John Fothergill and His Friends: Chapters in Eighteenth-Century Life* (London: Macmillan and Company, 1919).

Gardner, W. J., *A History of Jamaica from its Discovery by Christopher Columbus to the Year 1872* (London: Frank Cass and Co.,1971).

Gilmartin, Kevin, "In the Theatre of Counterrevolution: Loyalist Associations and Conservative Opinion in the 1790s," *Journal of British Studies*, 41/3 (July 2002): 292–328.

Gleadle and Richardson (eds), *Women in British Politics, 1760–1860; The Power of the Petticoat* (London: Macmillan Press, 2000).

Grant, Charlotte, "The Choice of Hercules: the polite arts and 'female excellence' in eighteenth-century London," in Elizabeth Eger, Charlotte Grant, Cilona O'Gallchoir and Penny Warburton, *Women, Writing and the Public Sphere* (Cambridge: Cambridge University Press, 2001).

Greaves, Richard L,"Seditious Sectaries or 'Sober and Useful Inhabitants?': Changing Concepts of Quakers in Early Modern Britain," *Albion*, 33/1 (2001): 24–50.

Green, Joseph J., "Jenny Harry, later Thresher (c. 1756–1784)," *Friends Quarterly Examiner*, 10th Month/1913: 559–82.

———, "Jenny Harry, later Thresher (c. 1756–1784) (concluded)," *Friends Quarterly Examiner*, 1st Month/1914: 43–64.

Guest, Harriet, *Small Change: Women, Learning, Patriotism, 1750–1810* (Chicago: University of Chicago Press, 2000).

Hart, Charles Henry. "Benjamin West's Family: The American President of the Royal Academy of Arts Not A Quaker," *Pennsylvania Magazine of History and Biography*, (1908).

Hart, Kevin, *Samuel Johnson and the Culture of Property* (Cambridge: Cambridge University Press, 1999).

Hedley, Olwen, *Queen Charlotte* (London: John Murray, 1975).

Hesselgrave, Ruth Avaline, *Lady Miller and the Batheaston Literary Circle* (New Haven: Yale University Press, 1927).

Hicks, Philip, "Catharine Macaulay's Civil War: Gender, History, and Republicanism in Georgian Britain," *Journal of British Studies*, 41/2 (2002): 170–98.

Hill, Bridget, *Republican Virago: The Life and Times of Catharine Macaulay, Historian* (Oxford: Clarendon Press, 1992).

———, *Women, Work and Sexual Politics in Eighteenth-Century England* (London: University College of London Press, Ltd.,1994).

Hill, George Birkbeck (ed). *Boswell's Life of Johnson* (6 vols, New York: Harper and Brothers, 1891).

———, (ed.), *Life of Johnson* (6 vols, New York: Bigelow, Brown and Co., 1921).

———, (ed.), George Birkbeck Hill, rev. by L. F. Powell, *Boswell's Life of Johnson*, (6 vols, Oxford: Oxford University Press, 1971).

Hudson, Nicholas, "From 'Nation' to 'Race:' The Origin of Racial Classification in Eighteenth-Century Thought," *Eighteenth-Century Studies*, 29/3 (1996): 258.

Hunt, Margaret, *The Middling Sort: Commerce, Gender and Family in England, 1680–1780* (Berkley: University of California, Press, 1996).

Hunt, Thomas (ed.), *The Medical Society of London, 1773–1973* (London: William Heinemann, 1972).

Hughes, Bernard and Therle, "An Artist in Needlework," *Country Life*, 105 / 2714 (1949): 138–9.

Hyde, Mary, *The Thrales of Streatham Park* (Cambridge: Harvard University Press, 1977).

Ifekwunigew, Joyce O., "Diaspora's Daughters, Africa's Orphans?" in Heidi Safia Mirza, ed. *Black British Feminism: A Reader* (London: Routledge, 1997).
Ingram, John H., *The Haunted Homes and Family Traditions of Great Britain* (London: W. H. Allen, 1884).
The Irish Friend: A Monthly Periodical Devoted Chiefly to the Interests of Friends, 2, 9 (September 2, 1839).
Jennings, Judith, *The Business of Abolishing the British Slave Trade, 1783–1807* (London: Frank Cass, 1997).
Justice, George L. and Tinker, Nathan (eds), *Women's Writing and the Circulation of Ideas: Manuscript Publication in England, 1550–1800* (New York, 2002).
Kemmerer, Kathleen Nutton, *"A neutral being between the sexes:" Samuel Johnson's Sexual Politics* (London: Associated University Presses, 1998).
Klein, Lawrence E., "Gender and the Public/Private Distinction in the Eighteenth Century: Some Question about Evidence and Analytic Procedure," *Eighteenth-Century Studies*, 29/1 (1995): 97–109
Landor, Walter N., "An Account of the Manor and Ancient Paris of Rugeley from the Days of the Saxons," Typescript, Rugeley Public Library.
Langford, John Alford (ed.), *A Century of Birmingham Life* (2 vols, Birmingham: E. C. Osbourne, 1868).
Lapsansky, Emma Jones and Verplanck, Anne A. (eds), *Quaker Aesthetics: Reflections on a Quaker Ethic in American Design and Consumption* (Philadelphia: University of Pennsylvania, Press, 2002).
Larson, Rebecca, *Daughters of Light: Quaker Women Preaching and Prophesying in the Colonies and Abroad, 1700–1775* (New York: Alfred A. Knopf, 1999).
Lewis, Judith S., *Sacred to Female Patriotism: Gender, Class, and Politics in Late Georgian Britain* (New York: Routledge, 2003).
Lloyd, Samuel. *The Lloyds of Birmingham* (3rd edn, Birmingham: Cornish Bros., Ltd., 1908).
———, *Some Account of Jenny Harry* (privately printed, 1912).
Lowe, Rachel, *Farm and Its Inhabitants* (privately printed, 1883).
Lustig, Irma S., "The Myth of Johnson's Misogyny in the *Life of Johnson*: Another View," in Thomas Crawford, ed, *Boswell in Scotland and Beyond* Glasgow: Association for Scottish Literary Studies, 1997).
McDowell, Paula, *The Women of Grub Street: Press, Politics and Gender in the London Literary Marketplace, 16778–1730* (Oxford: Clarendon Press, 1998).
Midgley, Claire, "Slave Sugar Boycotts, Female Activism and the Domestic Base of British Anti-Slavery Culture," *Slavery and Abolition*, 17/3 (1996): 142.
Millar, Oliver, *The Later Georgian Pictures in the Collection of Her Majesty the Queen* (2 vols, London: Phaedon Press, 1969).
Moore, Rosemary, *The Light in Their Consciences: The Early Quakers in Britain, 1646–1666* (University Park: Pennsylvania State University Press, 2000).

Myers, Sylvia Harcstack, *The Bluestocking Circle: Women, Friendship, and the Life of the Mind in Eighteenth-Century England* (Oxford: Clarendon Press, 1990).

Nickalls, John, "Some Quaker Portraits: Certain and Uncertain," *Journal of the Friends Historical Society*, Supplement 29 (Autumn, 1958): 1–18.

Nussbaum, Felicity, "Women and race: 'a difference of complexion,'" in Vivien Jones, ed. *Women and Literature in Britain, 1700–1800* (Cambridge: Cambridge University Press, 2000).

Oldfield, J. R., *Popular Politics and British Anti-Slavery: The Mobilisation of Public Opinion against the Slave Trade, 1787–1807* (London: Frank Cass, 1998).

"Our bibliographers: Morris Birkbeck," *Journal of the Friends Historical Society*, 8/1 (March 1911): 11

Pocock, J. G. A., "Catharine Macaulay: patriot historian," in Hilda L. Smith, ed., *Women writers and the early modern British Political Tradition* (Cambridge: Cambridge University Press, 1998).

Pointon, Marcia, *Hanging the Head: Portraiture and Social Formation in Eighteenth-Century England* (New Haven: Yale University Press, 1993).

———, "Quakerism and Visual Culture, 1650 – 1800," *Art History*, 20/3 (1997).

Powell, W. Raymond, "Charlotte Fell Smith, Friend, Biographer and Editor," *The Journal of the Friends Historical Society*, 60/2 (2004); 113–42.

Prochaska, Frank, *Royal Bounty: The Making of a Welfare Monarchy* (New Haven: Yale University Press, 1995).

Rogers, Katharine M., *Feminism in Eighteenth-Century England* (Urbana: University of Illinois Press, 1982).

Royle, Edward and Walvin, James, *English Radicals and Reformers* (Lexington: University Press of Kentucky, 1982).

Shepherd, Verne A., "Trade and Exchange in Jamaica in the Period of Slavery," in Hilary McD Beckles and Verne Shepherd, eds. *Caribbean Slavery in the Atlantic World: A Student Reader* (Princeton: Marcus Weiner Publishers, 2000).

Shteir, Ann, *Cultivating Women, Cultivating Science: Flora's Daughters and Botany in England, 1760–1860* (Baltimore: Johns Hopkins Press, 1996).

Shoemaker, Robert B., *Gender in English Society 1650–1850: The Emergence of Separate Spheres?* (London: Longman, 1998).

Sisman, Adam, *Boswell's Presumptuous Task: The Making of the Life of Johnson* (New York: Farrar Straus Giroux, 2001).

Stephen, W.B. (ed.), *Victoria County History of Warwickshire*, vol. 3, *The City of Birmingham* (London: Oxford University Press, 1964).

South, Helen Pennock, "Dr. Johnson and the Quakers," *The Bulletin of the Friends Historical Association*, (Spring 1955): 19–42.

Sox, David, "Sydney Parkinson (1745–1741): Quaker artist with Cook's *Endeavour* voyage," *Journal of the Friends Historical Society*, 59/3 (2002): 231–5.
Swain, Margaret. *Embroidered Georgian Pictures* (Princes Risborough, Buckinghamshire: Shire Publications Ltd., 1994),
——, *Figures on Fabric: Embroidery design sources and their application*, (London: Adam and Charles Back, 1980).
Taylor, Barbara, *Mary Wollstonecraft and the Feminist Imagination* (Cambridge: Cambridge University Press, 2003).
Thomas, Peter D. G., *John Wilkes: A Friend to Liberty* (Oxford: Clarendon Press, 1996).
Vickery, Amanda, *The Gentleman's Daughter: Women's Lives in Georgian England* (New Haven: Yale University Press, 1998).
——, (ed.), *Women, Privilege, and Power: British Politics 1750 to the Present* (Stanford: Stanford University Press, 2001).
Wain, John, *Samuel Johnson: A Biography* (New York: Viking Press, 1974).
Warner, Pamela, *Embroidery: A History*, (London: B. T. Bashford, Ltd., 1991).
Weis Charles McC. and Pottle, Frederick, (eds), *Boswell in Extremes, 1776–1778* (New York: McGraw Hill, 1971).
White, William, *Friends in Warwickshire in the 17th and 18th Centuries* (3rd edn, London: Edward Hicks, 1894).
Williams, Carolyn D., "Poetry, Pudding, and Epictetus: The Consistency of Elizabeth Carter," in Alvaro Ribeiro and James G. Basker, eds, *Tradition in Transition: Women Writers, Marginal Texts, and the Eighteenth-Century Canon* (Oxford: Clarendon Press, 1996).
Williams, Eric, *Capitalism and Slavery* (New York: Capricorn Books, 1966).
Woolley, James D. "Johnson as Despot: Anna Seward's Rejected Contribution to Boswell's *Life*," *Modern Philology*, 70/2 (1972): 140–45.
Yeo, Eileen Janes (ed.), *Radical Femininity: Women's Self-Representation in the public sphere* (Manchester: Manchester University Press, 1998).

Index

Note: page numbers for illustrations are indicated by italics

abolition of slave trade 3, 4, 87–8, 93, 99, 105, 106, 148
abolition of slavery 105, 106, 131, 173
"Addressed to the Amiable M. B, with a Set of Paints" 108–9
American Revolution 3, 4, 54, 73, 83, 86, 87, 121
Anglicans 2, 13, 23, 42, 53, 56, 107, 136
animal magnetism 102–3, 158
anti-Semitism 66, 84, 146
associative social space 49, 51, 81, 87

baptism 13, 14, 38, 53, 124, 156, 166
Barclay, Robert 10, 13, 14, 160
  Apology for the True Christian Divinity 8, 9, 11, 12, 28, 43, 51, 57, 65, 129
Barnard, Hannah 145–6, 147–8
Barnes, Surrey 54, 56, 58
Bath 54, 78, 81, 87, 100, 138
Batheaston 81, 138
Binns, Jonathan 39, 41
Birkbeck, Morris Sr. 109–10, 145–6, 148, 154
Birkbeck, Morris Jr. 148
Birkbeck, William 16
Birmingham 4, 9, 12, 27, 34, 35, 38, 39, 51, 80, 81, 122, 130, 138, 145, 156
Blakes, Ann Junior 146
Bluestockings 53, 105, 131
Bone Pick'd 125–7
Boswell James 2, 4, 5, 49, 73, 78, 89, 100, 101, 104, 112, 121, 132, 167–8, 172
  Account of Corsica, 40

death, 61, 134
declaration of loyalty 131–2
dinner 15 May 1776 50–51
dinner 15 April 1778 59–68
Harry, Jane 62–3
Knowles, Mary 40, 59, 63, 86. 110–111, 140
Knowles, Thomas 86
Life of Johnson 4, 89, 111–15, 121, 131, 134, 165
  2nd edition 133, 140
  3rd edition 134, 139
  4th edition 145, 155
  5th, 6th, 7th, 8th editions 166
  Croker edition 166–7
  Hill edition 170–71
No Abolition of Slavery 131
Principal Corrections 132–3
Seward, Anna 88, 92–3, 133–4
Boswell, James (son) 134, 155, 166
botany 12, 108–9, 135–6
Braithwaite, Anna and Isaac, 149
Brighthelmstone 75, 100, 108, 138
Bristol 82
British Library 140, 156, 160
Brocklesby, Dr. Richard 94
Bunhill Fields 95, 160, 166
Buxton 101, 131, 138

Calder, Dr. John 43, 44
Cadell, Thomas 155, 166
Capper, Anne Fry 68, 157, 158, 159, 160, 168
Capper, Jasper 53, 62, 68, 157, 158, 168
Carey, George Saville 137
  The Balnea 138

Carter, Elizabeth 20, 23
Catholics 2, 14, 15, 101, 124, 125, 126, 127
Charlotte 35, 36, 36, 38, 39, 40, 73–4
childbirth 27, 31, 32–3, 41–2, 87, 158
Christie, Thomas 102
Church and King 122, 127, 131
Churchill, Charles 17, 23
Clarkson, Thomas 125, 130
Clericus 12–14, 22, 38, 146, 156
Cobb, Mary 100
Compendium of a Controversy on Water-Baptism (1771) 38
Compendium of a Controversy on Water-Baptism (1776) 53,127
Compendium of a Controversy on Water-Baptism (1805) 156, 166, 168, 169
Croker, John Wilson 93, 114, 167, 170

Davies, William 155, 166
Deists 2, 65, 93, 121, 122, 127, 128
Deverell, Mary 53
Devonshire House Meeting 42, 83, 147
Dialogue Between Dr. Johnson and Mrs. Knowles 139–40
Dialogue Between Mrs. Knowles and Dr. Johnson 155, 156
Dillwyn, George and William 137
Dilly, Charles 40, 49, 53, 59–67, 87, 89, 100, 110, 139, 155
Dilly, Edward 39–40, 44, 49, 50–51, 53, 59, 60–61, 67, 87, 88, 92
domesticity 1, 27, 34, 43, 173

Edinburgh 39, 40, 41, 42, 50, 75, 88, 100, 102
Eliot, John 157–8
engravings 150, *152, 153*

fame 2, 3, 4, 27, 38, 73, 85, 86, 101, 104, 132, 133, 150, 156, 161, 168, 173
Farmer, Mary; *see also* Lloyd, Mary Farmer 29, 30, 31, 32–3, 34, 79, 159
fashion 10, 80–81, 156

Fell, Margaret 8, 28
Fell, John 16, 38, 39, 41
Fell, Sarah 16, 38
Foote, John 32–3, 41
Forster, William 42
Fothergill, John 41, 42, 108–9
Fox, Charles James 106, 131
Fox, George 7, 8, 9, 11, 13, 14, 28, 36, 64, 122, 124, 126, 128
French Revolution 3, 4, 121–2, 129–31, 147, 173
Friends *see* Quakers 7
Fry, Jonathan 15–16, 68

Galton, Samuel Sr. and Jr. 145
gender, 1, 2, 78, 82, 102, 124, 128–9, 132, 139, 145, 146, 147, 165, 168, 169, 173
Gentleman's Magazine 4, 64, 86, 88, 110, 115, 116–17, 121, 122–3, 123–4, 125–7, 127–8, 132, 134, 135, 139, 154, 155, 170
George III 1, 17, 35, 36, *37*, 38, 39, 40, 52, *56*, 73–4, 169, 75, *76*, 86, 101, 121, 130, 137
Gracechurch Street Meeting 86, 137
Granville, Harriet Delabere 92
Graham, Catharine Sawbridge Macaulay; *see also* Macaulay, Catherine Sawbridge 87, 129
Letters on Education 115, 116, 138
Graham, William 87, 139

Harry, Jane *see also* Thresher, Jane Harry 2, 4, 49, 54, 56, 58, 74–5,79–80, 82, 83, 99, 110, 112, 113, 116–17, 140, 167, 169, 172
Gentleman's Magazine 122–3
Johnson, Samuel 59, 62–9
Knowles, Mary 55, 56–7, 64–8, 79–80
Knowles, Thomas 56
politics of complexion 55, 73, 82
Quakers 56
Reynolds, Joshua 57
Seward, Anna 90

Harry, Margaret 54, 55, 56
Harry, Mrs. 54, 82, 83
Haverford College Library 151, *152*, *153*
Hayley, Eliza 81, 85–6
Hayley, George 85
Hayley, Mary Wilkes 52, 53, 85–6, 87, 173
Hayley, William 81, 85, 94, 102
Hibbert, Thomas 54, 55, 56, 57, 58, 64, 82, 90, 92, 171
Hibbert, Thomas Jr. 82
Hoare, Samuel and Sarah 136
Howard, Robert and Luke 157–8, 165–6
Hunter, Anne Home and John 101

Jamaica 54, 82, 83
Jenkins, James 15, 16, 17, 27, 28, 68, 79, 81–2, 83, 86, 95, 103, 125, 145, 146–8, 158, 159, 160, 161
Jenyns, Soame, *A View of the Internal Evidence of the Christian Religion* 61
Jews 2, 14, 15, 66, 84, 124, 125–6, 127
Johnso-mania 99, 103
Johnson, Samuel 2, 4, 5, 49, 55, 73, 78, 100, 101, 104, 110, 121, 132–3, 167–8
  death 61, 88
  Dialogue between Dr. Johnson and Mrs. Knowles 139–40
  Dialogue between Mrs. Knowles and Dr. Johnson 155
  dinner 15 April 1778 59–68
  Gentleman's Magazine 122–3
  Harry, Jane 59, 62–3, 74
  Knowles, Mary 52, 64–8, 124
  Lady's Magazine 128–9
  Lady's Monthly Museum 150
  Pilkington, Mary 155
  politics 50, 51
  Quakers 49, 51, 64, 91–2, 99
  women 51, 53, 60, 64, 65, 114–15, 171
Seward, Anna 89–92
sexuality 112

Kendal, John 17, 20, 21, 22, 23
Knowles, George 41–2, 73–4, 100, 107, 130, 158, 166, 169, 173
Knowles, Mary Morris; *see also* Morris, Mary 29–30, 34–5, 41, 79, 81, 94, 136, 147–8, 167–8
  "Addressed to Amiable M. B. with Set of Paints" 108–9
  American Revolution 54, 84
  Barnard, Hannah 147–8
  Birmingham 34, 35, 38
  Bone Pick'd 125–7
  Boswell, James 40–41, 63, 89, 100, 110–11, 132–3
  botanical art 108–9, 135–6
  Calder, John 42–3, 44
  Capper, Ann Fry 68, 157, 158, 159, 160
  Capper, Jasper 53, 68, 157, 158
  Capper, Mary 53–4
  Charlotte 36, 38, 40
  "Child of Candour" 139–40, 165
  childbirth 31–2, 32–3, 158
  Compendium of a Controversy on Water-Baptism (1771) 38
  Compendium of a Controversy on Water Baptism (1805) 156, 166, 168, 169
  death 61, 158–61
  Dialogue Between Dr. Johnson and Mrs. Knowles 139–40
  Dialogue Between Mrs. Knowles and Dr. Johnson 155, 156
  Dilly, Charles 87, 100
  Dilly, Edward 40, 44, 50, 51, 59, 60
  dinner party 15 May 1776 50–52
  dinner party 15 April 1778 64–8
  domesticity 30, 34, 43
  dress 78, 80, 81, 121, 125–7
  Edinburgh 41
  Eliot, John 157
  engravings *152*, *153*
  fame 2, 3, 4, 38, 40, 44, 52, 56, 73, 101, 121, 133, 150, 160, 161,
  Farmer, Mary 29–30, 32–3, 34, 158
  French Revolution 121–2, 129–31

Gentleman's Magazine 88, 110, 115, 116–17, 121, 122, 123–8, 133, 135, 154
George III 36, *37*, 38, 73–4, 137
Graham, Catharine Macaulay 87
Harry, Jane (Thresher) 64–8, 79–80, 83, 87–8
Hayley, Eliza 81, 85–6
Hayley, Mary Wilkes 85–6
Hayley, William 85–6
Hoare, Samuel and Sarah 136
Howard, Robert 157, 158
Hunter, Anne Home 101
Jenkins, James 29, 68, 81–2, 147–8, 158, 159
Johnson, Samuel 52, 78
Knowles, George 41–2, 73–4, 100, 107, 130, 158, 166
Knowles, Rachel 32, 34
Knowles, Thomas 29, 31, 34
Lady's Magazine 129
Lady's Monthly Museum 149, 150–51, 155, 156, 160
"Lamentation of Timothy Tattle" 80
Lee, William 50
liberty 3, 4
    political 39
    slaves 105
    "warlike liberty" 74
    women 49, 60, 112–13
Life of Johnson 111–14, 134, 140
Linwood, Mary 138
Lloyd, Mary Farmer 79, 147–8, 149, 157, 160
London 41–2
"Lord North and the Quaker" 83–4
Lort, Susannah Norfolk 101
marriage 29, 31, 34, 95, 99
Matthews, William 78, 160
Mildenhall 30
"Minister and Quaker" 84
Morris, Alice 28, 34, 34–5
Morris, Esther 31, 32, 33, 34, 35
Morris, Joseph 30–31
Morris, Thomas 123

needle painting of George III 1, 36, *37*, 75, *76*
Nichols, John 110, 115–16
non-Quakers 33–4, 53, 78, 81
"On Fashion" 80–81
patriot 50, 52, 161
pacifism 93, 102, 173
Paine, Thomas 136
patronage 38–9
Phillips, James 103, 130
Pilkington, Mary 154–5
Piozzi, Hester Thrale 104
political participation 38–9, 74, 94, 106, 137, 161
Price, Richard 87
Quakerliness 27, 73, 78, 82, 99, 108, 159
Rack, Edmund 78
religious views 31–2, 33, 42–3, 57–8, 61, 62, 65–7, 99, 122, 125–7, 146–7, 156–7, 159–60
"Reply to a Love Letter" 138–9
Reynolds, Joshua, 57
Romney, George 85
Sael, G. 110, 134
Savery, William 137, 154
self-doubt 5, 145, 159, 161, 174
self-portrait 1, 75, *77*, 171
self-representation 1, 73, 75, 99, 117
"Sent with Drawing" 109
Seward, Anna 59, 68 85, 89–92, 93, 105, 107, 131
sociability 30, 42, 56, 94
social text 31, 84, 106, 127
Sprigg, Nathaniel 55
stage coach dialogue 130
"To Ann Blakes, junior" 146–7
"To Friend Pope" 135–6
"To T. and I. D." 35
travels in Europe 41
Verses 156–7
Wakefield, Gilbert 148–9
West, Benjamin 35, 137
widowhood 95, 99–101
Woods, Joseph 103, 158, 160

"Written in Terrors of Childbirth" 31–2
"Wrote by MK before birth of child" 31–2
Knowles, Rachel 32, 34
Knowles, Thomas 28, 29, 31, 34, 35, 39, 40, 41, 42, 53–4, 56, 58, 59, 73, 75, 78, 79, 83, 85, 86, 87, 84, 95, 99, 105, 107, 160

Lady's Magazine 121, 127–8
Lady's Monthly Museum 149–50, 150–51, *152*, 155, 156, 160, 165, 169
"Lamentation of Timothy Tattle" 80
Lee, Arthur 50, 87
Lee, William 50, 87
Letter from a Clergyman to M. Morris 53
Lettsom, John Coakley 27–8, 41, 42, 50, 55, 83, 94–5, 137
Leyden 27, 41
liberty 3, 14, 39, 60, 80, 99, 161
　African slaves 105–6
　America 50
　Christian liberty 14
　English 121
　religious liberty 57
　"warlike liberty" 74
　women's liberty 29, 49, 60, 61, 63, 67, 112–13, 172
Library of the Religious Society of Friends, London 16, 89, 123, 139, 140, 150, 156, 166
Lichfield 4, 9, 11, 59, 62, 84, 85, 88, 94, 100, 107, 109, 129
Life of Johnson see Boswell, James
Lindsay, Theophilus 42–3
Linwood, Mary 138, 149, 155
literary coterie 49, 52, 67, 101, 115
Lloyd, Charles Sr. and Jr. 79
Lloyd, Mary Farmer *see also* Farmer, Mary 79, 147–8, 149, 157, 160
Lloyd, Sampson II 12
Lloyd, Sampson III and Rachel 12, 51, 79, 80, 130, 149
London, 4, 16, 31, 39, 41, 43, 49, 50, 52, 53, 54, 55, 56, 57, 58, 59, 73, 75, 79, 81, 83, 86, 87, 89, 94, 100, 101, 107, 109, 111, 117, 125, 127, 130, 134, 137, 146, 157
London Abolition Committee 105, 106, 136, 137
Lord North, 52, 73, 83–4, 87
"Lord North and the Quaker" 83–4
Lort Michael 101, 103–04
Lort, Susannah Norfolk 101, 103
Lythall, Esther Morris *see also* Morris, Esther 34
Lyttleton, Thomas 151–2

Mackenzie, [first name unknown] 150. *156*
Malone, Edmond 110–11, 134, 139, 155, 166
Macaulay, Catharine Sawbridge *see also* Graham, Catharine Sawbridge Macaulay 17, 18, 28, 40, 51, 54, 78, 139
　Observations on a Pamphlet Entitled Thoughts on the Causes of the Present Discontents 39
marriage 1, 20, 27, 28–9, 99, 109, 138–9
Marsillac, Jean de 130
Mary, 1, 171
"Memoirs of M. M. spinster of this parish" 19–21, 22, 23, 38, 50
Moore, Hannah 105
Matthews, William 78, 160
Mayo, Rev. Dr. 59, 61
Medical Society of London 42, 43
Mildenhall 28, 29, 30, 33, 34, 35
Miller, Sir John and Lady Ann Riggs, 81
Montagu, Elizabeth Robinson 53
moral agency 49, 64–5, 68, 91, 93
Morris, Alice 10, 28, 34–5
Morris, Charles 124
Morris, Esther *see also* Lythall, Esther Morris 10, 31, 32, 33, 34, 166
Morris, Esther Storrs *see also* Esther Storrs 9, 10, 159, 160
Morris, Joseph 10, 15, 30–31, 166
Morris, Mary *see also* Knowles, Mary Morris 7, 9, 10, 12, 28

ancestors 7–9
botany 12
Clericus and Lavinia 12–14
Compendium of a Controversy on Water-Baptism (1776) 53, 127
dress 27–8
education 10–11, 20
Jenkins, James 15–16
Kendal, John 17, 20, 22, 23
Knowles, Thomas 28
letter to John and Sarah Fell 16–22
Letter from a Clergyman to M. Morris 53
Lettsom, John Coakley 27–8
liberty 14, 18
Lloyds 12
marriage 20
"Memoirs of M. M. spinster of this parish" 19–21
"Pudding Making Mortal" 21–2
Quakerliness 16
radical views 17–18
religious views 14–15
self-representation 17, 22–3
Seward, Anna 11, 22
sexual desire 19
sociability 16, 22
social texts, 15, 22
youth 11–12
Morris, Moses 9, 10, 35
Morris, Richard 9, 145, 159
Morris, Thomas 124–7, 168
motherhood 1, 107

needle painting 1, 35–6, *37*, 38, 40, 52, 56, 75, *76*, *77*, 138, 150, 171
New Lights 145, 147
New Testament 14, 33, 55, 61, 62, 66, 102, 128
Nichols, John 110, 115, 116
No Abolition of Slavery 131
Nottingham 127

"On Fashion" 80–81
Old Testament 31, 32

pacifism *see* Quakers and Knowles, Mary Morris
Paine, Thomas 122, 129, 136
patriot 18, 50, 52, 161
patronage 27, 38–9, 44
Peel Meeting 137, 157–8, 160
Penn, William 36, 54, 84, 130
Percy, Thomas Bishop 103–04
perfectibility 29, 122, 148
Phillips, James 103, 130
Pindar, Peter (Dr. John Woolcot) 94, 103
Pilkington, Mary 154–5, 169
Piozzi, Hester Thrale; *see also* Thrale, Hester 99, 103–4, 112, 132, 140
Pitt, William (the Elder) 18, 23
political participation 1, 2, 3, 52, 74, 84, 94, 106, 161, 173
politics of complexion 2, 49, 54, 55, 73, 82
Pope, Margaret and Robert 135
Price, Richard 3, 87, 106
printwork 35
"Pudding Making Mortal" 21–2, 23

Quakerism 7, 10, 12, 90, 92
Quakerliness 2, 5, 7, 10, 11, 12, 16, 27, 35, 73, 78, 80, 82, 99, 108, 121, 125, 146, 156, 157, 159, 160, 165, 166, 172
Quakers 1, 2, 3, 7, 8, 9, 10, 27, 74
    art 15, 36, 75, 136, 150
    dress 80–81, 124–5, 126–7, 146
    Harry, Jane 56
    internal tensions 8, 27, 79, 145–9
    Johnson, Samuel 50, 64–8, 92
    marriage 20, 28–9
    pacifism 12, 54, 73–4, 135, 145
    women 7, 8, 15, 17, 20, 51, 82, 146

Rack, Edmund 54, 78, 87
radical 50, 80, 84, 87, 105, 129, 148
    self-representation 1, 7, 22, 73, 75, 117, 171
    women 2, 3, 105, 129
"Reply to a Love Letter" 138–9

Index

Reynolds, Esther Morris, Margarette and Richenda Elizabeth 171
Reynolds, Joshua 57–8
Robinson, Elihu 146
Romney, George 85
Royal Academy of Art 57, 74, 138
Royal Collection 1, 171
Royal College of Physicians 42
Rugeley, Staffordshire 9, 10, 11, 33, 43, 53, 68, 85

Sael, G. 110, 132, 133, 134–5, 140
Savery, William 137, 154
self-doubt 5, 145, 159, 161, 174
self-representation 1, 7, 22, 73, 75. 117, 145
"Sent With Drawing" 109
Settle, Yorkshire 16, 27, 41, 109
Seward, Anna 2, 4, 11, 12, 22, 23, 59, 68, 81, 92, 94, 99, 100, 101, 104, 155, 166, 167–8, 169
   American Revolution 62
   Boswell, James 88, 133–4
   dinner 15 April 1778 59–68, 73, 78, 89–92, 93, 112–15, 139
   French Revolution 121, 122, 129
   Harry, Jane 87
   Johnson, Samuel 88
   Knowles, Mary 84–5, 87, 93, 100–101, 102, 104, 105, 107–8, 131
   Knowles, Thomas 84–5, 95
   Life of Johnson 111, 112, 115–16
   political participation 94, 106, 131
   Quakers 125
Seward, Thomas 11, 59, 104
sexual desire 19–20, 131
Shackleton, Richard and Mary 81
Sheridan, Charles Francis, *Account of the late Revolution in Sweden* 59
Sikes, Grace Jenkinson 7, 8
Sikes, Sarah *see also* Storrs, Sarah Sikes 8
Sikes, William 7, 8
slave 39, 121
slavery 14, 50, 83, 88, 105–6, 131, 133

Smith, Thomas 83–4
sociability 5, 30, 42, 56, 94, 172, 173
social networks 1, 3, 56, 93, 94, 101
social text 2, 15, 22, 84, 92, 106, 127
Society for the Encouragement of Arts, Manufactures and Commerce 74–5, 88
Sprigg, Nathaniel 54, 55, 57–8, 62, 67, 82, 90
Staffordshire 4, 9, 11, 52, 100
Storrs, Esther; *see also* Morris, Esther Storrs 8, 9
Storrs, Sarah Sikes; *see also* Sikes, Sarah 8
Storrs, William 8
subordination 131, 133
"sutile pictures" 52, 103–4, 112, 132
Swedenborg, Emmanuel 78

Tatler 11, 20, 28
Thrale, Henry 52
Thrale, Hester; *see also* Piozzi, Hester Thrale 52, 101, 111, 151, 170
Thresher, Jane Harry; *see also* Harry, Jane 87–8, 105, 171, 174
   Gentleman's Magazine 88
Thresher, Joseph 83, 88
"To Ann Blakes, junior" 146–7
"To Friend Pope" 135–6
"To T. and I. D." 35
toleration 2, 5, 7, 8, 11, 23, 59, 67, 92, 126, 172

Verses (by Mary Knowles) 156–7
Voltaire, François 10, 18

Wakefield, Gilbert 148–9
Warwickshire 4, 35, 92, 94
Wedgwood, Josiah 105
West, Benjamin 35, 36, 137
Whalley, Thomas Sedgewick 85
Whig 39–40, 50, 52, 63, 87, 106, 113, 124, 129
widowhood 99–101
Wigginshill, Warwickshire 10, 28

Wilkes, John 3, 17, 18, 23, 50, 51, 52, 53, 85, 86, 87, 111, 124
Williams, Helen Maria 93, 102
Wilson, Deborah (mother and daughter) and Rachel 16
Wollstonecraft, Mary 23, 29, 122, 129, 173
Wolseley, William 100, 151, 154
women 17, 29, 49, 74–5, 88, 99–101
   Johnson, Samuel 51, 114–15
   liberty 29, 49, 60, 61, 63, 67, 105, 112–13, 161, 172
   political participation 3, 38–9, 52, 74, 84, 106, 161, 173
   public gaze 85, 154
   radicals 2, 73, 80, 93
   spiritual equality 61, 64

Woods, Joseph 95, 103, 158–9, 160, 161
Woolman, John 106
"Written in Terrors of Childbirth" 31–2
"Wrote by MK before birth of child" 31–2

Yearsley, Ann 105

Zoffany, Johann 36, 37